SETTLER REGIMES IN AFRICA AND THE ARAB WORLD

The Contributors

ADNAN ABU-GHAZALEH is Professor of History at State University of New York at Plattsburg.

PETER ANYANG'-NYONG'O is Fellow in Political Science at the University of Chicago.

DANIEL BERRIGAN is a poet and peace activist.

ANDRÉ DIRLIK is Associate Professor of History at Military College of St. Jean.

HASSAN HADDAD is Professor and Chairman of the Department of History at St. Xavier College.

STEPHEN HALBROOK is Associate Professor of Philosophy at the Tuskegee Institute.

HATEM I. HUSSAINI, formerly Assistant Professor of Government at Smith College, is with the Arab Information Center.

KEMAL H. KARPAT is Professor of History at the University of Wisconsin.

ALICE K. KURODA is Lecturer in Sociology at the University of Hawaii.

YASUMASA KURODA is Professor of Political Science at the University of Hawaii.

WALTER LEHN is Professor of Linguistics at the University of Minnesota.

RUTH B. MINTER is a member of the Southern Committee on Southern Africa.

WILLIAM MINTER is the author of *Portuguese Africa and the West*.

NEVILLE RUBIN is Lecturer in African Law at the London School of Oriental and African Studies.

EDWARD W. SAID is Professor of English and Comparative Literature at Columbia University.

ERIC SELLIN is Professor of French Literature at Temple University.

ISRAEL SHAHAK is Professor of Chemistry at the Hebrew University.

RICHARD P. STEVENS is Professor of Political Science at Lincoln University.

FAWAZ TURKI is the author of *The Disinherited*.

JAMES J. ZOGBY is Assistant Professor of Philosophy at Shippensburg State College.

AAUG Monograph Series: No. 4

SETTLER REGIMES IN AFRICA AND THE ARAB WORLD:
THE ILLUSION OF ENDURANCE

edited by
Ibrahim Abu-Lughod
Baha Abu-Laban

THE MEDINA UNIVERSITY PRESS INTERNATIONAL
WILMETTE, ILLINOIS
1974

First published in the United States of America in 1974 by the
Medina University Press International
P.O. Box 125
Wilmette, Illinois 60091

Copyright © 1974 by the Medina University Press International
LCC: 74-77249
ISBN 0-914456-06-7 (cloth edition)
ISBN 0-914456-07-5 (paper edition)
All rights reserved.

Ibrahim Abu-Lughod is Professor of Political Science and Associate Director of the Program of African Studies at Northwestern University.
Baha Abu-Laban is Professor of Sociology at the University of Alberta.

CONTENTS

Foreword
   Ibrahim Abu-Lughod and Baha Abu-Laban   vii

PART I: COLONIAL SETTLEMENT: IDEOLOGICAL AND
      INSTITUTIONAL BASES
   The Biblical Bases of Zionist Colonialism
     Hassan Haddad   3
   The Philosophy of Zionism: A Materialist Interpretation
     Stephen Halbrook   20
   The Ideological Foundations of Settler Regimes: The Portuguese in Africa
     William Minter   31
   The Jewish National Fund
     Walter Lehn   43

PART II: RESPONSE TO SETTLEMENT
   Ottoman Immigration Policies and Settlement in Palestine
     Kemal H. Karpat   57
   The Algerian Response to Settlement
     André Dirlik   73
   The Palestinian Response to Zionist Settlement: A Cultural Dimension
     Adnan Abu-Ghazaleh   81
   The Palestinian Revolt of the 1930s
     James J. Zogby   94

PART III: SETTLERS AND NATIONALS: ALIENATION
AND LIBERATION
  Alienation of the Palestinian in the Arab World
    Fawaz Turki   119
  Alienation and Intellectual Invisibility of Algerian Nationals: The Writer's Vision
    Eric Sellin   125
  Education of Freedom Fighters in Mozambique
    Ruth B. Minter   136
  Socialization of Freedom Fighters: The Palestinian Experience
    Yasumasa Kuroda and Alice K. Kuroda   147

PART IV: INTERNATIONAL IMPACT
  The Impact of Zionism and Israel on the Political Orientation and Behavior of South African Jews
    Neville Rubin   165
  Smuts and Weizmann: A Study in South African–Zionist Cooperation
    Richard P. Stevens   173
  The Impact of the Middle East Conflict on African Orientations and Behavior
    Peter Anyang'-Nyong'o   187
  The Impact of the Arab-Israeli Conflict on Arab Communities in the United States
    Hatem I. Hussaini   201

PART V: ARABS AND JEWS: POSSIBILITY OF CONCORD
  Responses to Settler Regimes
    Daniel Berrigan, S.J.   223
  Arabs and Jews
    Edward W. Said   235
  Equal Justice for Every Human Being
    Israel Shahak   247

Index   253

FOREWORD

This collection of essays originated with the Sixth Annual Convention of the Association of Arab-American University Graduates, Inc., which was held in Washington, D.C., October 19–21, 1973. Approximately fifty papers were presented at this convention, the theme of which was "National Liberation and Settler Regimes: Africa and the Middle East." The selected essays contained in this volume were revised for publication on the assumption that they would appeal to a broad range of audiences interested in the study of the internal dynamics of settler regimes, and the interrelationships and confrontations between "settlers" and nationals. In addition to the fact that they were written by recognized scholars and specialists, these essays should be of interest in that they encompass recent research evidence on a topic both timely and of social and political significance.

Coincidentally, the Sixth Annual Convention was held in the shadow of the ongoing Arab-Israeli war of October, 1973. Viewed from the perspective of the world-wide struggle against oppression, this war manifests once more the inherent contradictions between colonialism, however garbed, and the basic human rights of colonized peoples. For over a generation, Zionism and imperialism have attempted, unsuccessfully, to liquidate the dispossessed Palestinians and to suppress the Arab people's struggle for national liberation. The tremendous mobilization of advanced technological resources against the Arab people has failed to shake their determination to extricate themselves, even at heavy sacrifices, from the shackles of Zionism and imperialism. Against such forces, the steadfast resolve of the Arab people appears to have been strengthened by an unyielding conviction that, ultimately, basic principles of human justice will prevail.

The convention program properly reflects emphasis on the comparative analysis of national liberation movements and settler regimes in Africa and the Middle East. The comparative approach assists in identifying common features of colonial systems and common responses to these systems by the colonized and the dispossessed. One of the themes which runs through several essays in this volume is the tendency for settler regimes to move toward exclusivism, exploitation, oppression, and racism. This is as much true of the Afrikaner regime in South Africa as the Israeli regime in Palestine; of the former French regime in Algeria as the current Portuguese regime in Angola and Mozambique. Significantly, these distinctive characteristics of settler regimes are intimately linked with ideological and religious precepts and numerous institutional structures designed to reinforce and perpetuate the subjugation of the national population.

Several essays in this collection address the ideological and religious foundations of the Afrikaner and Portuguese settlements in Africa and the Zionist settlement in Palestine. Taken together, these essays expose the role of belief in racial superiority and manifest destiny in the colonialist position. This belief serves to justify the settlers' claims to the land and to a superordinate position in the system. Such claims are further buttressed by negative images of the nationals. The essays dealing with the images of Africans and Palestinian Arabs as projected in the literature of white and Zionist settlers in Africa and Palestine reveal striking similarities: the national population is typically characterized as childish, irresponsible, and incapable of carrying the torch of civilization. Such images are not much different from those which many white Americans hold of Afro-Americans—a recognizably oppressed group in American society. The attribution of such negative qualities to nationals legitimizes for the settlers their view of the nationals as objects of pity, exploitation, and, if necessary, destruction, and also provides an insidious basis for negative self-images among the nationals themselves. In short, the religious and/or cultural heritage of the settlers facilitates assertion of self at the expense of virtual denial of others. This theme, among others, also appears in the essays by the Reverend Daniel Berrigan, Edward Said, and Israel Shahak.

The tenacious flourishing of settler regimes in Africa and the Middle East is made possible not only by elitist ideologies and institutional mechanisms which subordinate nationals and facilitate their exploitation but also by active support from external sources, notably Europe. Several participants at the convention noted that the subjugation of nationals in Palestine, South Africa, Rhodesia, Angola, and Mozambique could not have continued for long without European and, particularly in the case of Palestine, American support. Given the upsurge of national liberation movements and the steps taken recently to integrate these movements at the international level, the continued efficacy of external support of settler regimes stands in question.

The colonial system and its oppressive social, economic, and political institutions have left an indelible mark on the life experiences of the national populations. Although the colonized peoples of Africa and the Middle East are articulated differently in their respective settler regimes, they all have come to share similar experiences, including discriminatory treatment, oppression, and human degradation. It is these experiential commonalities which may help explain similarities in reactions to the colonial system. Several essays in this work delineate a wide range of spheres, including the social, economic, political, cultural, and psychological, in which responses to the colonial experience are expressed. From the perspective of the settlers, it is understandable that the most threatening response is the rise of national liberation movements and related cultural and institutional supports. However, not only does national liberation appear to be a logical and frequent outcome of oppression, but also, as the Pakistani scholar Eqbal Ahmad reflected at the convention, liberation movements constitute the only hope for the subjugated and the dispossessed to alleviate the extraordinary misery and human degradation which they have suffered.

As an educational organization concerned with the dissemination of knowledge about matters of vital concern to the Arab world as well as the Arab-American community, the AAUG has followed the practice of publishing the main proceedings of its annual conventions. The first five conventions resulted in the following publications: *The Arab-Americans: Studies in Assimilation; The Palestinian Resistance to Israeli Occupation; The Arab World: From Nationalism to Revolution; The Arabs Today: Alternatives for Tomorrow;* and *The Middle East: Five Perspectives.*

In addition to this volume, which contains nineteen essays, the Sixth Annual Convention resulted in three other publications of general public interest at this time. All three of these works were published in the AAUG Information Papers series. The essays by the Reverend Daniel Berrigan, Edward Said, and Israel Shahak, which appear in this volume, were published earlier as Information Papers No. 11, entitled *Arabs and Jews: Possibility of Concord.* The papers presented by Caesar Farah, Carolyn Lobban, and Richard Lobban, dealing with issues concerning the integration of various groups into their respective communities in the Arab world, were published as Information Papers No. 12, entitled *Problems of National Integration in the Arab World.* Finally, the papers delivered by Ayad Al-Qazzaz and Ibrahim Oweiss, dealing with selected aspects of the military and economic institutions in Israeli society, were published as Information Papers No. 13, entitled *Two Studies on Israel.*

This work and the three related Information Papers are products of a collective effort within the AAUG. We wish to acknowledge the contributions of those whose essays are presented in this book and in the Information Papers, and of the other participants who presented papers, appeared on panels or forums, or served as chairpersons or commentators, at the convention. We wish also to acknowledge the valuable editorial help of Ms. Linda Norris.

For their contributions to the success of the convention, we should like to express our deep appreciation to Flora Azar, M. Cherif Bassiouni, William J. Gedeon, George Hishmeh, Hassan Hussaini, Hatem I. Hussaini, Abdeen Jabara, Levon Keshishian, Fauzi Najjar, Ibrahim Oweiss, Wafiya Shafey, Sami Shihadeh, Sam Zaitoun, and Faith Zeadey.

IBRAHIM ABU-LUGHOD
BAHA ABU-LABAN

PART I: COLONIAL SETTLEMENT: IDEOLOGICAL AND INSTITUTIONAL BASES

Hassan Haddad

THE BIBLICAL BASES OF ZIONIST COLONIALISM

THEOPOLITICS OF ISRAEL

THE IDEALS, GOALS, STRATEGY, AND TACTICS of Jewish settlement in Palestine may correspond, in some respects, to those of settler regimes elsewhere. But, unlike other settler regimes, Israel claims to be the restoration of a state that had temporarily been disrupted. To study other settler regimes, one would have to refer mainly to the socioeconomic and political conditions prevalent in the West in the last three or four centuries. To study the Jewish settler regime in Palestine, however, one must concentrate on its theopolitical aspects. The concept of return, of redress, and of reclamation of an ancient, but still valid, title to a specific land is central to the Zionist movement. This concept is firmly anchored in the Bible, giving it an aura of finality and uncontestability and, in Zionist minds, setting it above legal and moral considerations.

The Bible (the Old Testament) contains the only available record of this ancient state, its origin, its ideology, and its prophetic and eschatological destiny. This collection of myths, legends, historical narratives, poems, and prophetic and apocalyptic pronouncements is primarily responsible for the beliefs, conditions, and attitudes that produced Zionism and eventually led to the occupation and transformation of Palestine. We can summarize these beliefs as follows. (1) The Jews are a separate and exclusive people chosen by their God to fulfill a destiny; the Jews of Europe in the twentieth century have inherited the covenant of divine election and historical destiny from the Hebrew tribes that existed more than three thousand years ago. (2) This covenant includes definite ownership of the Land of Canaan (Palestine) as a patrimony of the ancient Israelites to be passed on to their descendants forever; no other people can lay a rightful claim to that land. (3) The occupation and settlement of this land is the fulfillment of the duty, placed collectively on the Jews, to establish a state for the Jews; the purity of the Jewishness of the land is derived from a divine command and is thus a sacred mission.

Accordingly, the settlement of Palestine, in addition to its economic and political motivations, acquires a romantic and mythical character. That the Bible is at the root of Zionism is recognized by all Zionists—religious, secular, nonobservant, and agnostic ones. Although Herzl's knowledge of the Bible may have been less than complete, his formulation of the ideas of the Jewish state do not conflict with the Bible at all. Moses Hess, who preceded Herzl and who is considered to be one of the fathers of the Zionist movement, recognized and preached the principle of interdependence of religion and nationalism in Jewish life. To him Jewish religion was, above all, Jewish nationalism.[1] Ben Gurion, often biblical in his writings and speeches, calls the Bible the "sacro-sanct title-deed to Palestine" for the Jewish people, "with a genealogy of 3500 years."[2] Others have called the Bible the Jewish national record. Abba Eban, in his popularized history of the Jews, brings out the concept of this unique history of the Chosen:

> The utter singularity of the Jewish history, its rebellion against all historic laws, its total recalcitrance to any comparative system of research, have all been brought home to me at every stage. . . . There is no other modern nation whose motives of existence and action require such frequent reference to distant days.[3]

Norman Bentwich points out:

> The awareness of the relevance of the Bible to present-day life permeates the schools of all sections in Israel and moulds their thought and expression. . . . The Bible represents the history and the thought of the biblical period with which modern Israel feels a close affinity.[4]

---

1. Hess, *Rome and Jerusalem: A Study in Jewish Nationalism*, trans. Meyer Waxman (New York, 1943).
2. David Ben Gurion, *The Rebirth and Destiny of Israel* (New York, 1954), p. 100.
3. Eban, *My People, The Story of the Jews* (New York, 1968), p. v.
4. Bentwich, "Judaism in Israel," in *Religion in the Middle East,* ed. A. J. Arberry (Cambridge, Mass., 1969), I, 76.

While most Zionist thinkers attempt to present Jewish nationalism as a modern movement based on conditions present in the ninteenth and twentieth centuries, the fact remains that this modern movement—ideologically, ethnically, and territorially—is based primarily on biblical Israel. The name *Zion* refers to the territorial description found in the Bible. The name *Israel* reflects the intertwining of racial and territorial considerations found in the Bible, in traditional Jewish beliefs, and in rabbinical literature. Consequently, when Zionists speak of their historic right to Palestine, they are referring to a history and to a historical philosophy found in the Bible and in the rabbinical literature. To deny the "historic right" of the Jews to Palestine is to challenge the scriptures. This argument has been used effectively against Jews as well as Christians who might have been inclined to oppose Israel.[5]

To advocates of Jewish nationalism, the books of the Bible (with the exception of the wisdom literature, which forms a small part of the whole) contain the necessary references to the political and territorial structure of Israel. The five books of the Torah (the Pentateuch), the most revered part of the Bible to most Jews, are concerned with the origin and conditions of the covenant that establishes Israel as the Chosen People and the Land of Canaan as the Promised Land. Because the state and the people are sacred, the conquest of Canaan is a religious duty. The law in the Torah is interpreted as a sign of the covenant between Yahweh and Israel. The Canaanites, being outside the covenant, could not be assimilated into the law or into Israel. In fact, the complete eviction and extermination of the Canaanites is strongly recommended, as we shall demonstrate later.

The historical books relate the attempt of the Hebrew tribes to establish their "first commonwealth." The high point in this ancient history, according to the biblical account, is the kingdom of David and Solomon, which has been the model and the ideal of Jewish nationalism throughout the ages.

The prophetic books of the Bible are concerned with why the covenant was not fulfilled. The destruction of the kingdom of Israel by the Assyrians, the impending danger to the kingdom of Judah, and the subsequent "Babylonian captivity" all required an explanation. The Prophets reproach Israel for being unfaithful to the covenant, primarily by "following after foreign gods"; but they also offer hope that Yahweh, who is ever faithful to his promises, will one day redeem the people of Israel, will bring them back to the Promised Land, will make them

---

5. See Willard G. Otoxby, "Christians and the Mideast Crisis," *Christian Century*, July 26, 1967, pp. 961 ff.

a great nation, and will frustrate their enemies.

Thus the Torah sets the divine basis for the exclusivist choice of Israel and its title deed to Palestine. The historical books record the attempts to bring about the fulfillment of the Jewish state as ordained by divine command. The Prophets rationalize the failure of this endeavor and project its fulfillment to a future date. Accordingly, the three pillars of Zionism are found in (1) the covenant of divine election and the title deed to Palestine, (2) the historical precedents of the Jewish state, and (3) the realization and fulfillment of the prophecies. Calling Zionist colonization of Palestine *aliyah* ("return") is a testimony to the primacy of the Bible to Zionism and to Israel.

Non-Zionist Jews who have spiritualized Judaism and the Bible beyond the level of ethnic nationalism cannot counteract this profusion of biblical texts concerned explicitly with Jewish nationalism and exclusivism. To sublimate a statement, even a biblical one, is much more difficult than to believe in it literally. Moreover, the poetic style of the Prophets of the Bible, the most important basis of spiritualized, denationalized Judaism, is not immune from ultranationalistic exploitation. It is, in fact, a great source of Zionist enthusiasm. Because this type of writing makes great use of the nationalistic terminology, it lends itself readily to the nationalistic aspirations of Zionism. Examples of biblical prophetic statements that can easily bolster the extreme nationalistic and militaristic character of the Jewish state are many. From Isaiah, the greatest of Israel's prophets, we have, for example, predictions about the future of Jerusalem and Israel that are considered topical and valid today:

> Foreigners shall rebuild your walls, and their kings shall be your servants. . . . For the nation and kingdom which refuses to serve you shall perish. . . . The few shall become ten thousand, the little nation great. I am the Lord: soon, in the fullness of time, I will bring this to pass [Isa. 60:10, 12, 22].
> Foreigners shall serve as shepherds of your flocks, and aliens shall till your land and tend your vines; but you shall be called priests of the Lord and be named ministers of our God; you shall enjoy the wealth of other nations and be furnished with their riches [Isa. 61:5, 6].[6]

This, of course, is based on a selective reading of the Bible; but there is an abundance of such verses.

In 1869, before the establishment of the Zionist movement, American Reform rabbis decided to take a bold step toward the spiritualization

---

6. All biblical quotations are from the New English Bible.

of the covenant. They declared, at the Philadelphia Conference, that "the messianic aim of Israel is not the restoration of the old Jewish state under a descendant of David."[7] Again, in 1885, they asserted: "We consider ourselves no longer a nation, but a religious community, and, therefore, expect no return to Palestine."[8]

While this attitude is prevalent among many Jews, a retreat from this position toward a more fundamentalist interpretation can be detected in American Reform Judaism. In 1937, when Zionism was capitalizing on the plight of the Jews in Nazi Germany, American Reform rabbis modified their stand on the separation between spiritual and political Israel: "We affirm the obligation of all Jews to aid in . . . upbuilding [Palestine] as a Jewish homeland.[9] In 1967 a Reform rabbi who asserted that he was non-Zionist (he objected to Ben Gurion's thesis that a good Jew should live only in Israel) was moved by the events of the Arab-Israeli June war to declare: "The destiny of the Household of Israel is a theopolitical matter now as it was in biblical times." He went on to describe, in theopolitical terms, the war that had just ended:

> That Monday afternoon when the war began and no news of what was taking place came through, there was black anxiety throughout the Jewish world. The question was not military—who should win. It was theological. Would God abandon the people of Israel again and allow the citizens of the State of Israel to be slaughtered by Arab armies? . . . It was not, then, only the Israeli armies who were on trial that day but, in very earnest, God himself.[10]

The ambivalent attitude of non-Israeli Jews stems from the biblical intertwining of the political and the spiritual in conceptualizing Israel. Israel as a state is, according to this point of view, a matter of religious concern to all Jews, regardless of their place of birth or residence. The rabbi explained:

> It is certain that neither of us [Jews and Israelis] realized how deeply we were still rooted in Jewish tradition until we all stood once again,

---

7. Full text of the declaration appears in *Yearbook of the Central Conference of American Rabbis*, I (1891), 117 ff.

8. *Ibid.*, pp. 120 ff.

9. Full text appears in *ibid.*, XLVII (1937), 97 ff.

10. Rabbi Eugene B. Borowitz, "Hope Jewish and Hope Secular," in *The Future as the Presence of Shared Hope*, ed. M. Muckenhirn (New York, 1968), p. 107. Rabbi Borowitz read his paper at a religious conference at St. Xavier College in Chicago in June, 1967, right after the Arab-Israeli war.

so unexpectedly, before the Western Wall of the Temple in Jerusalem. Irony of ironies, it is that archaic symbol which, more than anything else, explains to agnostics and liberals, to secularists and the non-observant, who the people of Israel is.[11]

Biblicism and archaism are the trademarks of Jewish settlement in Palestine, in spite of the modernity of Israeli society, industry, and the Israeli military establishment. All segments of Israeli society, and a large number of non-Israeli Jews, have succumbed to biblicism in explaining and justifying Israel. Some extreme Israeli and Jewish thinking, in the category of national atavism, calls for the restoration of the Temple; the adoption of the Mosaic Law in its entirety, including the sacrifice; and the re-establishment of the Aaronic priesthood. Liberals, on the other hand, moved by humanitarian considerations, do recognize that the indigenous inhabitants of the land may have some rights; but these liberals do not relinquish their basic belief in the exclusive historical right of the Jews to the land of Israel as defined in the Bible. Arie Eliav, considered a liberal Zionist because he speaks out for the rights of the Arabs in Israel, remains faithful to the biblical territorial definition of the Jewish state:

> In stating [that the Arabs also have rights], I do not negate or detract one whit from the full historical rights of the Jews to the undivided Land of Israel—that is, the Land of the Twelve Tribes.[12]

Complete disregard for human rights when it comes to the possession of the Holy Land is apparent in Ben Gurion's statement on the subject. The Zionist leader, in a biblical spirit, distinguishes between human rights in general and the specific rights of Zionists in claiming Palestine: "The rights to Palestine do not, as in other countries they do, belong to the existing settlers, whether they be Jews or Arabs. The crux is the Right of Return of Jewry Dispersed."[13] This distinction between Israel and the rest of the world, between the rights of Israel and legal rights in general, is a basic biblical outlook and is bolstered by the belief in the primacy of the Bible over human thinking, and the primacy of the suprarational concepts of the Chosen People and the Promised Land. The promise, the choice, the covenant are sacred, producing

---

11. *Ibid.*, p. 109.

12. Eliav, *The Promised Land*. English summary of the book in *Foreign Policy*, no. 10 (April, 1973), pp. 62–72.

13. Ben Gurion, *Rebirth and Destiny of Israel*, p. 38.

a sacred historical right. Justice and human rights are in the realm of the profane. The conquest of Canaan under Moses and Joshua, the attempt of Ezra and Nehemiah to establish a Jewish state within the Persian Empire, and the Zionist colonization of Palestine all fall into this category of suprarational actions that are above legal and moral considerations. Whether or not Zionists are practicing religious Jews, the biblical attitude toward the state, the land, and the people who should and who should not live on it permeates their thoughts and their actions.

Abba Eban, a modern and moderate Zionist, makes no apology for the conquest of Canaan as related by the Bible.

> The Bible does not represent the Israelite entry into Canaan as a conquest by an alien people. The process is described as the return of a tribe who, in the distant but unforgettable past, had dwelled in the land. The people who now returned had never seen the Promised Land but they had dreamed of it for generations. This home had been vivid in their memory as the only place in which their divine mission could be fulfilled.[14]

While this is a description of something that occurred more than three thousand years ago, Eban is undoubtedly drawing a parallel with the story of modern Israel. The myth is legitimized as the basis of the historical and legal right of European Jews to Palestine. Eban is making the point that Zionist Israel's occupation of Palestine is not a conquest by aliens. He alludes to "the distant but unforgettable past," to the "now returned," to the home "vivid in their memory," and, last but not least, to the "divine mission" that had to be fulfilled.

THE HOLY LAND

On the question of land-ownership, biblical literature is relatively free of controversy. The territorial element of Zionism is the least ambiguous of all the issues that confront Jewish nationalism. While the question of peoplehood (Who is a Jew?) may be open to complex biblical interpretation, and the problem of dealing with the indigenous population may be subject to some moral considerations, the right to the land is so basic that it is hardly contested. *Eretz Israel,* as defined in the Bible, is not an ambiguity.

Although the boundaries of the Promised Land vary throughout

---

14. Eban, *My People,* p. 17.

the Bible, the locality of that land is constant. Whether it is defined as from Dan to Beersheba and from the desert to the sea[15] or, more often, from the Euphrates to the Nile,[16] Jerusalem is the center around which these circles of varying size are drawn.

Territoriality in the Bible is raised above political, economic, and strategic considerations, and becomes a theological imperative. Abba Eban's statement, quoted above, reveals the romantic and religious basis of the conquest of Palestine, the only place in which the divine mission of Israel can be fulfilled.

With the influence of the Bible, Jerusalem has acquired a great importance. Although this holds true for Christians and Muslims, nothing can equal the romantic and mystical attachment that Jews have developed for the city. Political Zionism had no alternative to Jerusalem and Palestine; no other territory proposed had the slightest chance of general acceptance.

The return to the land becomes, in the Bible, the ultimate sign of God's compassion for the Jews, and heralds the coming of the golden age:

> When these things have befallen you, the blessing and the curse . . . if you turn back to Him . . . then the Lord your God will show you compassion and restore your fortune. He will gather you again from all the countries to which he has scattered you. Even though He were to banish you to the four corners of the world, the Lord God will gather you from there, from there he will bring you into the land which your forefathers occupied and you will occupy it again [Deut. 30:1–3].

"God will not come to the heavenly Jerusalem," goes a rabbinical saying, "till Israel has come to the earthly Jerusalem." Without the land, the covenant has no earthly basis, and an important part of the Torah and the Prophets becomes meaningless. Rabbi Wolfe Kelman, chief executive officer of the International Association of Conservative Rabbis, commenting on a proposed Vatican document concerning Judaism, welcomed in particular the document's "recognition of the reality of the State of Israel," its assertion that Jewish fidelity to the old covenant between God and the people of Israel is "linked to the gift of land, which, in the Jewish soul, has endured as the object of aspiration that Christians should strive to understand and respect."[17]

---

15. See Judg. 20:1; 2 Sam. 3:10; 1 Kings 4:25; 2 Chron. 30:5.
16. See, for example, Gen. 15:18; Deut. 1:7; Num. 34:1–16.
17. *Christian Century*, January 24, 1970, p. 39.

In view of this attitude toward the land of Palestine, settlement there becomes an act of piety, of righteousness, of religious fulfillment, an act above legal and humanistic considerations. Rabbi Nissim, chief rabbi of Israel in 1968, made the following statement:

> The Land of Israel was, with its borders, defined for us by Divine Providence. Thou shalt be, says the Almighty, and there it is; no power on earth can alter that which was created by him. In this connection it is not a question of law or logic; neither is it a matter of human treatment or that sort of thing.[18]

According to the Bible, the promise of land to Israel is an irrevocable act of God, not subject to abrogation. Even the sins of the people of Israel do not nullify their claim to the land.

> It is not because of your merit or your integrity that you are entering the land to occupy it; it is because of the wickedness of these nations that the Lord God is driving them out before you and to fulfill the promise which the Lord made to your fathers, Abraham, Isaac and Jacob. Know then that it is not because of any merit of yours that the Lord your God is giving you this rich land to occupy; indeed you are a stubborn people [Deut. 9:5–6].

The Canaanites, the inhabitants of the land, were driven out because of their supposed wickedness. Modern Zionists update this argument to the effect that the Palestinian Arabs have not used the land properly. But no transgression of any kind counts against the "children of the covenant."

Another text makes the land the property of Yahweh, therefore putting a restriction on its sale: "No land shall be sold outright, because the land is mine [says the Lord], and you are coming into it as aliens and settlers" (Lev. 25:23). This text is the basis of the mandate of the Jewish National Fund, which is to purchase, develop, and settle lands as the "inalienable property of the whole Jewish people," with restrictive covenants on the purchases so that Arabs may not buy or rent them.[19] Zionist policy was to acquire land in Palestine and to prohibit its resale. In 1937 Ben Gurion declared: "No Zionist can forgo the smallest portion of the Land of Israel."[20] This spirit guides the

---

18. Reported in the Israeli daily *Hayom*, June 7, 1968.

19. Abraham Granott, *Agrarian Reform and the Record of Israel* (Mystic, Conn., 1956), p. 27. See Constitution of the Jewish Agency, Art. 3 d, in *ibid.*, p. 53.

20. In his speech to the Twentieth Zionist Congress, Zurich, August 15, 1937.

policy of the state of Israel toward the occupied territories. This policy, which adheres closely to the biblical injunction against dispensing with property within the Promised Land or withdrawing from any territory conquered by force of arms within the designated boundaries of *Eretz Israel*, is in conformity with a direct order from Yahweh: "Every place where you set foot is yours. I have given it to you, as I promised Moses" (Josh. 1:3; 14:9).

Given this biblical background, one can see that Israel is not likely to withdraw from Jerusalem or to relinquish the West Bank or the Golan Heights (they both fall within the biblical boundaries of the Promised Land), but that it may reluctantly pull out partially—or even totally, if forced—from Sinai, which is not clearly included in the biblical promise.

The Bible presents many versions of the geographical extent of the Promised Land. The least extensive is "from Dan to Beersheba." This corresponds roughly to the boundaries of Palestine when it was carved from geographical Syria under the British Mandate. However, this definition of the land exists only in the historical books of the Bible; it is never expressed as a goal for the greater Israel as defined by the covenant in the Torah. "From Dan to Beersheba" is, rather, a factual description of the extent of the territory that the Israelite tribes inhabited during the time of the judges.[21]

The Promised Land that is described in Deuteronomy is much more extensive, and it is to be occupied on direct orders from Yahweh:

> The Lord our God spoke to us at Horeb and said, "You have stayed on this mountain long enough; go now, make for the hill country of the Amorites, and pass on to all their neighbors in the Negeb, and on the coast, in short, all Canaan and the Lebanon as far as the great River, the Euphrates. I have laid the land open before you; the land which the Lord swore to give to your forefathers Abraham, Isaac and Jacob, and to their descendants after them" [Deut. 1:6–8].
> Every place where you set the soles of your feet shall be yours. Your borders shall run from the wilderness to the Lebanon and from the River, the River Euphrates, to the Western Sea [Deut. 11:24].

This plan for greater Israel came close to realization during the reign of David and Solomon, according to the biblical books of Samuel, Kings, and Chronicles. The kingdom of David and Solomon thus represents

---

21. See Judg. 20:1; 2 Sam. 3:10, 17:11, 24:2; 1 Kings 4:25; 1 Chron. 21:2; 2 Chron. 30:5. See also maps and text of Aharoni and Avi-Yonah, "The Land that Remains," in *Macmillan Bible Atlas*, 1970, p. 69.

the golden age of Israel as a political entity and is the model and goal of Jewish nationalism. This was true for Ezra and Nehemiah in the sixth and fifth centuries B.C. and is equally true for Zionists in the twentieth century.

Herzl's idea of the geographical extent of the Jewish state was derived from the biblical romance of the Davidic kingdom. It was a fundamentalist Christian Zionist, the Reverend Mr. Hechler, chaplain to the British embassy in Vienna, who gave Herzl the biblical definitions of the boundaries for the prospective state. Herzl writes in his diaries:

> Hechler unfolded his Palestine map in our [train] compartment and instructed me by the hour. The northern frontier is to be the mountains facing Cappadocia, the southern, the Suez Canal. Our slogan shall be: "The Palestine of David and Solomon."[22]

This is a liberal interpretation of the biblical text. It does, however, illustrate the extent to which Zionist expansionism can use biblical material to establish its claims. The Bible, in this case, can accommodate the ambitions of a militarily strong Israel to lay claim to all Syria.

A recent Israeli best-seller, *Eretz Gedolah L'Am Gadol* [A great country to a great people], written by labor leader Zwi Shiloach, contains aspirations for future Israeli expansion and domination which mirror the ancient biblical geopolitical plan:

> A renewed covenant between the nation Israel and the Land of Israel can again become the source of enthusiasm, inspiration and self-sacrifice to the high ideals of Zionism. . . . Zionism always believed in a great Jewish nation and in a great Jewish country. . . . Today the Jewish nation is considered a small nation, and only a part of it finds itself in our Fatherland. But who says that it is ordained for the Jews to be forever a small and poor nation? . . . The Jewish nation is really one of the great nations of the world. . . . Once a real peace treaty is signed in Baghdad, it will put an end to the idea of a United Arab Nation. . . . Egypt will become a true African nation and strictly an African nation, and the Jewish nation, in returning to its homeland, will develop together with the northern Arab nation and the interests of the Middle East.[23]

This kind of talk might have been considered the ranting of a chauvinist if not for its conformity to biblical precedents. The covenant between

---

22. *The Diaries of Theodor Herzl*, ed. Marvin Lowenthal (New York, 1956), p. 124.

23. Quoted in a letter from Moshe Menuhin to *Middle East Perspective*, August, 1973, p. 6.

the people and the land is close to literal biblicism. The territorial ambitions of this text conform to the formula "from the Euphrates to the Nile" and to the slogan of Hechler and Herzl. The expected peace treaty will be signed in Baghdad, which is outside—not in Damascus, which is within—the territorial claims of greater Israel.

THE CURSE OF CANAAN

In comparing Zionist and South African racial policies, Erskine Childers quotes Patrick Keatley: "One cannot help feeling . . . that in their heart of hearts, the white Rhodesians bear a wordless wish . . . that the Africans would disappear."[24] Childers, implying that Zionists have a similar "wordless wish" to see the Palestinians disappear, does not take into consideration the biblical material concerning Israelite settlement in the Land of Canaan. These texts provide that wish with words. Thousands of words express the wish that the Canaanites would disappear, and thousands more recommend their annihilation.

The greatest measure of biblical wrath and fury is directed, not against those who enslaved, captured, or exiled the Jews, but against the inhabitants of the Promised Land, be they Canaanites, Jebusites, Hittites, or any other people. The Bible argues that the presence of the Canaanites in the Promised Land could threaten the political structure of the Chosen People and could possibly undermine the cultural and religious character of Israel. The "holy seed" must have a holy state, uncontaminated by the *goyim*.[25] I. F. Stone recognized this fact and its relevance to the plight of the Palestinian refugees at the hand of the modern Israelis. After the war in 1967, he wrote:

> The Bible is still the best guide to it. Nowhere else can one find a parallel for its ethnocentric fury. Nowhere that I know of is there a word of pity in the Bible for the Canaanites whom the Hebrews slaughtered in taking possession.[26]

The biblical "final solution" to the Canaanite question was complete annihilation. Canaanite civic, cultural, and religious institutions were

---

24. Childers, "The Wordless Wish: From Citizens to Refugees," in *The Transformation of Palestine*, ed. Ibrahim Abu-Lughod (Evanston, Ill., 1971), p. 165.

25. See Ezra 9:1–2. The books of Ezra and Nehemiah are devoted to the problem of *aliyah* and the purity of the race.

26. *New York Review of Books*, June, 1967.

to be condemned and destroyed. The example of the conquest of Jericho, which is described in the Book of Joshua, reveals a cruelty that was to be a recommended policy in dealing with the conquered towns of Canaan: "Everything in it belongs to the Lord, no one is to be spared." The Israelites thus destroyed everything in the city; they put every living thing to the sword, men and women, young and old, and cattle, sheep, and asses (Josh. 6:17, 18, 21). The Torah and the historical books contain scores of examples of such cruelty.

In case total destruction was not possible, total boycott—economic, social, and cultural—was recommended as a religious duty. Joshua's directives to the leaders of Israel on this subject are explicit:

> Be on your guard then, love the Lord your God, for if you do turn away and attach yourselves to the peoples that still remain among you, and intermarry with them and associate with them and they with you, then be sure that the Lord will not continue to drive those people out to make room for you [Josh. 23:11–13].

This text leaves no doubt about the religious nature of the abuse of the Canaanites. Loving the Lord and hating the Canaanites are closely linked. If narrowly interpreted, such biblical texts make racial prejudice almost an article of faith.

The origins of this genocidal policy are to be found in the Torah as direct commands of Yahweh given through Moses. The rationale of such a policy was that the worship of the one true God demanded that no foreign worship be allowed to contaminate it, that the "holy race" in a "holy land" should be free from the "abominations of the Canaanites." Moses, giving his instructions to the Israelites as they were about to enter the Promised Land, says:

> "You must drive out all its inhabitants as you advance. . . . If you do not, . . . any whom you leave in possession will become like a barbed hook in your eye and a thorn in your side. They shall continually dispute your possession of the land, and what I meant to do to them I will do to you." [Num. 33:52, 53].

The most extreme orders to commit genocide are found in Deuteronomy. Moses is instructing the people:

> "When the Lord your God brings you into the land which you are entering to occupy and drives out many natives before you—Hittites, Girgashites, Amorites, Canaanites, Perizzites, Hivvites, and Jebusites, seven nations

more numerous and powerful than you—when the Lord your god delivers them into your power and you defeat them, you must put them to death. You must not make a treaty with them or spare them. You must not intermarry with them, neither giving your daughters to their sons, nor taking their daughters for your sons; if you do, they will draw your sons away from the Lord and make them worship other gods. Then the Lord will be angry with you and will destroy you quickly. But this is what you must do to them: pull down their altars, break their sacred pillars, hack down their sacred poles and destroy their idols by fire, for you are a people holy to the Lord your God; the Lord your God chose you out of all nations on earth to be his special possession [Deut. 7:1–6].

The laws of modern Israel regarding marriage and economic, political, and social contact with the Arabs of Palestine reflect the bias of this text. It is difficult to argue that this modern policy was not directly inspired by the biblical example.

The laws of war that the Book of Deuteronomy prescribes are most savage. They fall into two categories: treatment of conquered cities outside the boundaries of the Promised Land, and treatment of conquered cities within the boundaries. The laws in the first category prescribe extreme cruelty; those in the second, total destruction (Deut. 20). These rules for conduct in conquest are reflected in the Deir Yassin massacre (April, 1948), as well as in many other incidents of cruelty exhibited, sometimes proudly, by Zionist armed gangs.

In the cities of the nations whose land the Lord your God is giving you as patrimony, you shall not leave any creature alive. You shall annihilate them—Hittites, Amorites, Canaanites, Perizzites, Hivvites, Jebusites—as the Lord your God commanded you, so that they may not teach you to imitate all the abominable things that they have done for their gods and so cause you to sin against the Lord your God [Deut. 20:16–18].

According to this text, the extermination of the Canaanites is a condition for the establishment of the commonwealth of Israel. It is ironic to note that the Nazis, in their attempt to exterminate the Jews and other "undesirable" elements in Germany, felt a sense of dedication to the realization of the Third Reich. Would not the great task of establishing the Third Jewish Commonwealth evoke such dedication in the dispossession and extermination of the Palestinians?

Any right of ownership, real or potential, that might conflict with this racially exclusive philosophy is suspect. The Book of Joshua tells of the Gibeonites, who wanted to make a treaty with the Israelites;

they said, as they presented their case, that they came from a distant land, not from within the boundaries claimed by the Hebrews. Joshua replied: "But maybe you live in our neighborhood; if so, how can we grant you a treaty?" (Josh. 9:7).

If the fact that the land had been cultivated and built up by others affected the claim at all, it was to make it more attractive.

> The lord your God will bring you into the land which he swore to your forefathers Abraham, Isaac and Jacob that he would give you, a land of great and fine cities which you did not build, houses full of good things which you did not provide, rock-hewn cisterns which you did not hew, and vineyards and olive trees which you did not plant [Deut. 6: 10].

These words must soothe the consciences of those who are exploiting stolen and confiscated property in Israel today. The report of the U.N. Conciliation Commission for Palestine estimates that in 1953 more than 30 per cent of the total area of Israel, and more than two-thirds of the cultivable land in Israel, belonged to Arab refugees who were prevented from returning home. One-third of Israel's Jewish population, according to the report, was then living on property belonging to absentee Arabs. Nearly all the olive groves, half the citrus groves, and ten thousand shops, businesses, and stores in Israel belonged to absentee Arab refugees.[27]

The totally uncompromising attitude toward the Canaanites finds a mythical origin in the Book of Genesis. The story goes that Canaan, father of the Canaanites, received an eternal curse upon him and his descendants because his father, Ham, had seen his own father, Noah, naked and drunk and had made fun of him. Noah, after sobering up, delivered a curse and a blessing: "'Cursed by Canaan, slave of slaves shall he be to his brothers' and he continued: 'Bless, O Lord, the tents of Shem; may Canaan be his slave.'" The legend sets the stage for the conquest of Canaan by the descendants of Shem, the Israelites. Ham, the one who had sinned, was not cursed because, as rabbinical interpretations explain, he had already received the blessing of God bestowed on the family of Noah.

The traditions of ancient Israel and the rabbinical literature elaborate on the theme of the Canaanite curse. From the apocryphal Book of

---

27. United Nations, General Assembly, *Progress Report of the Conciliation Commission for Palestine*. For a full discussion of land alienation, see John Ruedy, "Dynamics of Land Alienation," in *Transformation of Palestine*, ed. Abu-Lughod, pp. 119–38; for a discussion of the UNCCP report, see p. 135.

Daniel and Susanna, we learn that it was a great insult to a Jew to be called "spawn of Canaan, no son of Judah." The word *Canaanite* came to mean, to the Israelites and the Jews, a scheming merchant, a liar, a cheat, and a swindler—a meaning similar to the one that Christian Europe attributed to the word *Jew*.

Just as the sins of Israel would not cancel the covenant between the Israelites and the Lord, so also the good deeds of the Canaanites could not redeem them from the curse. "Many of the sons of Canaan were worthy of being ordained as rabbis; but the guilt of their father barred them from such a career."[28] Another talmudic text explains the philosophy behind the dispossession of the Canaanites.

> Canaan exemplified to his sons the life worthy of slaves. When Noah divided the earth among his sons, Palestine fell to the lot of Shem. Canaan, however, took possession of it, notwithstanding the fact that his father and his children called his attention to the wrong he had committed. They therefore said to him: "Thou art cursed, and cursed will thou remain before all the sons of Noah, in accordance with the oath which we took before the Holy Judge and our father Noah."[29]

But the Canaanites remained on the land and flourished. The kingdoms of Israel and Judah were influenced greatly by Canaanite culture and religion, which was passionately denounced by the Yahwist prophets. The demise of the kingdom of Israel (traditionally believed to contain ten of the twelve tribes of Israel) left the kingdom of Judah facing a crisis of extinction. To this period of crisis, culminating in the "Babylonian captivity," and to the attempts to "return" under Ezra and Nehemiah, is attributed the extreme chauvinistc and genocidal tendencies found in the biblical books, especially in Deuteronomy. At that point in history, the Jews (of the tribe of Judah) claimed to inherit the blessing and the patrimony of all the Israelite tribes.

The mission of Ezra and Nehemiah, in addition to rebuilding the Temple, was to make sure that the "holy race" was not contaminated by the abominations of the Canaanites. The "returning" Jews refused the help offered them by some of their neighbors. "Let us join you in building," they pleaded, "for like you we seek your God, and we have been sacrificing to Him even since the days of Esarhaddon king of Assyria who brought us here" (Ezra 4:1–2). As for the Amorites and the Arabs, the book of Nehemiah states that they were told: "You

---

28. *Yoma* 87 a, quoted in *Jewish Encyclopedia*, s.v. "Canaan."
29. *Jubilee* x, quoted in *ibid*.

have no stake, or claim, or traditional right in Jerusalem" (Neh. 2: 20).

The wrath of Ezra extended the curse of Canaan to

> the people of Israel, including priests and Levites [who] have not kept themselves apart from the foreign population and from the abominable practices of the Canaanites, the Hittites, the Perizzites, the Jebusites, the Amorites, the Egyptians . . . [who] have taken women of these nations as wives for themselves and their sons, so that the holy race has become mixed with the foreign population [Ezra 9:1, 2].

He deplored this practice because it made the Holy Land unclean.

> [It] is a polluted land, polluted by the foreign population with their abominable practices, which have made it unclean from end to end. Therefore, do not give your daughters in marriage to their sons, and do not marry your sons to their daughters, and never seek their welfare or prosperity [Ezra 9:11-12].

According to Ezra, the condition for accepting these erring Jews into the fellowship of the "holy race" was to "dismiss those women and their brood, for in this there will still be hope for Israel" [Ezra 10: 2, 3]. Nehemiah, in turn, sought to renew the covenant for the "returning" Jews by inviting them to take an oath of renewal. The first article of that oath was to maintain the purity of the race by strict adherence to the ban on intermarriage (Neh. 10:30).

By promoting and executing plans for the third *aliyah* to establish the Third Jewish Commonwealth, Zionism has established itself firmly in the biblical tradition of Deuteronomy, Ezra, and Nehemiah. It has acquired unilaterally the right of ownership to Palestine—an absolute right, not subject to history, law, or humanitarianism. It has adopted wholly the biblical blessing and the biblical curse: the blessing reserved for the "holy race," the Chosen People; and the curse placed on the indigenous *goyim*, be they Canaanites or Palestinians.

Stephen Halbrook

THE PHILOSOPHY OF ZIONISM: A MATERIALIST INTERPRETATION

THE IDEALIST INTERPRETATION of Zionist philosophy appears to explain the creation of the Israeli state in terms of a two-thousand-year-old spirit among Jews of the Diaspora which caused them to long for a return to Zion, or the Holy Land. Such an outlook is based on a religious ontology. It would seem more in keeping with modern scientific methodology to analyze Zionism as a set of ideas bound to the concrete social situation in which they emerged.[1] The early Zionist, Moses Hess, was in accord with Marx, Mannheim, and others who have treated the sociology of knowledge (or, more precisely, of ideas) according to the epistemological thesis that ideas constitute a superstructure over—and, in the final analysis, are derivatives of—material bases. The critical analysis made by a dialectical materialist eschews a mechanical economic determinism, contending more broadly that the relation of individuals to the means of production and the form of their participation

---

1. "Zionism" refers here to the political Zionism of Theodor Herzl as it appears, for example, in the Biltmore Program of 1942. That program demanded a majority Jewish state in Palestine and the expulsion of the majority Arab population from its own national area, a process the program praised as having already "written a notable page in the history of colonization" (Walter Laqueur, ed., *The Israeli-Arab Reader* [New York: Bantam, 1970], p. 78). This usage excludes the cultural Zionism of the humanists Buber and Magnes, the poets Bialik and Tchernihorsky, and others whose Jewish philosophies opposed or were unrelated to the statist, racist, and colonialist features embodied in political Zionism.

in socioeconomic structures shape their beliefs and attitudes and lead to the formation of their class *Weltanschauung*—in short, that ideologies are expressions of latent or manifest functional class interests interacting dialectically in the struggle between classes.[2] The ideology of Zionism lends itself particularly well to materialist analyses because Theodor Herzl, Zionism's leading philosopher and early organizer, defined rather explicitly the social, political and economic benefits which would accrue to a variety of classes in the process of Zionist colonization and statization of Palestine.

Defined primarily in terms of production, and with reference to technological development, the classes and worlds which Hess, Herzl, and later Zionist philosophers anticipated would gain most radically by the creation of a Jewish state in Arab Palestine might be categorized thus: in the developed capitalist world (First World), the European imperialist bourgeoisie, the European-Russian ruling classes, and the Zionist economic elite; and in the underdeveloped world (Third World), the Arab absentee landlords, the Israeli settler bourgeoisie, and the settler-workers' aristocracy.

THE DEVELOPED CAPITALIST WORLD (FIRST WORLD)

The European Imperialist Bourgeoisie
The essence of Zionism was created before the birth of Herzl by

---

2. A materialist analysis of the Jewish question is provided in Abram Leon, *The Jewish Question: A Marxist Interpretation* (New York: Pathfinder Press, 1970), which touches on Zionism only briefly. The methodology employed below might be broadly defined as "Marxist"; however, the term might be confusing for the reason that Marx and Engels retained a Hegelian, European-oriented outlook similar to that of Hess, viewing Western conquests in the Arab world (as in the Afro-Asian worlds in general) as progressive and civilizing. In modern times negative critiques of the imperialist, racist, and bourgeois elements of Zionism seem to be represented by their authors as distinctly Marxist, whereas these critiques might be more accurately depicted as Bakuninist, Leninist, or Fanonist. Primary and secondary material on this question is available in Shlomo Avineri, ed., *Karl Marx on Colonialism and Modernization* (Garden City, N.J.: Doubleday, 1968); Avineri, "Modernization and Arab Society," in *Israel, the Arabs and the Middle East,* ed. Irving Howe and Carl Gershman (New York: Bantam, 1972); Stephen P. Halbrook, "The Marx-Bakunin Controversy" (Ph.D. diss., Florida State University, 1972); and Halbrook, "Lenin's Bakuninism," *International Review of History and Political Science,* VIII (February, 1971), 88–111. On the other hand, Marx's characterization of religion's function as an opiate by which the ruling class lulls the masses into submission, as well as his approach to the Jewish question, suggests that the religious, antiassimilationist, and antisocialist aspects of Zionism are in contradiction to Marxism. Se Karl Marx, *Early Writings,* ed. T. B. Bottomore (New York: McGraw Hill, 1963), pp. 1–40.

non-Jewish European colonialists who held that Jewish colonization of Palestine would offer to the European empires a loyal outpost to guard the routes to the East and to suppress Arab nationalism, and that the new colony would provide Europe with raw materials and markets. Ernest Laharanne, the private secretary of Napoleon III during the period of growing French intervention in Syria, promised in 1860 that all Europe would support Jewish acquisition of Palestine from Turkey: "European industry has daily to search for new markets as an outlet for its products. . . . The time has arrived when it is imperative to call the ancient nations back to life, so as to open new highways and byways for European civilization."[3] Moses Hess recommended this and other arguments by European colonialists, concluding:

> After the work on the Suez Canal is completed, the interests of world commerce will undoubtedly demand the establishment of depots and settlements along the road to India and China, settlements of such a character as will transform the neglected and anarchic states of the countries lying along this road into legal and cultivated States. This can occur only under the military protection of the European powers.
>
> [To the Jews:] A great calling is reserved for you: to be a living channel of communication to the primitive people of Asia. . . . You should be the mediators between Europe and far Asia, open the roads that lead to India and China—those unknown regions which must ultimately be thrown open to civilization.[4]

The material advantages that the Jewish colonization of Palestine would provide the European imperialist bourgeoisie were sufficiently apparent that Herzl, without being aware of Hess's work, made a similar argument in his classic *Der Judenstaat* (1896):

> If His Majesty the Sultan were to give us Palestine, we could in return undertake the complete management of the finances of Turkey. We should there form a part of a wall of defense for Europe in Asia, an outpost of civilization against barbarism. We should as a neutral state remain in contact with all Europe, which would have to guarantee our existence.[5]

---

3. Laharanne, *The New Eastern Question* (1860), quoted in Moses Hess, *Rome and Jerusalem* (1918; reprint ed., New York: Bloch, 1945), pp. 135–36. For earlier plans for Jewish colonization of Palestine, see Lotta Levensohn, *Outline of Zionist History* (New York: Scopus, 1941), pp. 56–62; Uri Avnery, *Israel without Zionists* (London: Macmillan, 1968), pp. 56–57; William Polk et al., *Backdrop to Tragedy* (Boston: Beacon, 1957), pp. 136–37.

4. Hess, *Rome and Jerusalem*, pp. 227–29, 139.

5. Quoted in Ludwig Lewisohn, ed., *Theodor Herzl* (Cleveland; World, 1955), pp. 254–55.

Herzl also contended:

> The [European] states would have a further benefit in the enormous increase of their export trade; for since the emigrant Jews "over there" would for a long time to come be dependent on European products, they would necessarily have to import them.[6]

Later, in his appeals to German empire-builders for aid, Herzl added that realization of Zionism would result in the profitable export to the colony of investment capital.

> The Grand Duke mentioned the demoralization which . . . existed among the Russian Jews who had emigrated to London.
> I said: "In order to govern them, we need a strong authority. This is precisely why it is indispensable that at the outset we obtain recognition from the Great Powers. . . .
> I then explained how only the *trop plein* [surplus] were to be drained off; how, too, fluid capital cannot be considered as tied to any particular country; and how, after this solution of the Jewish problem, it would stream back. [*Lowenthal notes:* Herzl's thought seems to be that an orderly withdrawal of Jewish capital from Europe would offer inducements for other capital, then invested abroad, to return home.] At present such capital was creating trouble for the home industry by financing cheap labor in remote lands. There was no need for it to bring the Chinese to Europe. Factories, simply, were built for them in China. Thus, agriculture having been imperilled by America, industry is being threatened by the Far East.
> To offset this situation, my movement can help on two fronts: through draining off the surplus Jewish proletariat, and through harnessing international capital.[7]

After the turn of the century Herzl turned to British imperial interests for aid in promoting Jewish colonization of Palestine. In 1902 he solicited the help of Cecil Rhodes, who, by participating in this new colonial

---

6. *Ibid.*, p. 298.
7. Herzl, *The Diaries of Theodor Herzl*, ed. Marvin Lowenthal (New York: Grosset & Dunlap, 1962), p. 120. Initially Herzl placed his hopes in Bismarck and the German imperialists to secure a chartered land company under a German protectorate, promising that a Jewish state would protect the proposed Berlin-Baghdad railroad, provide a new overland route to Asia via a railway connecting the Mediterranean to the Persian Gulf, and extend German influence in the Middle East (*ibid.*, p. 122).

enterprise, would "have the satisfaction of making a good profit."[8] To Lord Rothschild, Herzl wrote: "You may claim high credit from your government if you strengthen British influences in the Near East by a substantial colonization of our people at the strategic point where Egyptian and Indo-Persian interests converge."[9] And of Colonial Minister Joseph Chamberlain, Herzl recalled: "He liked the Zionist idea. If I could show him a spot among the British possessions which was not yet inhabited by white settlers, then we could talk."[10] Following the strategy of the Jameson raid in South Africa, the two projected the colonization of Cyprus, El Arish, and Sinai as bases for the conquest of Palestine, which would be ruled by the white Jewish minority until the Arabs could be expelled.

While Palestine remained the ultimate goal, Herzl considered the colonization of European and Russian Jews in other nonwhite territories, appealing to Britain for Uganda, to Portugal for Mozambique, to Belgium for the Congo, and to Italy for Tripoli. In sum, Zionism was seen to be in the interests of the European imperialist bourgeoisie, including both its non-Jewish and its Jewish members. Finance capital would profit from the export of investment funds; industrial capital would conquer new markets, natural resources, and cheap labor; and merchant capital would win new commercial routes on land and sea, all protected by the white Jewish settlers and the empire militaries.

The European-Russian Ruling Classes

Claiming that Zionism solved the social question simultaneously with the Jewish question,[11] Herzl clarified that his approach to class struggle in the First World was based on the European bourgeois colonial *Weltanschauung* prevalent in the last two centuries. Cecil Rhodes had argued that social revolution in Europe could be nipped in the bud by encouraging the rebellious poor to become colonists. As privileged white settlers, they might well support imperialist counterrevolution if they were living in Asia or Africa. Herzl assumed that this method of repressing class war in Europe and Russia (which was to become the Second World) was particularly suited to exploited Jews. Oppressed as Jews by anti-Semitism and as workers (if they were employed) by

---

8. Herzl, *The Complete Diaries of Theodor Herzl*, ed. Raphael Patai (New York: Herzl Press, 1960), p. 88.

9. *Diaries*, ed. Lowenthal, p. 371. Edmond de Rothschild, a financial backer of Rhodes's African expeditions and diamond-mining concerns, financed the British government's purchase of Suez Canal shares.

10. *Ibid.*, p. 377.

11. *Ibid.*, p. 45.

monopoly capitalism, yet urbanized and educated, this group provided actual or potential support for popular revolution. But they could be diverted from such activity by their emigration or deportation to distant lands like Palestine, Argentina, and Uganda. That Zionism was an ideology to prevent Jewish participation in revolution, and not a revolutionary solution to the Jewish question, is further suggested by its dependence on anti-Semitism, which diverted Jews from class struggle in alliance with the non-Jewish oppressed to a war based on a false consciousness generated by (both Christian and Jewish) religious myths and fictitious racial differences, the effect of which was to perpetuate and enhance the power of the non-Jewish as well as the Jewish European and Russian ruling classes.

Despite his agreement with the anti-Semites that all Jews (exploiters and exploited alike) were one people, Herzl did not ignore the class struggle within Jewry. He claimed that rich Jews, unlike poor Jews, "experience nothing of anti-Semitism, although they are actually and mainly responsible for it." Nonetheless, Herzl began to pardon anti-Semitism, which "will do the Jews no harm. I hold it to be a movement useful for the development of Jewish character."[12] Partly a product of anti-Semitism, Zionism, in turn, encouraged and cooperated with anti-Semitism.[13] Zionism was the "final solution" for the lower-income Jews who played leading roles in the revolutionary underground in Russia or who emigrated to Germany, Britain, and the United States, where they became slum-dwellers, continued their militant traditions, and produced world-renowned revolutionaries who advocated unity with the non-Jewish oppressed for the overthrow of tsarism, European reaction, and the non-Jewish and Jewish bourgeoisie (e.g., the anarchists Aaron Lieberman and Emma Goldman). In both East and West the Jewish proletariat opposed Zionism as a bourgeois, counterrevolutionary ideology.[14]

12. *Ibid.*, pp. 5, 6, 10.

13. Herzl derived his ideas on Jews from anti-Semitics, originally treating the Jewish question after perusing Dühring's anti-Semitic work, and later anti-Semitics (e.g., Eichmann) derived their ideas on Jews from Herzl. For Herzl's views on anti-Semitics, see *ibid.*, pp. 27, 34, 89, 91, 101–2, 103, 436, 451; see also Hannah Arendt, *Eichmann in Jerusalem* (New York: Viking, 1963); Meyer Barkai, ed., *The Fighting Ghettos* (New York: Tower, 1962), pp. 19–31.

14. For an overview of Jewish revolutionary and anti-Zionist agitation in Britain around the turn of the century, see Rudolph Rocker, *The London Years* (London: Robert Anscombe, 1956). See also Louis Greenberg, *The Jews in Russia* (New Haven: Yale University Press, 1944), Vol. I, chaps. 11, 12, 13; Isaac Deutscher, *The Non-Jewish Jew* (London: Oxford University Press, 1968), pp. 61, 66–67; Arie Bober, ed., *The Other Israel: The Radical Case against Zionism* (Garden City, N.J.: Doubleday, 1972), pp. 152–53.

From its beginnings in Herzl's vision, Zionism rested on an alliance with anti-Semites to drain off the "surplus" population of poor and radical Jews and thereby preserve the status quo; this "final solution" was meant for lower-income Jews, not for upper-income Jews, who would remain in the First World and who (along with upper-income non-Jews) would experience economic improvement. Herzl went so far as to agree with tsarist pogrom-organizers to repress information on the massacre of Jews at Kishinev in exchange for tsarist aid to Zionism, which would check (revolutionary) Jewish nationalism and drain the revolutionary parties of the Jewish personnel who would emigrate to Palestine.[15] The self-avowed counterrevolutionary character of Zionism was expressed in its refusal to support oppressed Jews in an attack on their anti-Semitic oppressors, which might have destroyed the existing socioeconomic and political structures of Europe and Russia, and, following World War I, in its struggle to overthrow revolutionary Russia in league with the anti-Semitic tsarists and the world imperialist powers.

The Zionist Economic Elite

A third class in the First World which constituted a major ideological source of Zionism might be designated as the Zionist economic elite and defined as the Jewish big bourgeoisie which supported and profited from a colony of poor Jews in the Third World. Plagued by a real or imagined conspicuousness as Jews, the members of this class saw the alleged anti-Semitism generated by Eastern European Jews who emigrated to Germany, England, and other Western countries, and who became competitors in the labor market with non-Jewish proletarians, as a detriment to the complete assimilation of the Jewish elite into the European ruling classes. Zionism was doubly a boon to this elite, for not only would its members be assimilated, but they would also derive material gains from the role they would play as Jewish capitalists in exploiting the labor, natural resources, and investment potential of a Jewish colonial state. Recognizing all Jews as *one people,* these most farsighted of the Jewish finance capitalists and entrepreneurs found Zionism to be an ideology to promote class collaboration, that is, to convince oppressed Jews that their interests lay, not in alliance with oppressed non-Jews, but in alliance with wealthy Jews. Nonetheless, the fact that class struggle existed among Jews in the same qualitative fashion as among members of any other group (whether Arab, European, or Gentile) was indicated by the revolts of the Jewish proletarian settlers

15. Herzl, *Diaries,* ed. Lowenthal, pp. 390–91, 395, 399, 403, 412–13.

against the economic monopoly of the Rothschild interests.

The finance capitalists Baron Maurice de Hirsch and Edmond de Rothschild promoted Jewish colonization in Argentina and Palestine respectively, and Herzl's initial and most persistent pleas for support for a Zionist state were addressed to and centered around these millionaires. The first draft of Herzl's *Der Judenstaat* was entitled *Address to the Rothschilds* and was meant for the private use of this family of banking magnates;[16] and Herzl reiterated that Hirsch or Rothschild must assume the highest position of leadership within the Zionist movement.[17] That Zionism was a classic European colonial (not specifically Jewish) solution to the Jewish question was indicated by Herzl's immediate goal: "The Jewish Company is conceived partly on the model of the great land-development companies . . . [and] will be set up as a joint-stock company, incorporated in England, under British laws and protection."[18] Zionist colonization would be an economic boon to the Jewish big bourgeoisie, which would remain in Europe. "The great financiers, moreover, will certainly not be asked to raise an amount so enormous out of purely philanthropic motives; that would be expecting too much. Rather may the promoters and stockholders of the Jewish Company look forward to considerable profit. . . . One million would produce fifteen millions; and one billion, fifteen billions."[19] In Herzl's conception, the Jewish big bourgeoisie in the First World would play the paramount role in organizing the economy of the colony.[20] Altruistic motives influenced the Jewish elite no more and no less than non-Jewish elites in their acts of colonization; and, as Rothschild remained from 1882 until his death, in 1934, the greatest single benefactor of the Zionist work in Palestine,[21] it may be assumed that one function of Zionism was to promote the material and ideological interests of the Rothschilds against those of the Jewish proletarian settlers and, above all, against those of the Arab peasantry. Rothschild maintained absolute control over the farms and agricultural produce of the Jewish settlers, who often revolted against his autocratic administration, charging him with "seeking to enslave the colonists and to extort profits for himself."[22] "Without me, Zionism wouldn't have succeeded,"

---

16. *Ibid.*, pp. 29 ff.
17. *Ibid.*, pp. 16, 24, 39, 181.
18. Quoted in Lewisohn, ed., *Theodor Herzl*, p. 256.
19. *Ibid.*, pp. 274, 284.
20. *Ibid.*, pp. 252, 258; Herzl, *Diaries*, ed. Lowenthal, p. 95.
21. Arthur Hertzberg, ed., *The Zionist Idea* (New York: Atheneum, 1969), pp. 401–3.
22. David Druck, *Baron Edmond Rothschild* (New York: Hebrew Monotype Press, 1928),

said Edmond de Rothschild, "but without Zionism my work would have been struck to death."[23] The class antagonisms upon which Zionism was based were further exemplified in the fact that the Balfour Declaration of 1917 was addressed to Lord Lionel Rothschild, head of the English finance family, which by then was the most powerful of all the branches of the House of Rothschild.[24]

THE UNDERDEVELOPED WORLD (THIRD WORLD)

The Arab Absentee Landlords

From its beginnings, Zionism was based on a principled alliance with Turk and Arab forces of reaction. In exchange for the land of Palestine as a Jewish colony, Herzl promised the Turkish imperialists (the earlier colonizers of Palestine) that the Jews would loyally defend the status quo against Arab revolutionary nationalism.[25] In addition to this political alliance, there was an economic alliance between the Zionist land-purchasers and -grabbers, and the absentee landlords in Turkey and Syria, who exploited the Palestinian and Syrian *fellahin* and who sold the land to the incoming settlers. Crushed by taxes, rents, and evictions, the Arab tenants who had worked the land migrated to the cities, where the Histadrut prevented them from working in the predominantly Jewish-owned commerce and industry.

The Israeli Settler Bourgeoisie

By the turn of the century it became clear that with the rise of state monopoly capitalism in Europe and Russia, the middle and petty bourgeois classes were being increasingly threatened. Borochov warned of the growing proletarianization of "the Jewish middle and petty bourgeoisie, with no territory and no market of its own. . . . Lacking any means of support in their struggle for a market, they tend to

---

pp. 20, 178–79; Barnet Litvinoff, *To the House of Their Fathers* (New York: Praeger, 1965), p. 120.

23. Quoted in Frederic Morton, *The Rothschilds* (New York: Atheneum 1962), p. 205.

24. E. C. Corti, *The Reign of the House of Rothschild* (New York: Cosmopolitan Book Corp., 1928), II, 414.

25. See Herzl, *Diaries*, ed. Lowenthal, pp. 159–60, 164, 176, 464. See also Hannah Arendt, "Zionism Reconsidered," in *Zionism Reconsidered*, ed. Michael Selzer (New York: Macmillan, 1970), p. 236; Avnery, *Israel without Zionists*, p. 51.

speak of an independent political existence of a Jewish state where they would play a leading political role."²⁶ Just as the non-Jewish and Jewish imperialist big bourgeoisie needed a new foreign market, the Jewish middle bourgeoisie needed its own domestic market, a national area where its domination could be established over vast labor resources (the Eastern Jews), raw materials, and commodity market outlets. Herzl argued that the capital of wealthy Jews would be rehabilitated in a new colony, for

> the establishment of industries will be promoted by a judicious system of duties, by the supply of cheap raw material, and by the creation of a bureau to collect and publish industrial statistics. . . . Industrialists will be able to apply to centralized labor agencies. . . . Parties of workmen will thus be systematically drafted from place to place like a body of troops.²⁷

In later years, after the establishment of the Israeli state, emphasis was also placed on exploiting the natural resources and agriculture of the Arab economies, which would provide a market for manufactured commodities from Israel.²⁸

The Settler-Workers' Aristocracy

The last and least class that Zionism would benefit was the settler working class, which would escape the competition from non-Jewish labor in Europe and Russia and would form a workers' aristocracy in Palestine. As Jews in a Jewish state, members of this class could suppress competition from Arab labor by racist unions and by intimidation and terror. Class collaboration was to apply only among the settlers; like the white workers of South Africa, the Jewish workers would be granted privileges to make them loyal to the settler bourgeoisie. Zionism was based on a class alliance whereby each class in the socioeconomic pyramid would tolerate its own exploitation by the class above as long as it could, in turn, exploit the class below. Herzl clarified this: "Those who are now desperate will go first, after them the poor, next the

---

26. "Our Platform" (1906), in *Zionist Idea*, ed. Hertzberg, pp. 361–63.
27. Quoted in Lewisohn, ed., *Theodor Herzl*, p. 272. See also *ibid.*, pp. 264–68.
28. "What we aspire to . . . is far more akin to the relationship between the United States and the Latin American continent" (Abba Eban, *The Voice of Israel* [New York, 1957], p. 63).

well-to-do, and last of all the wealthy."[29] Zionist colonization was to be carried out by Jewish workers, who would have no use for Arab workers unless there were swamps to be drained, swamps infested with poisonous snakes as well as the mosquitoes that transmit malaria.[30] Thus the colonized class, which has been described as the "Jews of the Jews," was the Arab *fellahin* (and the Oriental Jews, as it is becoming increasingly clear in a state dominated by an Occidental Jewish elite); and material privileges and racist ideology have insured that each time the Arab masses have rebelled—in 1920–21, 1929, 1933, 1935–39, 1948, and more recent times—the Zionist workers' aristocracy has sided with colonialism against national self-determination. While the Jewish working class in Palestine and Israel has derived manifest short-run gains, it may be that their long-run interests would have been better served had they remained in the First World and overthrown their exploiters rather than serve the non-Jewish and Jewish imperialists and colonialists, whose ideologists stressed the religious and racist aspects of Zionism in order to exploit the prejudices of oppressed and uneducated Eastern Jews.

While material rewards among sectors of Israeli society have been derived from the exploitation, expulsion, and genocide of the Palestinian Arab majority, the inevitable guerrilla revolutionary response of the *fedayeen*, provoked by Zionist colonization and statization, has, by its outbursts of insurrection, its commando campaigns, and its terrorist activities, lowered the quality of life among Israeli settlers, who pay dearly for their expansion and terrorism. Since all classes (even the bourgeois class) of the Israeli settler society live in a warfare, garrison state, with all the human and material costs that aggressive militarism entails, it might well be that in the final analysis the principal beneficiaries of Zionist theory and practice are not the Israeli settlers but the non-Jewish and Jewish elite classes in the First World.

---

29. Quoted in Lewisohn, ed., *Theodor Herzl*, p. 244. See also *ibid.*, pp. 252–53.

30. See Jessie Sampter, ed., *Modern Palestine* (New York: Hadassah, 1933), p. 109; Herzl, *Diaries*, ed. Lowenthal, p. 280.

William Minter

THE IDEOLOGICAL FOUNDATIONS OF SETTLER REGIMES: THE PORTUGUESE IN AFRICA

ANY OPPRESSIVE SOCIAL ORDER is normally surrounded by an ideological smoke screen which, in describing and justifying that order, both reveals and obscures its contours. Ideology thus has a dual relationship to the social reality on which it is based—on the one hand revealing the perceptions of that reality as they are expressed by the defenders of the social order, who wish to justify their position to others, and on the other hand concealing and distorting that same reality in order to make it more acceptable. The analysis of a particular ideology, then, involves as well an analysis of the reality on which it is based, the social order it is intended to defend. This paper presents a brief sketch of Portuguese colonial rule in Africa and then examines several themes of the Portuguese colonial ideology as it is currently expressed, in an effort to discover what these themes reveal and what they conceal about this system of colonial domination.

The Portuguese colonial empire in Africa consists of two small territories—Guinea (Bissau) and the Cape Verde Islands, and the islands of São Tomé and Príncipe—and two much larger ones, Angola and Mozambique. Guinea (Bissau) and Cape Verde have together a population of approximately one million; São Tomé and Príncipe, a population of about one hundred thousand. The population of Angola is almost six million, and that of Mozambique over eight million. The combined population of Angola and Mozambique considerably exceeds the estimated population of Portugal itself, which is about nine million. This empire is ruled by the Portuguese government in Lisbon, under a regime which came to power in 1928 and which has maintained a fascistlike dictatorship over Portugal for more than forty years. The Portuguese constitution terms the "overseas territories" part of the national territory of Portugal itself and denies their right to any existence as separate countries. Although under recent constitutional changes the "states" of Angola and Mozambique have "legislative assemblies" elected, in part, by local voters, effective power remains in the hands of the colonial administration, which is under the authority of the overseas minister in Lisbon.

In Angola and Mozambique the upper strata of the population consist of European settlers (almost entirely of Portuguese origin), estimated at 400,000 in Angola (7 per cent of the population) and 200,000 in Mozambique (3 per cent of the population). Although a Portuguese presence along the coast of Angola and Mozambique stems from the original Portuguese voyages of almost five hundred years ago, settlement in such large numbers is very recent. Portuguese authority over the territories of Angola and Mozambique was not solidified until early in this century, and even as late as 1940, Portuguese settlers numbered only 44,000 in Angola and 27,500 in Mozambique. The settler population is concentrated in the cities and towns, constituting one-third of the population of the Angolan capital, Luanda, for example.

Most of the Africans in each country live in the rural areas, where they cultivate the traditional crops of a subsistence economy and also produce some goods for sale, the marketing of which is controlled by Portuguese firms and government agencies. The Africans also supply the labor for the Portuguese-owned plantations (and for those owned by companies from Western Europe and the United States as well) and for the mines (in which Portuguese capital is secondary to European, American, and South African capital). A smaller number of Africans hold jobs in light manufacturing or service industries, in the lower levels of the colonial administration, or in other urban firms, but the best jobs are, as a rule, occupied by Portuguese settlers. In Mozambique, more than 100,000 African men, under an arrangement between the Portuguese and South African governments, go to South Africa each year to work in the mines at wages which, as low as they are, exceed what they could earn at home.

In Angola, in Mozambique, and in Guinea (Bissau), Portuguese rule is challenged by African liberation movements which control certain areas, and by guerrilla fighting which is spreading in each country. In Guinea (Bissau) the forces of the African Party for the Independence of Guinea and Cape Verde (PAIGC) have occupied almost the entire territory, have recently acquired a significant antiaircraft capability, and are preparing to declare themselves an independent state. In Mozambique the guerrillas of the Mozambique Liberation Front (FRELIMO) have recently penetrated as far south as the central and strategic province of Manica and Sofala, and FRELIMO-liberated areas farther to the north are firmly established. In Angola the Popular Movement for the Liberation of Angola (MPLA) has sustained a guerrilla struggle for over a decade, in the face of very serious obstacles, and has established large liberated areas in eastern Angola. Portuguese counterinsurgency strategy has included the standard approaches used by the United States in Indochina, such as regrouping the population in "strategic hamlets" and establishing "free-fire zones" for indiscriminate bombing and raids by ground troops. This strategy has also included, and dramatically so in recent years, the attempt to Africanize the military at the lower levels and to incorporate a limited number of Africans into token positions of authority within the colonial order.

In the course of the wars that Portugal has fought in resisting African independence, another feature of that country's colonial rule has become clear—namely, its dependence on the economic and military support of other, more developed, capitalist countries, a pattern of support in which Portugal serves as junior partner. Portugal benefits from the military aid that it receives from other countries in NATO (above all, France, West Germany, Britain, and the United States). Meanwhile, the expanding strategic sectors of the economies of Angola and Mozambique are fueled by capital from those same countries. South Africa, also, is expanding its close economic links with the Portuguese territories, particularly with Mozambique, and has expanded military cooperation to include the posting of South African soldiers to aid the Portuguese army in Angola and Mozambique.

This, then, in very summary terms, is the social reality to which the following ideological themes relate.[1] The themes to be discussed are derived primarily from the recent speeches of Premier Marcello Caetano of Portugal, successor to the long-time ruler Salazar. Together, these themes give a picture of the present stance of Portugal's colonial regime.

---

1. For suggested readings on "Portuguese" Africa, see the recent list in *Southern Africa: A Monthly Survey of News and Opinion* (June–July, 1973), pp. 39–41. For an analysis showing the reality behind the Portuguese claims of nonracialism, see C. R. Boxer's *Race Relations in the Portuguese Colonial Empire, 1415–1825* (Oxford: Clarendon Press, 1963).

The Unity of the Portuguese Nation

The first, and a very prominent, theme is the inalienable unity of the Portuguese nation, including the "overseas provinces." Thus Premier Caetano, in rejecting the possibility of discussions with the "terrorist movements," dismissed the idea of handing over to them "the administration of territories which the Constitution, history, and national feeling enjoin on [the Portuguese government] to maintain as an integral part of Portugal."[2] One of the fundamental principles of the Portuguese colonizing tradition, wrote Caetano in 1951 (after his experience as minister of the colonies, in 1944–47), was political unity of the national territory.[3] In a speech of September 27, 1970, Caetano spoke of the reasons for defending the overseas provinces: "because there are there millions of Portuguese, black and white, who trust in Portugal, who want to continue to live under our flag and enjoy our peace."[4] Portugal is considered to be a multicontinental nation; all the inhabitants of the Portuguese territories should be proud to be Portuguese, and those who do not consider themselves so can be regarded only as traitors.

The primary beneficiary of this ideological theme, which justifies the continued domination of Portugal's African territories by the Portuguese central government, is the ruling class of Portugal. Independence under progressive African regimes would lead to the reorientation of trade patterns and the appropriation of Portuguese economic enterprises in Africa, as well as to the loss of the *raison d'être* of the Portuguese military leadership and colonial administration. Even independence under a settler-dominated regime or a compliant neocolonial African one would cause some reorientation: few Portuguese enterprises would be able to compete with foreign capital, which would no longer have reason to take on junior partners from Lisbon. Accordingly, political ties must be maintained in order to guarantee privileges to Portuguese economic interests; the precise shape of those political ties may change, however, as in the recent constitutional revision, permitting greater scope for administrative autonomy and providing for representation of those local interests (settlers and perhaps some few Africans) whose position of privilege rests on their collaboration with the Portuguese regime.

---

2. Marcello Caetano, *The Only Road Open to Us Is to Defend Our Overseas Provinces,* January 15, 1973 (all translations are my own).

3. Caetano, *Colonizing Traditions: Principles and Methods of the Portuguese* (Lisbon: Agência Geral do Ultramar, 1951), p. 31.

4. Caetano, *E na linha das reformas profundas que temos de prosseguir,* September 27, 1970.

The fact that continued privilege for local Portuguese interests rests on the military power supplied in large part by the central government, and directed entirely by that government, counters the tendency of the settlers to reject unity and move toward some form of independent, settler regime. There is persistent talk of a UDI in Angola or in Mozambique, and resentment that local interests are not adequately taken into account by Lisbon, but any attempt by settler groups to carry a plan for independence into action must founder on continued military dependence on Portugal. In spite of Portuguese efforts to make the military more locally dependent, both financially and in terms of manpower, any prospective settler regime would, without support from Lisbon, be extremely vulnerable to advances by the African liberation movement. And the military manpower of white South Africa is by no means sufficient to fill the gap. Whatever moves toward autonomy are taken, therefore, must be confined to limits set in Lisbon; and those limits will be set according to the estimates made by Portuguese ruling circles of the reliability of the local forces to which "autonomy" is being granted, and of the possibilities for retaining a dominant position by more subtle means. So far, those limits are narrow indeed; and the unity of the Portuguese nation is more dominant a theme, in ideology and in political reality, than the autonomy of the individual territories.

WHITE SUPREMACY

The second theme is the continued importance of white initiative and the impossibility of rule by the black majority. In 1954 Caetano wrote: "The blacks in Africa have to be directed and organized by Europeans, but they are indispensable as aids to them"[5] (as opposed to the possibility, mentioned earlier in his book, of simple extermination). In more recent speeches the theme is more subtle, but still unmistakable. On January 11, 1973, Caetano spoke of the necessity of building a society of racial harmony, the only road "that will prevent painful dramas in those countries south of the equator where there are large numbers of white settlers, whose efforts have set up cities, industries, and enterprises which cannot last without their presence and support, in the absence of the spirit that gave them birth."[6] Before the arrival of Portugal, Caetano proclaimed in another speech, the overseas provinces were "desolate territories, here and there peopled by the most

5. Caetano, *Os Nativos na Economia Africana* (Lisbon: Coimbra Editora, 1954), p. 16.
6. Caetano, *The Only Road*.

primitive tribes without any notion of nationality." It was the Portuguese who brought civilization and progress, and it is necessary that they continue in their present role. In impassioned terms Caetano rejects the possibility of majority rule:

> In the demagogic clamor of the attackers of Portugal one hears that Africa is for the Africans, that the government must belong to the majorities. We here are faced with a racism covering itself with a weak cloak of democracy. Why not admit the existence of white Africans? Why is it necessary to ignore the fact that in African countries the majority does not possess the democratic spirit, nor is it accustomed or disposed to putting into practice the governmental patterns of the Western type? Why must one close one's eyes to the reality that these majorities neither have the mentality nor possess the techniques or the capital that would permit a true independence able to advance human development and the development of natural riches?[7]

The point of this theme, clearly, is to maintain white rule in Africa. Portions of a confidential document that General Kaulza de Arriaga, former Portuguese commander in Mozambique, sent to the high command in Lisbon in 1966 have been smuggled out of Portugal and made public. Here the theme is stated more bluntly:

> We will only be able to maintain white rule in Angola and Mozambique, which is a national objective, if white settlement is at a rhythm which accompanies and at least slightly exceeds the production of evolved blacks.
> . . .
> If we journey from north to south, it appears that the latitude has some influence on the races of man. We see that the races, as we descend in latitude, acquire certain characteristics which, in relation to the actual parameters of modern life, are inferior. First we see the Nordics, very developed; . . . the Latins, much less enlightened; afterward we pass to the Arabs, much worse than we are; and we end with the blacks.[8]

Such sentiments obviously are not suitable for public expression by a Portuguese regime which claims to practice no racial discrimination; and perhaps the former university professor Caetano is not so crude, even in private, as this general. But the point is clear: power must not be turned over to the majority in the "overseas provinces."

This denial of the principle of majority rule is consistent with the

7. Caetano, *E na linha.*
8. *Angola Bulletin* (published in Amsterdam by the Angola Comité), February, 1972.

general political basis of the Portuguese regime, which began to speak favorably of "democracy" only to make itself appear more acceptable to members of the Western alliance. The present Portuguese state restricts democracy by limiting the franchise to those who can meet literacy and property requirements, by supporting an official fascist party, and by allowing only those who are "competent and motivated by the desire to improve things" to comment on and discuss government policy.[9] To support the principle of majority rule, irrespective of degree of civilization, would undermine the basis of the state in Portugal itself and, if carried out consistently, even within the hypothetical context of a unified multicontinental Portugal, would lead to domination by the combined population of the two largest overseas provinces, Angola and Mozambique. It would also, of course, undermine the position of the privileged settler strata in Angola and Mozambique. Therefore majority rule must be denied; and African participation in whatever power is given to local authorities must be carefully regulated to prevent "uncivilized" elements from gaining power and acting against Portuguese interests.

The role that white settlers are expected to play was discussed at a 1969 Portuguese conference on counterinsurgency (from which selected documents have been received and published by the Angola Comité, in Amsterdam). In speaking of the whites in Angola, a report of one study group noted that they have "the responsible and important task of playing a decisive role in the socioeconomic progress of the second group [the Africans], so that the latter may integrate themselves in a culture with more developed institutions."[10] To implement this, another report suggested, it was important to increase the number of Europeans, so that more Africans, regrouped into "strategic hamlets," could profit from European leadership.

ASSIMILATION OF AFRICANS

The Portuguese ideology, as defined so far, shows both striking differences and basic similarities when compared with that of the other white regimes in Africa, South Africa and Rhodesia. The emphasis on unity of the nation (including Africans) is directly contrary to the South African emphasis on apartheid, or separateness, of the different

9. Caetano, *Não há liberdade contra a lei*, April 8, 1970.
10. *Angola: Kolonie van een Diktatuur (geheime portugese rapporten over de contra-subversie)* (Amsterdam: Angola Comité, 1973), p. 54.

ethnic groups as different nations, and contrary as well to the tendency of the Rhodesian regime to move in that direction. Yet the common emphasis on white leadership reveals that all three are opposed to African majority rule, and that they support, in theory and in practice, white supremacy. A third theme of Portuguese colonial ideology defines a method of preserving that supremacy, a method that differs substantially from those of its white partners. That theme is assimilation and equal treatment as "Portuguese" for those Africans who meet the appropriate standards of civilization and loyalty.

In Caetano's speech of January 15, 1973, he points out that

> the central government is also responsible for the observance of the individual rights of all the classes of population of the overseas provinces, without any discrimination. The juridical equality of all Portuguese citizens must be paralleled, everywhere and at all times, by social mingling. If, at any time, local tendencies toward segregation were to be manifested or revealed, they would be inexorably combated by the intervention of the central authorities, should the necessity arise. We shall not give up our policy of racial fraternity; we shall not turn our backs on our intention to continue with the setting up of multiracial societies; we shall be absolutely intransigent as to the maintenance of one sole statute for Portuguese people, of whatever race or color they may be.[11]

It is this aspect of Portuguese policy, so dramatically different from the policies of the neighboring white regimes, that is emphasized again and again in Portuguese propaganda to the world. And, superficially, this contrast is indeed striking. It is best placed, however, in the light of the blunt comments of General Kaulza de Arriga:

> Since there is little possibility for evolving all the blacks—thanks be to God—it is very possible, in fact it is almost certain, that we can place white settlers, if we work hard, in such quantities that they will establish an equilibrium between themselves and those blacks who are becoming evolved. . . .
>
> Therefore multiracialism has to be authentic, and has to keep itself authentic, even though in its shadow we may need to lightly put the brakes on the development of the black peoples. Then we have to convince this folk that we are developing them at an adequate rate.[12]

This same Portuguese general has been responsible for greatly increasing

11. Caetano, *The Only Road*.
12. *Angola Bulletin*, February, 1972.

the number of Africans drafted into the Portuguese army in Mozambique and was still commander there when the new legislative assembly was elected, with a slight majority of Africans (all candidates were picked by the government party). Nevertheless, the advances of FRELIMO would seem to indicate that the general's persuasiveness is hardly enough to convince the African people of Mozambique that they are "being developed at an adequate rate."

The contrast between the theme of assimilation and the social reality is also apparent in a report from Angola, a confidential document written by Dr. Alfonso Mendes, director of the Labor Institute in Angola. Convinced that the policy of assimilation and development of the African population has to be pursued more seriously in order to advance the counterinsurgency effort and deny recruits to the liberation struggle, he portrays the actual situation in frank terms. After noting "a wide and deep gap between the two population groups," he deplores the fact that this may lead to black racism. He points to

> the existence of grave "social lags," which are the origin of cracks through which subversive forces penetrate, with their mission of disruption, to win the sympathy of the malcontents. And in the case of Angola, these malcontents may constitute more than 90 per cent of the entire population![13]

Mendes' comments on some more particular problems are most revealing with regard to the role that the African is to play within Portugal's civilizing scheme. He notes "the immense discrepancy between the standard of living of the African population and that of the population of European origin." His solution is

> to spread the idea that this discrepancy results from the Africans' lack of education, their smaller desire to work, and their doubtful spirit of enterprise. . . . We must create a propaganda which guides the population and directs their attention toward the joint task of economic development.

To remedy various abuses of authority, he suggests reforms, including raising African wages, permitting African workers more mobility, stimulating the birth of a black bourgeoisie, and, in general, devoting more attention to winning over the African population. With respect to the personal attitudes of the Portuguese settlers, he notes that "individuals of European origin deliberately and maliciously insult the

---

13. *The "Mendes" Report* (Amsterdam: Angola Comité, 1972), p. 11.

Africans, in their daily contact, with attitudes based upon an unmistakable hostility." Mendes' proposed solution is to "develop a propaganda campaign directed to encouraging mutual understanding between both groups."

Thus the Portuguese theme of assimilation indicates a policy of trying to win over, and bring more effectively within the Portuguese nation, a limited number of Africans. That policy is based to some extent on a social reality which, in contrast to that of South Africa, permits the incorporation of such selected individuals. The principle of equal opportunity and nondiscrimination is officially approved, and public disagreement with it is not acceptable. But the application of the principle founders on the reality of white privilege; and the limits to which Portuguese officials push this principle are set by the necessity to defend that privilege. The officials may well be ready to sacrifice some particular settler interests if they think that by doing so they will be strengthening the resistance to African rule. Some forces within Portugal may even contemplate the existence of future neocolonial local regimes in the overseas provinces, controlled by the black bourgeoisie they are trying to foster. But such hopes are limited by the reality. Just as any settler-based regime would have to continue to depend on Portugal to put down the liberation struggle, so also would any Portuguese-fostered neocolonial regime. Moreover, the independent weight of any black bourgeoisie is, to date, so small that the chances that any such regime will be more than an obvious puppet of settler and metropolitan Portuguese interests are almost nil. Those few Africans who are recruited are those who are willing to exist within the existing structure of white privilege as prominent exceptions—to be, in Caetano's words, "collaborators who will continue to improve institutions and make them work even better so as to defend the interests of all; to avoid the predominance of one class, one tribe, or one race over the others; and to keep careful watch over the lives, the property, and the progress of them all."[14] In spite of this rhetoric, it is the whites who now have property and progress and what political power there is for the population of a colony of a dictatorship. Assimilation and nondiscrimination as themes are designed to deny that fact, and to win over or neutralize foreign critics and as many as possible of the African population. Those Africans not won over (according to the Portuguese, a very small number) are to be dealt with by other counterinsurgency measures carried out by the Portuguese police and military: surveillance; establishment of strategic hamlets and free-fire zones; use of bombs, napalm, defoliants;

14. Caetano, *The Only Road.*

torture—all the techniques used in a war of repression against an entire people.

ANTICOMMUNISM AND ANTITERRORISM

A fourth theme, and the last to be dealt with in this paper, is to identify the liberation movements as terrorist, and to raise the spectre of a communist conspiracy against Western society. Thus Caetano's speech of January 15, 1973, refers to "terrorist groups, whose sole motivation is to spread violence and to be the tool of foreign interests." Speaking of the penetration, even within Portugal, of subversives, he refers to "a world climate of conflict which on every side has put into question—above all, among the youth—the foundations of social order and the legitimacy of our civilization."[15] General Kaulza de Arriaga, putting it in strategic terms, writes in a Portuguese army journal of May, 1973, of "communist neoimperialism," which is preparing a battle for the strategic region of southern Africa, the fall of which would lead eventually to communization of the world. "The war which we are conducting and carrying on," he says, "is imposed on us from abroad, and is a part of the struggle in process between the West and communist imperialism, which uses, as its principal instrument, neoracism."[16]

Thus the defense of the Portuguese colonial presence in Africa is conveniently placed within a framework congenial to Portugal's allies, South Africa and the other Western countries. The order that Portuguese rule brings is presented as necessary for the preservation of Western values against the linked threats of black rule and communist domination. To date, Portugal's allies seem to be convinced, judging from the support which has helped Portugal maintain its position in Africa. As long as the alternative is either continued Portuguese presence or the installation of progressive African regimes in Angola and Mozambique, those allies can be expected to stick with Portugal. The anticommunist theme holds some dangers for Portugal, however, for at some point Portugal's allies may decide that Portuguese colonialism is a losing cause, a hopeless anachronism, and they may seriously begin to search for some way to install compliant African regimes which would replace Portugal in defending their interests.

15. Caetano, *E na linha.*
16. *Jornal do Exército* (Lisbon), May, 1973.

For the present, however, the theme of anticommunism, antiterrorism, and "defense of the West" is an accurate indicator of the close collaboration of other Western powers in defending Portuguese colonialism, and of the involvement of Western capital in profiting from the continued Portuguese presence. At the same time it deflects attention from the primary base for resistance to Portuguese colonial rule, the African peoples themselves, and seeks to portray the struggle as illegitimate aggression against Portugal. "What I cannot understand," says Caetano, "is why we should be accused of disturbing the peace, when we are merely engaged, in our own country, in defending ourselves from acts of aggression prepared, supported, and encouraged by foreign powers."[17]

Thus each of the themes of Portuguese colonial ideology discussed in this paper reflects the interests of those who benefit from continued Portuguese colonial rule: the Portuguese ruling class, the Portuguese settlers in Angola and Mozambique, the foreign powers for whom Portugal provides stability in exchange for military and economic support. The talk of unity of the Portuguese nation indicates the central role of the Portuguese ruling class. The defense of the necessity for white initiative ensures the settlers that their leading role will not be questioned. The theme of assimilation and nondiscrimination seeks to hold out to some Africans the promise of a share in the benefits obtained from exploiting the African masses. And the theme of anticommunism sets the whole repressive venture of maintaining Portuguese colonialism within the context of preserving the interests of the capitalist powers against the threat of instability and revolution. What is missing, of course, systematically obscured from view, is the struggle of the African peoples under Portuguese rule to win freedom and determine their own destinies, to build a future free of exploitation.

---

17. Caetano, *The Only Road.*

Walter Lehn

THE JEWISH NATIONAL FUND

IN THE EXTENSIVE LITERATURE on Zionist colonization of Palestine and the consequent and continuing conflict, one rarely finds more than a passing reference to the role of the Jewish National Fund (JNF). Yet in 1948 the JNF was the largest private (i.e., nongovernmental) land-owner in Palestine, holding title to 933,000 dunams,[1] on which 85 per cent of the Jewish settlements or establishments were located. Clearly, the JNF was one of the major instruments in implementing the Zionist objective—establishment of a Jewish state. In light of this

---

1. Abraham Granott, *Agrarian Reform and the Record of Israel* (London, 1956), p. 28; 1 dunam = 1,000 square meters = .2471 acres. According to Granott, at the beginning of 1948, Jews owned 1,734,000 dunams; of this, 933,000 were held by the JNF, and the balance by other, including private, owners. The 1,734,000 figure is not impressive if we note that this represented only 6.59 per cent of mandate Palestine's total land area of 26,323,000 dunams (exclusive of Transjordan). Granott generally rounds figures to the closest 1,000, a practice that will be observed in this paper also.

No attempt is made in this paper to reconcile varying figures on land-ownership given in different sources. Granott's figures are accepted because of his long and close association with the JNF (from 1919 until his death, in 1962), and because his figures agree substantially with those given elsewhere. See, for example, Government of Palestine, *Village Statistics 1945: A Classification of Land and Area Ownership in Palestine* (Jerusalem, 1946), reprinted with explanatory notes by Sami Hadawi (Beirut, 1970); and United Nations, General Assembly, *Report of the Ad Hoc Committee on the Palestinian Question*, 1947. Useful interpretive studies are Sami Hadawi, *Palestine: Loss of a Heritage* (San Antonio, 1963); and John Ruedy, "Dynamics of Land Alienation," in *The Transformation of Palestine*, ed. Ibrahim Abu-Lughod (Evanston, Ill., 1971), pp. 119-38.

fact, the absence of detailed studies of the JNF is surprising. This paper is a contribution toward filling this lacuna.

Establishment of the JNF

At the last session of the First Zionist Congress in Basel, in August, 1897, Hermann Schapira proposed the establishment of an organization to redeem the land of Palestine.[2] This redemption, in his view, could be effected only by Jews owning, living on, and cultivating the land. To achieve these ends would require (1) an appropriate organization and (2) large sums of money. "Let us suppose," he said, "that our forefathers had placed any sum of money, however small, in trust for the benefit of future generations; why, we should now be able to acquire immense tracts of land. And what our ancestors failed to do, that it is incumbent upon us to do for ourselves and for those who shall come after us."[3] Schapira proposed that a fund be established to collect money from Jews all over the world, that this be saved until a large sum had accumulated, and that two-thirds of it then be used to purchase land in Palestine for Jewish settlement. The remaining one-third would be used for settlement and development of the settlements. The land, however, was not to be sold to the settlers; title to it was to be held by the fund in perpetuity as the property of the Jewish people. In short, the land was never to be sold but only leased to Jewish settlers for periods not exceeding forty-nine years. Schapira further stipulated that the fund was to be under the control of the Zionist organization proposed by Theodor Herzl. Although Schapira's proposal was applauded, and apparently was supported by Herzl,[4] no action was taken at this congress, and Schapira did not live to see establishment of the fund.

---

2. See Israel M. Biderman, *Hermann Schapira: Father of the JNF,* Zionist Personalities Series, Jewish National Fund, Vol. II (New York, 1962); Maximilian Hurwitz, "The Father of the National Fund: A Biographical Sketch of Hermann Schapira," in *Eretz Israel: Jubilee Volume of the Jewish National Fund* (New York, 1932), pp. 24–29; *Encyclopedia of Zionism and Israel,* 1971 (henceforth *E.Z.I.*), s.v. "Schapira, Hermann (Zvi)," "Jewish National Fund."

3. "The Jewish National Fund: Its Origin, Object, History and Achievements," in *Eretz Israel,* p. 31.

4. Herzl's account of the First Zionist Congress makes no mention of Schapira's address or proposal; see *The Complete Diaries of Theodor Herzl,* ed. Raphael Patai (New York, 1960), pp. 574–97.

In December, 1901, at the Fifth Zionist Congress in Basel, Johann Kremenetzky, one of Herzl's friends and supporters, took up Schapira's proposal in a somewhat revised form and presented it for action. With strong support from Herzl and Max Nordau, but with opposition from many delegates (who argued that it was a mistake to purchase land before there were settlers prepared to cultivate it), the Jewish National Fund (Keren Kayemet Leisrael) was voted into existence, with the stipulations that no purchases were to be made until the sum of £200,000 had been raised, and that the funds were to be used (as distinguished from the 1897 proposal) "exclusively for the purchase of land in Palestine and Syria."[5] The JNF became active immediately, although initially on a small scale. Its headquarters was established in Vienna, and Kremenetzky was named head.[6] In 1902, three fund-raising devices were put in use: blue collection boxes for the home, JNF stamps,[7] and, for large contributors, inscription of their names in the Golden Book (now on exhibit at JNF headquarters in Jerusalem).

The arguments attending the creation of the JNF concerned primarily the tactics of colonization. The view of Herzl and most of his associates on the Smaller Actions Committee (later, the Zionist Executive) of the World Zionist Organization (WZO) was that colonization rights, i.e., a charter, should be secured first, followed by land purchases and settlement. Accordingly they viewed the small settlements in Palestine by the Lovers of Zion groups as experimental and were opposed to the establishment of more until, in the words of the 1897 Basel program, "a home in Palestine [had been] secured by public law."[8] Others, especially the Russian Zionists, saw this approach as belittling the

---

5. Quoted from the proceedings of the congress in A. Granovsky (later Granott), *Boden und Siedlung in Palaestina* (Berlin, 1929), p. 183. The original reads: "ausschliesslich nur zum Landkaufe in Palaestina und Syrien." For accounts of the Fifth Congress, see Anna Nordau and Max Nordau, *Max Nordau: A Biography* (New York, 1943), pp. 172–77; Herzl, *Diaries*, ed. Patai, pp. 1187–93; Alex Bein, *The Return to the Soil: A History of Jewish Settlement in Israel* (Jerusalem, 1952), p. 16.

6. The headquarters was later moved to Cologne (1907), then to The Hague (1914), and finally to Jerusalem (1922). Following Kremenetzky, the JNF was headed by Max Bodenheimer (beginning in 1907), a provisional committee (1914), Nehemia de Lieme (1919), Menachem Ussishkin (1921), an executive committee (1941), Abraham Granott (1945), and, currently, Jacob Tsur (1956).

7. These fund-raising stamps, overprinted "post," were used as postage stamps in the early days of the state of Israel and were sold for this purpose on the streets as early as May 9, 1948; Terence Prittie, *Eshkol: The Man and the Nation* (New York, 1969), pp. 130–31.

8. Quoted in J. C. Hurewitz, *Diplomacy in the Near and Middle East: A Documentary Record* (Princeton, 1956), I, 209.

significance of these early settlements and argued for the opposite, or "practical," approach, i.e., to continue with and increase land purchases and settlement, and to negotiate for political rights later, essentially a policy of proceeding by *fait accompli*. These arguments continued, even after the establishment of the JNF, until the Sixth Zionist Congress in Basel, in August, 1903. At this congress the advocates of the practical approach won the debate, aided in no small way by the widespread opposition on the part of many delegates to the British East Africa settlement proposal, which Herzl appeared to support since he did not favor its outright rejection. The previous decision not to make any land purchases until a substantial sum of money had been raised was modified, and the JNF was authorized to begin to buy land whenever a majority of its board of directors so decided; its expenditures, however, were not to exceed 75 per cent of its capital, the remainder being held as a reserve.

In 1905, as a consequence of this decision, the first JNF purchases were made. By 1907 three large areas had been acquired: 4,000 dunams near Tiberias, 2,000 near Lydda, and 6,400 directly south of Lake Tiberias, a total of 12,400 dunams.[9] Since under Ottoman law these lands (designated *miri*) could not be left uncultivated without their being liable to revert to the state, and since leasing them to Palestinian Arabs was unacceptable, in part because long-term tenants could legally establish a claim to continued possession, the World Zionist Organization, having embarked on a program of land acquisition, had no alternative but to begin settlement at once and to regularize the legal status of the JNF. The JNF was registered in Britain in 1907 under the Companies Act as Keren Kayemet Leisrael Limited, "an association limited by guarantee and not having a capital divided into shares."[10] Further, since the WZO had no organization in Palestine capable of overseeing settlement, the Eighth Zionist Congress (The Hague, August, 1907) decided to open a Palestine Office in Jaffa, which began operation in early 1908. At the same time the WZO founded a land-purchasing and development company. It was registered in Britain as the Palestine Land Development Company Limited, with a capital of £50,000 in £1 shares. The company was to serve private individuals, as well as the JNF, as central land-purchasing agency. By this means, it was hoped, speculation would be checked and random and unsystematic purchases of small and/or scattered parcels of land unsuitable for large-scale colonization would be avoided. The company made its first purchases

9. Bein, *Return to the Soil*, p. 23.
10. Quoted in *E.Z.I.*, s.v. "Jewish National Fund."

in 1909 and, in time, became the principal purchasing agent for the JNF.

The expenses of the Palestine Office were paid largely by the JNF, which also provided assistance and loans to settlers. Although the JNF was severely criticized for these departures from its land-purchasing mission, it defended them on the ground that its charter "provided for investment in any project that would further the rebuilding and resettlement of Palestine."[11]

Another milestone in the history of the JNF occurred in London in July, 1920, when the Zionist conference held there decided to establish an immigration and colonization fund of £25,000,000 to be known as Keren HaYesod. The following year it was registered in Britain as the Palestine Foundation Fund Limited, like the JNF, an association limited by guarantee and not having a share capital.[12] As the central financial institution, it was to seek the participation of all Zionist and non-Zionist Jews, and was to derive its income principally from an annual tax paid by all Jews. At least 20 per cent of its funds were to be turned over to the JNF. Of the remainder, one-third was to be spent on colonization and two-thirds invested in "permanent national institutions or economic undertakings."[13] This fund, like the earlier Palestine Land Development Company, represented an attempt—not wholly successful—to restrict the activities of the JNF to its original purpose: land acquisition.

LAND POLICY OF THE JNF

Beginning in 1921, the JNF developed what Abraham Granott calls "a rational and considered land policy," and extensive acquistions were begun. As a consequence, JNF holdings increased, from 16,000 dunams in 1914, to 197,000 in 1927, and to 370,000 in 1936.[14] The new land policy was dictated by several considerations. Land for agricultural settlement remained the first objective, but strategic security and national political objectives also became important. However, the three objectives—agricultural, strategic security, and national political—did not always prescribe the same tactics. The first two suggested large, or

---

11. Quoted in *ibid.*
12. *E.Z.I.*, s.v. "Keren Ha Yesod." See also Ben Halpern, *The Idea of the Jewish State*, 2d ed. (Cambridge, Mass., 1969), p. 190.
13. *E.Z.I.*, s.v. "London Zionist Conference."
14. Granott, *Agrarian Reform*, pp. 28, 31.

small contiguous, acquisitions; the third, on the other hand, suggested acquisitions in border areas—hence, at times, the acquisition of widely separated parcels of land. In time the third objective became the major one; and after the Peel Commission in 1937 recommended partition, "it became JNF policy to acquire land in areas excluded from the proposed Jewish state and to form settlements there." [15]

In accordance with the policy enunciated by the British government in the 1939 White Paper new land-transfer regulations for Palestine (effective from May, 1939) were published in February, 1940, virtually prohibiting Jewish land purchases (in Zone A, 63 per cent of Palestine) or severely restricting them (in Zone B, 32 per cent). In only a small free zone (5 per cent of Palestine) were there no restrictions on land acquisition.[16] The regulations, however, appear to have had little effect on the JNF, which increased its holdings from 473,000 dunams in September, 1939, to 835,000 in September, 1946. Of these new acquisitions, 270,000 dunams (79 per cent) were in Zone A or Zone B, 75,000 formerly owned by Jews and 195,000 by Arabs, including nonresident Lebanese and Syrians. Some of these acquisitions were undoubtedly in violation of the regulations, testimony to the effectiveness of the JNF in pursuing its objectives and to the laxity of enforcement of the regulations by the mandate government.[17]

The 1947 U.N. partition recommendation demonstrated the wisdom of JNF policy. In the words of Granott:

> The frontiers [i.e., the 1949 armistice lines] of the new State, which march in so curiously winding a fashion, were largely determined by the success of the Jews in creating *faits accomplis*. All those parts to which the Jewish settler had penetrated were included within the State, whereas those where

---

15. *E.Z.I.*, s.v. "Jewish National Fund"; Granott, *Agrarian Reform*, pp. 34–35. The so-called stockade and tower settlements were begun during this period.

16. *Palestine Gazette*, February 28, 1940. See also Robert John and Sami Hadawi, *The Palestine Diary: 1914–1945* (New York, 1970), pp. 332–34; and George Kirk, *The Middle East in the War*, Royal Institute of International Affairs Survey of International Affairs, 1939–46 (London, 1952), pp. 232–35.

17. *E.Z.I.*, s.v. "Jewish National Fund"; Keren Kayemet Leisrael, Ltd., *Report for 5700–5706 (1939–1946)*, submitted to the Twenty-second Zionist Congress, Basel, Switzerland, December 9, 1946 (Jerusalem, 1946), pp. 14–21 (henceforth *JNF Report 1946*). Among the methods used to circumvent the regulations, a common one practiced from the early settlement days was to have the land registered in the name of an individual residing in Palestine, but not holding Palestinian citizenship, who would give the JNF an irrevocable power of attorney. British and South African Jews were willing to help in this manner. See Amos Elon, *The Israelis: Founders and Sons* (New York, 1971), p. 94.

they were not strong enough, or did not have time to plant stakes, remained for the most part outside. Proof of this is seen in a comparison of the two proposals for the Partition of Palestine, of 1937 and 1947. . . . Developments during the . . . ten years are reflected in the boundaries drawn in the United Nations Partition plan of 1947. . . . Thus the various objectives—national policy, security, and strategy—were linked through land acquisition with the settlement objective, all being welded together into a united, systematic, purposeful, and far-seeing policy.[18]

Since title to the land purchased by the JNF was to be held in perpetuity "as the inalienable property of the Jewish people,"[19] use of the land required the development of a system of long-term leasing, the lessor being the JNF. The land could be leased for specified purposes for periods up to forty-nine years, at the end of which the lessee could renew the lease for a similar period, a total of ninety-eight years. Under these circumstances, the lease itself had considerable value and could, subject to the lessor's approval, be sublet, sold, mortgaged, bequeathed, or given as a gift. Rent, paid annually, was assessed at 2 per cent (agricultural) or 4 per cent (urban) of the value of the land; the lessor had the right to make periodic reassessments of the land and to raise the rent accordingly. The lessor had the further rights, which could be exercised at its discretion, to inspect the property, to decrease the amount of land held, and to take back the land if the lessee was held to have violated the terms of the lease. In the latter instance the lessee might, depending on the nature of the violation, receive compensation for improvements he had made.[20]

All of these terms, including the lessee's rights, were subject to one overriding condition, made explicit in the lease: the lessee must be Jewish. Accordingly, the land could not be leased to a non-Jew, nor could the lease be sublet, sold, mortgaged, given, or bequeathed to anyone but a Jew. Non-Jews could not be employed on the land or even in any work connected with cultivation of the land. Violation

---

18. Granott, *Agrarian Reform*, pp. 37–38. Similar claims can be found repeatedly in JNF literature; see, for example, Herbert Freeden, "The JNF in 25 Years of Statehood," in *1973 JNF Handbook: Israel's 25th Anniversary*, ed. I. M. Biderman (New York, 1973), p. 2.

19. Constitution of the Jewish Agency for Palestine (adopted August, 1929), Art. 3, quoted in John Hope Simpson, *Palestine: Report on Immigration, Land Settlement and Development* (London, 1930), p. 53. See also Halpern, *Idea of the Jewish State*, p. 195.

20. Abraham Granott, in *The Land System in Palestine: History and Structure* (London, 1952), pp. 315–26, gives the most detailed account of the system of JNF leasing. He

of this term of the lease rendered the lessee liable for damages to the lessor, and the third violation gave the lessor the right to abrogate the lease without compensation to the lessee.[21]

Since the JNF eventually became the largest private land-owner in Palestine, holding title by 1948 to 53.8 per cent of the Jewish-owned land, its practices were adopted by, or, at times, imposed on, other Jewish land-owners.[22] Hence, the result of JNF activity was—as noted by John Hope Simpson in 1930—that the "land has been extraterritorialised. It ceases to be land from which the Arab can gain any advantage either now or at any time in the future." This was "not only contrary to the provisions . . . of the Mandate, but . . . in addition a constant and increasing source of danger to the country."[23] In spite of these and subsequent criticisms of the JNF (e.g., that of the 1946 Anglo-American Committee of Inquiry), and in spite of repeated Palestinian Arab protests, nothing was done by the mandate government to prevent the JNF from continuing to place restrictive covenants on its land. This practice continues to this day in Israel, where the JNF remains the second-largest land-owner, the largest being the state.

The period since 1948 has seen several important developments. In the first place, the JNF has greatly increased its landholdings. Under agreements negotiated in January, 1949, and October, 1950, the JNF bought from the government of Israel 2,374,000 dunams of so-called abandoned land. By April, 1954, the JNF held title to about 3,500,000 dunams in Israel.[24] In the second place, there has been a gradual shift in the emphasis and activities of the JNF from land acquisition to (1) land reclamation, (2) road-building,[25] (3) various forms of assistance to new settlements, including well-drilling and construction of dams and irrigation systems, and (4) large-scale afforestation. The JNF's

---

does not, however, explicitly state the condition that all of this applies only to Jews.

21. See Simpson, *Palestine*, p. 53.

22. *Ibid.*, p. 55. See also Uri Avnery, *Israel without Zionists: A Plea for Peace in the Middle East* (New York, 1968), p. 85.

23. Simpson, *Palestine*, pp. 54, 55.

24. Granott, *Agrarian Reform*, pp. 107–12. For a detailed and documented account, written by an Israeli Arab attorney, of post-1948 developments with regard to acquisitions of Arab-owned land, see Sabri Jiryis, *The Arabs in Israel: 1948–1966* (Haifa, 1966; Beirut, 1968), pp. 55–90.

25. Since 1967 it has also financed road-building in occupied territories. A highway through the West Bank, linking Jerusalem with the Upper Jordan Valley, with the JNF providing half the cost, was begun in November, 1972. See Terence Smith, "Israel Is Quietly Building a Highway on West Bank," *New York Times*, February 20, 1973.

fund-raising, information, and education activities have, of course, continued without change.

In 1960 the JNF and the Israeli government reached an agreement clarifying the relationship of the JNF to the state. Under this agreement, based on legislation enacted by the Knesset in July, 1960, two bodies were established: (1) a government land authority, headed by the minister of agriculture and responsible to a board of thirteen (seven representing the government and six the JNF), to manage, in accordance with a uniform policy, all state and JNF lands, and (2) a development authority, set up within the JNF, headed by a representative of the JNF, and responsible to a board of thirteen (seven representing the JNF and six the government), to oversee all land development, including reclamation and afforestation. The agreement further recognized that each party would retain title to its lands, and that the JNF would continue to be under the control of the WZO and would "continue its work of information, education and fund-raising in Israel and in the Diaspora."[26] Thus, through the JNF, as through the Jewish Agency, the WZO shares with the state of Israel a curious sort of condominium over what was once known as Palestine.[27] Probably the most significant consequence of this agreement was that the restrictive JNF policies regarding the sale and leasing of land were applied to all state lands,[28] which, together with JNF lands, constitute 90 per cent of the land in Israel. The implications of this for non-Jewish Israeli citizens, and for any eventual settlement of the conflict, are obvious.

---

26. Jacob Tsur, *Old Concepts and New Realities* (Jerusalem, 1962), pp. 9–17 (quotation is from p. 16). For some current details of fund-raising, see the UPI dispatch from New York, "Private Gifts to Israel Dwarf Official U.S. Aid," *Los Angeles Times,* September 3, 1973; Robert Silverberg, *If I Forget Thee O Jerusalem: American Jews and the State of Israel* (New York, 1970), pp. 232–33; Samuel Halperin, *The Political World of American Zionism* (Detroit, 1961), pp. 270–78.

27. WZO control of the JNF is exercised through the latter's Board of Directors. The chairman of the Zionist Executive, who is simultaneously chairman of the Executive of the Jewish Agency for Israel, serves on the JNF board as a governor with veto power over decisions of the board. In addition, the board has a chairman and a deputy chairman and (in 1972) twenty-two members elected by the Zionist Congress. Both the size of the board and the directness of its election by the delegates to the congress have varied over the years. Control of the JNF by the WZO, however, in accordance with Schapira's original proposal, does not appear to have changed. See "The Board of Directors of the Jewish National Fund," *JNF Report 1946,* p. 5; and *Israel Government Year Book 5732 (1971–72),* p. 343.

28. Tsur, *Old Concepts and New Realities,* pp. 11, 15. For the effect of this agreement on Arab citizens of Israel, see John K. Cooley, "Israeli Arabs Do Well, but . . . ," *Christian Science Monitor,* May 3, 1973.

Conclusion

In conclusion, the achievements of the JNF in redeeming the land of Palestine, for which purpose the organization was established, can be evaluated only within the larger context of the conflict for control of Palestine. Such an evaluation falls beyond the scope of this brief report. Suffice it to say that according to JNF sources, the JNF made its first purchases in 1905 and, by 1948, after forty-three years of land acquisition, held title to 933,000 dunams, representing 3.54 per cent of the total land area of mandate Palestine (exclusive of Transjordan). In view of the fact that from October, 1920 (date of reopening of the land-registry offices in Palestine under the British civil administration), to May, 1939 (date of the restrictive land-transfer regulations), a total of nineteen years, there were no legal impediments to JNF activities, and in view of the fact that the impediments after May, 1939, were obviously not very effective—since the JNF acquired almost half of its pre-1948 holdings (460,000 out of 933,000 dunams) during this period—the extent of its land acquisition is hardly impressive.

An interesting and by no means irrelevant question concerns the vendors of land to the JNF. Granott estimates that of all land owned by Jews (including the JNF) in 1947, 57 per cent had been purchased from large Arab land-owners, 16 per cent from the government, churches, and foreign companies, and 27 per cent from the *fellahin*.[29] However, the only detailed information he provides does not seem to support his estimates. The statistical department of the Jewish Agency provided details on former owners of Jewish-owned land as of March, 1936. According to this, 52.6 per cent had been purchased from large absentee land-owners, 24.6 from large resident land-owners, and 13.4 per cent from various sources such as the government, churches, and foreign companies, making a total of 90.6 percent. This leaves only 9.4 per cent acquired from small Palestinian farmers; and 40 per cent of this (25,741 out of 64,201 dunams) had been acquired during 1891–1900, i.e., before the JNF was established.[30] It seems fair to conclude, therefore, that the JNF was not at all successful in purchasing land from small Palestinian land-owners. Nevertheless it was precisely these Palestinian Arabs who eventually paid the highest price for JNF efforts to redeem the land of Palestine. That they accordingly feel a deep and abiding sense of injustice is surely less than surprising.

At the present time, although the redemption of the land of Palestine

---

29. Granott, *Land System*, p. 278.
30. *Ibid.*, p. 277, Table 32.

envisaged by Schapira nearly eighty years ago appears to have been largely completed, it has not been accomplished by the means he intended. The JNF deserves only limited credit; the largest share belongs to military conquest.

PART II: RESPONSE TO SETTLEMENT

Kemal H. Karpat

OTTOMAN IMMIGRATION POLICIES AND SETTLEMENT IN PALESTINE

The Ottoman state was subject to profound demographic changes in the nineteenth century. During the first half of the century, and well into the 1860s, the Ottoman population either decreased or stagnated. Then it actually began to increase, mainly because large groups of Muslims, forced to abandon their ancestral homes in the Balkans and in Russia, settled in Ottoman territories, especially in Anatolia and northern Syria.

These two phases in the demographic history of the Ottoman state, although fundamentally different from each other, are intimately related in their impact upon the population policy of the government. I am fully convinced—after considerable research in the Ottoman archives—that a greater understanding of the demographic changes in the Ottoman state would cast a new light on the rise and the social and political transformation of states in the Middle East. In fact, I have come to believe that a demographic historical study of the Middle East in the nineteenth century would change many of our present views about the sociopolitical history of the area.

I must stress, furthermore, that any study of a single section of the Middle East prior to 1916 without reference to the general policies or the other areas of the Ottoman state is bound to be one-sided and incomplete. Demographic changes in this area, including the Ottoman settlement policies, can be judged accurately only within a framework that includes population movements throughout the Ottoman territory, as well as the government's general policy toward settlement and immigration. Thus, the Circassian Muslims arriving from the northern Caucasus in the 1860s were settled in the Balkans, Anatolia, Syria, and even sections of northern Palestine, as part of a general policy which must be viewed as a whole. The Muhacirun Komisyonu, established in 1860 specifically for settlement purposes, issued a series of orders that applied throughout the lands under Ottoman rule. Ottoman documents from the first half of the nineteenth century refer to the general area west of present-day Iraq as Syria, and, later in the century, to the mutasarriflik of Jerusalem and to Lebanon. Consequently, many decisions regarding Syria apply also to Palestine.

The significance of the population problems of the Ottoman state will become evident only after a demographic picture of the entire state is presented in full. I do hope to publish such a study in the near future. For the purpose of this communication, I shall limit my observations to the general settlement policies of the government and to settlement schemes concerning western Syria and, specifically, Palestine. Moreover, I shall leave out most of the information concerning the emigration of Syrians and other groups from the Ottoman state to the Americas, although this matter was also of major concern to the government.[1]

THE CALL FOR SETTLERS, 1800–1860

The Muslim population of the Ottoman state living in the Balkans, Anatolia, and northern Syria began to decline rapidly after 1800. At the same time, the non-Muslim population began to grow, especially in southwestern Anatolia and in sections of Syria, because of economic incentives as well as exemptions from military service. Moreover, the schools opened by the non-Muslim communities and by Western missions provided the Christian groups with a distinct qualitative educational superiority over the Muslims. The decline in the Muslim population was caused chiefly by the casualties suffered in a series of long wars with Russia in 1812, 1827, 1853, and 1877, in the Serbian uprisings in 1804, and 1815, in the Greek uprising in 1821–29, and in a series

---

1. Some of the information in this paper was presented in a different context at the meeting of the American Association for the Advancement of Slavic Studies in Dallas, March 15–18, 1972. The paper was titled "Population Movements in the Ottoman State and Modernization: The Bulgarian and Circassian Migrations, 1858–80."

of other rebellions. Disease, famine, and lack of health services increased the losses in human life.

The Muslims' situation was further aggravated by a relative stagnation in the economy, particularly in the agricultural sector. The change in the land-ownership system, the registration of lands as private property on the basis of deeds issued in the past by sipahis (administrators of timar lands) and by ayans, the endless litigations concerning land-ownership, the efforts of the bureaucracy to prevent usurpation of state lands, and the lack of a fully established market economy all combined to produce this stagnation in the agricultural sector. Large tracts of excellent arable land remained uncultivated. The dismal situation of agriculture resulted in a decrease in state revenue and had a further negative effect on the growth rate of the Muslim population. It must be mentioned that beginning roughly in the 1850s, the percentage of the non-Muslim population in port towns seemed to increase rapidly, while the Muslim population became predominantly rural.

In an effort to remedy the economic situation and to increase its own revenues by revitalizing agriculture, the Ottoman government sought the advice of various agricultural experts. These experts advised, and some of the high Ottoman officials agreed, that Ottoman agriculture would improve and state revenues increase only if there were adequately trained manpower to cultivate the land. Moreover, the demand for agricultural commodities, mostly from abroad, was so great as to force the government to seek immediate measures to increase rural production. This demand was stimulated greatly by the Crimean War (1853–56), and it seemed that it would continue to increase. Indeed, the Paris treaty of 1856, and the acceptance of the Ottoman state in the comity of European nations, seemed to augur well for the economic future of the Ottomans, although the ensuing trade relations benefited mostly the Europeans and their business agents in the Ottoman state. At any rate, the Paris treaty was a psychological turning point in Ottoman relations with Europe, for it recognized the Ottoman state as equal to European states, regardless of its different religion and the wars of the past.

The population policy adopted by the Ottoman government in 1857 was the result of the economic, political, and psychological conditions mentioned above. On March 9 of that year, the government issued, through the High Council of the Tanzimat, a decree on immigration and settlement which was sanctioned by the sultan.[2] The decree declared

---

2. Ottoman Archives; Foreign Ministry (henceforth F.M.); *Idare*, or Administrative, usually referring to internal communication (henceforth I, within parentheses); 127,

that immigration into the Ottoman state was open to anyone who would agree to give his allegiance to the sultan, to become a subject of the sultan, and to respect the country's laws. It stipulated further that "settlers will be protected against any infringement of the religion they profess and will enjoy religious freedoms like all other classes of the Empire's subjects" (Art. 3). If the locality in which the immigrants established themselves did not have chapels or churches for their rites, they "could ask and obtain from the imperial government the permission to build the needed chapels." The government promised to give the settlers, free of charge, the best arable lands owned by the treasury, and to exempt them from all taxes and military service for six years if they settled in Rumelia, and for twelve years if they settled in Asian domains (Art. 4, Art. 5, Art. 6). The immigrants could not sell the land for twenty years. Those who decided to leave the country would return the land to the government. Each family desiring to settle in Turkey would compile a list of the names and professions of its members, and indicate the capital or wealth that the family possessed. All this was to be submitted to the Ottoman government through its legations and consulates abroad. Each family applying to settle on Ottoman domains needed to possess at least 60 mejidie, or about 1,350 francs (Art. 13).

This decree was translated and published in major European journals so that a large number of people would become acquainted with the Ottoman immigration policy. Government representatives abroad, who were almost immediately swamped with inquiries, asked the government for details and precise instructions. On December 9, 1857, Ali Pasha, the minister, in a letter to the Turkish ambassadors, ministers, and consuls in London, Paris, Vienna, St. Petersburg, Madrid, The Hague, Berlin, Brussels, Turin, Naples, Leghorn, and Corfu, advised them not to hurry because there was a series of measures to be taken before the decree could be carried out.[3] Nevertheless, he insisted that the government was firm in its decision to implement its original decree.

The European response to the decree was overwhelming. Inquiries and applications came from every corner of Europe. Alexandre Baggio of Turin asked for a concession of land in Albania. He had established a company and had even acquired a boat to carry the agricultural commodities that would be produced on his land to European markets.[4]

---

the file number. The second number, if any, indicates the office number; the date of the document is sometimes included. The decree is in F.M. (I), 127.

3. *Ibid.*

4. F.M. (I), 177, 627, November 17, 1859.

He was offered land near Silistra, on the Danube, but the project failed to materialize because Baggio did not have sufficient capital. Also, a large number of families from Tuscany, in Italy, showed interest in immigration and asked for information.[5] A certain Philipp Olkonski from Lodz asked about immigration into Palestine, since he had heard that the "emperor" of Turkey offered land and travel expenses to those who wanted to settle in that country.[6] The Compte d'Haussville, president of the Committee for the Protection of Alsace-Lorrainers, inquired about the possibility of acquiring land in order to establish French colonies in the Ottoman state "similar to the German colonies founded in Jaffa and Haifa."[7] The committee had already established such colonies in Algeria. Aziz Pasha, the governor of Cyprus, had encouraged him to do so, he declared. Dormann Gasparini, who submitted official papers to prove his status as citizen of the canton of St. Gallen, as officer in the Swiss army, and as former member of the penal court, was interested in migrating to Turkey. He expressed the view that Turkey was a rich country that did not have good land-cultivators. Gasparini guaranteed the immigration of 2,000 Swiss but asked that the terms prohibiting sale of the land be shortened. He proposed several schemes of settlement, with and without government support.[8] Thomas Lames, British consul in Larnaca, Cyprus, demanded land, some 130,000 dunams,[9] in order to settle 300 Irish families on the island, but his death put an end to his plans, despite his brother's determination to take over the project.[10]

News of Ottoman land grants seems to have spread far and wide. German families living as far east of Berlin as Prussia demanded information about immigration and showed keen interest in settling in Turkey. J. Oxford Smith, the Ottoman consul in New York, wrote several letters requesting information about the liberal immigration policy of the government, and indicating that he had read notices about the policy in the *European Times*. He wrote that "there are many

---

5. F.M. (I), 177, April 14, 1857.
6. F.M. (I), 587, 60786/214.
7. F.M. (I), 177, June 4, 1875.
8. F.M. (I), 177, 10059/99, February 4, 1864.

9. The official size of a dunam, according to the High Council of the Tanzimat, is the following: a dunam consists of 1,600 archines, and each archine consists of 7 square meters. Thus a dunam corresponds to 11,200 square meters, or 1,200 square meters larger than a hectare. F.M. (I), 177, 2283, March 23, 1859. But see above, p. 43, n. 1.

10. F.M. (I), 177, 6885/36, February 12, 1863.

industrious, steady men who would like to take up residence in that land, especially Syria and Palestine, if they can obtain land and be protected in the cultivation of it. . . . The cultivation of cotton is one principal object in view." Smith also inquired "whether persons of color who are natives of this country or others are included in these conditions." Fuat Pasha replied that as far as blacks were concerned, they would have the same rights, since the "imperial government does not establish any difference of color or other in this respect."[11]

The demands and inquiries about migration to and settlement on Ottoman domains continued to reach Turkish representatives abroad. Thus a group of 2,000 families of German origin who were established in Bessarabia informed the Ottoman consulate in Odessa that they, too, desired to settle in Turkey.[12] Moreover, they wrote that if their demand was met favorably, more than 18,000 families, and possibly half of the German colonies located in southern Russia, would settle in the Ottoman state.[13] Similarly, a number of families from the island of Malta demanded permission to settle in Tripoli, in North Africa, and possibly elsewhere.[14]

It is interesting to note that the decree of 1857 did not incite immediate interest among the Jews of Europe. This is especially significant in view of the fact that beginning in 1839, with the establishment of the British consulate in Jerusalem (the first European representation in the Holy City), the British made strenuous efforts to stimulate the settlement of Jews in Palestine. The British had planned to install and protect the Jews in Palestine in the hopes of creating there a group friendly to themselves, a group that would check and balance the Russian influence among the Orthodox Christians, and the French influence among the Maronites. The Church of Scotland had even developed plans to convert the Jews to Christianity but had to give up proselyting after strong protests were lodged in England. Nevertheless, the Protestants covertly continued their conversion efforts for a long time.

The settlement of Jews in Palestine has a long history. In 1846, Isaac Altaras, a merchant from France, and Moses Montefiore, the British financier who also enjoyed the friendship of the sultan in Istanbul, both of them deeply distressed with the situation of Jews in Russia, discussed the settlement of these Jews in Palestine. By 1847, the Russians

11. All communications with Smith are in F.M. (I), 177, 2097, August 17, December 7, 1858, and February 2, 1859.
12. F.M. (I), 177, 2384, March 19, 20, 1872.
13. *Ibid.*
14. F.M. (I), 24971/96, June 9, 1869.

had received from the British consul in Jerusalem a plan to transfer the Russian Jews who were residing in Palestine to British consular protection because many of them had stayed in Jerusalem more than one year, in violation of the Russian law, and therefore remained without protection. The Russians balked, apparently expecting that the British scheme would somehow produce a long-range solution so that all the Jews in Russia would emigrate to Palestine and free the tsarist government from one of its perennial problems.[15] But the Jews did not emigrate. The Crimean War of 1853, the Ashkenazim's distrust of the English, Tsar Alexander II's promised reforms which, it seemed, would lead to better days for minorities and especially for Jews, and the desire of many prosperous Jewish merchants of Russia to be assimilated into the Russian culture are possibly some of the reasons which prevented Jewish mass emigration to Palestine in the 1850s and 1860s. Indeed, the idea of remaining in Russia found advocates among many of the newly enriched upper-class Jews. For instance, Baron Joseph Grunzberg, a financier of Jewish origin who built the Russian railway system, established, in 1863, the Society for the Spread of Enlightenment among Jews in Russia, with the purpose of assimilating them into the Russian culture. However, that very year Tsar Alexander, vexed by the revolt of the Poles, reversed his liberal policies and began to oppress minorities. The Jews, as usual, suffered the most. At the same time, following the Crimean War, the Jews of Crimea, who were of a different group, addressed a joint petition to the sultan and were allowed to migrate to and settle on Ottoman domains.[16]

The persecution of the Jews in Russia contrasted sharply with the tolerance and protection accorded them by the Ottoman government. A letter of April 27, 1876, signed by J. M. Montefiore on behalf of the Jewish Committee in London, and asking the sultan in Istanbul to intervene on behalf of some Yemeni Jews who were being mistreated by locals there, shows very well the difference between Russian and Ottoman treatment of Jews. Montefiore, president of the board of the Jewish Committee, mentions an imperial firman of November 16, 1840, which His Imperial Majesty

---

15. I have studied the British views on the migration of Jews in the consular reports in the British Public Record Office in London. I shall touch only lightly on this aspect of the problem. A good but incomplete collection of these consular reports concerning the Jewish question in Palestine may be found in A. M. Hyamson, *The British Consulate in Jerusalem: 1838–1914*, 2 vols. (London, 1939). See also I. Margalith, *Le Baron de Rothschild et la colonisation jurve en Palestine* (Paris, 1957).

16. See letter in A. C. Eren, Turkiye'de Göç ve Göçmen Meseleleri (Istanbul, 1966), pp 55 ff., 90–115.

has most graciously confirmed, guaranteeing my coreligionists the most ample protection for their person and property. Moreover, this Board has gratefully observed the readiness with which the Turkish government on all occasions interferes to throw its protection around my coreligionists who may happen to be the victims of fanaticism or intolerance.[17]

Population Movements and Change After 1860

The demographic changes in the Ottoman state after 1860 were conditioned by political and military events occurring in the northern section of the realm. The policy of the government toward immigration and settlement changed in response to these political and military conditions. Russia's occupation of the Caucasus area inhabited by Muslims of Circassian, Turkish, and Iranian origin was undertaken in 1796–1829. In 1859, after two decades of exhaustive war in the mountains, the Russians finally captured Sheyh Shamil, the leader of the Circassian Muslims, who were struggling to maintain the independence of their lands. Subsequently, the Russians advanced southward along the coast of the Black Sea to Anapa and Sukumkale, both of which were administrative centers and strongholds of Circassian Muslims. Then the Russian army turned inland to face the Circassian tribes which had fought against it under Sheyh Shamil. The Russians demanded that the Circassians settle north, in the marshes of Kuban, and serve in the Russian army, or that they simply convert to Christianity.[18] Caught at this time in one of its periodic fits of nationalism and Orthodox proselytism of its numerous religious and ethnic minorities, Russia regarded the Circassian tribes as backward and took it upon itself to "civilize" them by conversion—forceful, if necessary—to Orthodox Christianity. The tribes rejected the Russian demands and, consequently,

---

17. F.M. (I), 555.

18. There is ample literature on the Circassian migrations. Extensive information can be found in *Islam Ansiklopedisi*, published in Turkey, s.v. "Kaukas," "Murid," "Cerkes," "Abaza," "Dagistan," and in *Encyclopedia of Islam*, rev. ed. See also John F. Baddeley, *The Russian Conquest of the Caucasus* (London, 1908). On population specifically, see A. P. Berzhe, "Vyselenie Gortsev s Kaukaza," *Ruskaia Starina* (Moscow), January and February, 1882; Great Britain, House of Commons, *Accounts and Papers*, 1860–78; V. Minorsky, "Transcaucasia," *Journal Asiatique* (1930); E. G. Ravenstein, "The Populations of Russia and Turkey," *Journal of the Royal Statistical Society*, XL (1877), *The Caucasian Review*, published in Munich, has a series of excellent articles and bibliographical references to Circassians. See also Marc Pinson, "Demographic Warfare—An Aspect of Ottoman and Russian Policy, 1854–1866" (Ph.D. diss., Harvard University, 1970); Great Britain, House of Commons, "Papers Respecting the Settlement of Circassian Emigrants in Turkey," June 6, 1864.

were attacked and massacred. This was a preplanned action intended to drive the Muslim Circassian population southward, into the Ottoman territory. In anticipation of this exodus, the Russians had negotiated a treaty with the Ottomans in 1860, whereby the latter agreed to accept 40,000–50,000 Circassian migrants. Short of manpower, the Ottoman government hoped to employ the migrants in road construction and cotton cultivation, and to bolster its armed forces.

The Circassian migration from the north soon took the form of a deluge, especially after 1863, when the Russian government began to settle the Cossack soldiers in Circassia. The tribes, anxious to escape the Russian pressures, migrated south, to Anatolia, in ever increasing numbers, by sea and by land. Although figures concerning the exact number of immigrants are not available, it is estimated that the total number of Circassian immigrants (there were, in addition, other Muslims in the Caucasus who were forced to migrate south) was 1.2–1.6 million. It is also estimated that some 500,000–600,000 Circassians died of various diseases or drowned in the Black Sea. In any case, about 1.1 million Circassians settled in the Ottoman state, mostly in Anatolia, where they were joined, after 1878, by their brethren from the Balkans. A number of them also settled in Syria and in Palestine, mostly in the Golan region and in the Nablus area.

The immigration of Muslims into the Ottoman territories accelerated after the Russo-Turkish War of 1877, when large areas inhabited by Muslims (predominantly of Turkish origin) were lost to Rumania, Bulgaria, Serbia, and Greece. Beginning in late 1877, approximately two million refugees poured into the Ottoman domains in a span of thirty years. These were established mostly in Thrace and Anatolia. As a consequence of all these migrations and territorial losses, the density of population in the remaining Ottoman territories increased. The percentage of the population that was Muslim also increased sharply, and, consequently, Sultan Abdul Hamid embarked on a government policy designed to meet the long-range aspirations and interests of this group. Indeed, from the 1880s the Ottoman government identified itself increasingly with a universalist Islamic viewpoint, despite a series of developing nationalisms among the various ethnic groups.

Meanwhile, in Russia, the pogroms and persecutions of the Jews were growing more severe. The Jewish middle and lower classes suffered most, especially after the Russian middle and lower classes, unable to share in the limited economic boom of the 1870s, directed their frustrations against the Jews. Moreover, the industrialization of Russia, though slow, left Jewish craftsmen unemployed. Beginning in 1870, and especially after the assassination of Tsar Alexander II, in 1881, and the subsequent rash of anti-Semitism, there was an increased wave of Jewish emigration from Russia. Most of the emigrants went to the United States. A very small part of this wave of Jewish emigrants entered the Ottoman state. These came from Russia as well as from Rumania. Rumania, while under Ottoman suzerainty (until 1878), had received many of the Jewish emigrants escaping from Russia; but, after winning independence in 1878, it considerably stiffened its already evident anti-Jewish attitude.

Jewish Immigration

The history of Jewish immigration into the Ottoman state, and notably into Palestine, is little known. Rather than repeat what is already known, I shall deal with some of the relatively unknown facts as extracted from the Ottoman archives. I shall deal in particular with Jewish requests to settle in Palestine and with the Ottoman government's reply to them. It is necessary, however, to emphasize once again that both the Jewish immigration into Turkey and the Ottoman government's reaction to it must be viewed in light of the Russian persecution of minorities and the influx of a large number of Muslim refugees into the Ottoman domains. The Ottoman government's policy toward immigration, and especially toward Jewish immigration, must be seen also as a reaction to nationalism in general and to Zionism in particular. Indeed, after 1880 the government viewed nationalism which had political aims as a potential threat to the multiethnic, multinational principle of state organization on which the Ottoman comity was based.

The Jewish interest in settling in Palestine, usually expressed by intellectuals and religious leaders, is clearly evident in a series of letters found in Ottoman archives. Among these is a letter from Rabbi Joseph Natonek of Budapest, dated October 21, 1876, and addressed to Sultan Abdul Hamid through Aleko Pasha, Ottoman ambassador in Vienna.[19] Natonek demanded permission to settle Jews in Palestine. His arguments in favor of settlement rested on two points: the first concerned the dangers threatening the Ottoman state, and the second, the potential of Jews to rejuvenate it. Natonek believed that the Russian government and its people hated the Turkish government (*Turkish* is his word). Russians used a religious tradition to justify the lowest actions against Turkey, such as inciting rebellion among Ottoman subjects and undermining their loyalty to the government. The Ottomans found themselves isolated in Europe because of race and religion. The occasional support

---

19. F.M. (I), 177, 47646/183.

of Europeans given to Turkey, according to Natonek, was not sincere but was stimulated only by fear of Russia. Consequently, Rabbi Natonek proposed to suppress the Russian danger by reinforcing the Ottoman state with a Jewish population distinguished by intelligence and wealth. The colonization of Palestine by European Jews would give the Ottoman Empire moral and physical rejuvenation, as has been the case in all countries where Jews have established themselves. According to Natonek, if a substantial contingent from among three million European Jews, but mostly from among Russian Jews, were allowed to settle in Palestine, it would weaken and embarrass Russia. Once Ottoman permission for settlement was granted, Russia would oppose it for economic and political reasons, and this would cause discontent and irritation among Jews desiring to emigrate. "They will become fanatical about migration, and this will create an inevitable conflict between them and the Russian government."[20] The emigration of Jews to Palestine would also have positive effects upon the attitude of Europeans, such as the Austrians, who feared the Slavs. All of this, reasoned Natonek, would enhance the power of the Ottoman state and would allow it to pursue an aggressive policy.

Natonek stressed the fact that the desire of the European Jews to settle in Palestine stemmed from their religious beliefs as well as from their desire to escape the hatred of Catholics, which still existed despite the progress that religious tolerance had registered. The Jews, if allowed to settle in Palestine, would be grateful to the Ottoman government for saving them from intolerance, and they would develop the country and would enrich the government by buying land and real estate. Natonek advised the Ottoman government to allow only capable and hard-working people to settle in Palestine and to exclude those who used religious pretexts to live off charity. Moreover, the rabbi suggested that a law be enacted to regulate relations between colonists and the native population.[21] The colonists would enjoy special freedoms—the greater the freedom, the faster the progress—including the right to travel to Europe to secure financial aid and to inform the European Jews that there was a place on earth where they could find relief from European intolerance.

The Ottoman government replied to Natonek by stating firmly that almost all lands in Palestine were occupied, and that the autonomy sought by Natonek was incompatible with the administrative principles of the state. The government called Natonek's attention to the fact

20. *Ibid.*
21. *Ibid.*

that immigration into the Ottoman state was open to all individuals who wanted to establish themselves permanently, and that there was a regulation for mass settlement which the Jews could use.[22] Another communication, transmitted to the government by the Ottoman legation in Washington, and mentioning the good will to be created by free migration among Europeans, suggested that approximately one million Jews out of the five million who were living in Europe be allowed to settle in Ottoman territories.[23]

The Ottoman government's position on immigration was clear. It would allow any individual, regardless of religion or nationality, to immigrate into Turkey, but it would restrict mass settlement—that is, it would not permit one ethnic or religious group to establish numerical majority in one specific area.[24] Several decrees to this effect were issued, in 1884, 1887, and 1888. Despite these clear instructions, individuals continued to propose mass settlement. Dr. Alfred Nossig of the Jewish Committee of Berlin, for instance, had a rather ambitious scheme for settlement in Palestine.[25] Furthermore, Alexander Lederbaum, director of the journal *Hamelitz* in St. Petersburg, addressed a letter to the Ottoman government citing the difficult situation of the Jews in Russia. He was

> overwhelmed by the demand coming from all corners of the vast Russian Empire to help those Jews who wanted to migrate to the hospitable land of the Ottoman Empire in search of a new homeland. Numerous Jewish families have already the happiness of finding an excellent shelter in Syria and Palestine.[26]

Lederbaum asked for land and boats to transport the Jews to Palestine. The Porte answered that mass immigration had been forbidden as early as 1884, and that presently there were large groups of Muslims from Russia who had been deprived of their homes and who needed to be resettled. Afterward, if land was left, Jews would also be taken care of.[27]

Beginning in 1890, the question of Jewish immigration into Ottoman

---

22. *Ibid.* All this information is in the same file.
23. F.M. (I), 346, 6078/126, November 16, 1891.
24. See note to German embassy on October 15, 1888, and the reference to it by the embassy. F.M. (I), 346, 1438/1624, July 18, 1900.
25. F.M. (I), 346, 6695/331, Berlin, October 12, 1909.
26. F.M. (I), 587, 99125/139.
27. *Ibid.*

territory superseded theoretical debate and became a reality. Large groups of Jews from Russia and Rumania sought to migrate to and settle in the Ottoman state using any means available. Escaping persecution, large groups of Jews arrived in Ottoman ports without passports and visas, and even without means of subsistence. The Ottoman consulates, in asking for instructions, reported that even larger numbers of Jews were gathering in Russian ports and were seeking to migrate to the Ottoman territory by any means possible.

Consequently, the cabinet in Istanbul held a meeting on August 1, 1891, and communicated its decision in the form of a circular letter from the Foreign Ministry to Ottoman representatives in St. Petersburg and Athens.[28] The letter said that

> in order to avoid the dangers [of disease] presented by the agglomeration of Jewish migrants, the imperial government has been compelled to take defensive measures in order to prohibit their landing in Turkey. Renew the order to your consulates to refuse them [Jewish emigrants] visas, and inform navigation companies that the imperial authorities have the order not to allow them to land, so that the navigation companies shall not accept them on board.[29]

It must be stressed that this stern order was a reaction and a reprimand to the Ottoman consulate in Odessa. The consulate had issued general visas to 165 Jews who possessed Russian citizenship, and they went directly to Palestine, presumably to settle there. The communication made it clear that the prohibition did not affect individual Jews who would come into the Ottoman state on business or who were immigrating as individuals.[30] Jewish immigrants continued to arrive in large numbers, and the Ottoman government felt compelled to send notes to several foreign embassies asking them to report the prohibition of mass immigration to the local navigation companies.[31]

The British government, in a verbal note, objected to this decision, which in their view was in variation with the first article of the capitulation given to England in 1675 and confirmed by the treaty of April 29, 1861, and the treaty of Berlin of 1878. The British acknowledged that the decision referred only to those who wanted to immigrate in large numbers, and not to those who wanted to immigrate as individuals.

---

28. F.M. (I), 346, 101693/170A, August 18, 1891.
29. *Ibid.*
30. F.M. (I), 346, 6749/1048, July 19–31, 1891.
31. F.M. (I), 346, 102208/95, October 9, 1891.

Nevertheless, the Jews from England traveled with their families and thus appeared to be in large numbers. The British asked for further explanation.

In a stern answer, the Ottoman government maintained its position and insisted that its prohibition was applicable only to large groups from abroad, or even from within the empire, who wanted to settle in one specific place, and that all these restrictive measures were taken with the public interest in mind.[32] Some Jews from Georgia and Bokhara, in central Asia, found a way to circumvent the prohibition by going to Batum and proceeding from there to Palestine. Once more the Ottoman embassy issued a memorandum stating that the mass immigration of Jews into Palestine was forbidden. However, individual three-month renewable visas could be issued to Jews who wanted to go to Palestine for pilgrimage purposes. The Porte asked that the condition of admission be indicated on the traveler's passport.[33] On the other hand, the Ottoman government gave limitless permission to Muslim families in foreign lands to migrate to and settle on Ottoman lands. In fact, in some cases it instructed the consulates to issue passports free of charge to needy migrants, as was the case with some Muslims from Dobruja, Rumania.[34]

The restriction of immigration into Palestine was reinforced by some administrative measures. The embassies of France, Austria-Hungary, Greece, Belgium, Germany, Russia, Great Britain, and Spain, in verbal communications to the Porte, indicated that the Ottoman cadastral authorities, especially in Syria and Palestine, were formally opposed to the transfer of rural and urban real estate to foreign subjects of Jewish faith. They demanded an explanation.[35] The Ottoman government, in reply, referred them to the law of Sefer 7, 1284, which regulated the transfer of property among individuals, and which insisted that this was strictly an internal matter.[36]

Thus far I have not found any extensive information in the Ottoman archives concerning the attitude of the Anatolian or Syrian native population toward the settlement of outsiders on their lands, that is, toward the settlement of Circassians, Germans, Jews, Turks from the Balkans, and others. The only available information is an exchange of notes between the Ottoman government and the German embassy

32. F.M. (I), 346, 102116/102, November 19, 1891.
33. F.M. (I), 346, 512/191, March 7–23, 1904.
34. F.M. (I), 973, 34109/209, August 22, 1899.
35. F.M. (I), 346, 6787-37/20, April, 1911.
36. *Ibid.*

concerning the German colony at Jaffa. According to the complaint of the embassy, the local population, as early as 1877, showed deep hostility toward the German settlers, forcing them to seek the protection of German and British authorities. The Porte assured the embassy that the safety of the German colonists would be maintained. But at the same time, the Ottoman government, in a lengthy memo, stated categorically that it could not accept the unchecked growth of foreign settlements, such as the German colony at St. Jean d'Akcre. This colony, according to the Ottoman note, had isolated itself religiously and ethnically from the rest of the population. "It should be noted," remarked the government, "that in Turkey there was never formed a population center consisting exclusively of foreigners who constituted a commune through their isolation."[37]

Conclusion

The conclusion to be drawn from the information presented in this paper is self-evident. The Ottoman government first adopted a very liberal policy toward immigration and settlement, placing no conditions with regard to the nationality, race, or religion of the immigrants. It was forced to change this policy after large groups of Muslims, forced out of Russia and the Balkans, flocked into Anatolia and occupied much of the vacant land. Moreover, the nationalist currents, and the danger of having one ethnic or religious group concentrated in one area and claiming it as its independent territory, posed an immediate threat to the idea of multiethnic, multireligious coexistence, which was the constitutional basis of the Ottoman state.

All of these developments, as well as a growing Pan-Islamism in the Ottoman state, led to a restriction of the originally liberal immigration policy. Muslim refugees were allowed, out of necessity, to settle en masse in Ottoman territories. Non-Muslims were allowed to immigrate only as individuals, although in some exceptional cases group immigration was also permitted. The Jews in the Ottoman state enjoyed absolute freedom of religion, culture, travel, and occupation. Until the 1870s, Jews, like other Ottoman subjects, were free to settle wherever they wanted. (After Thessaly was left to Greece, a large group of Thessalian Jews asked for and received permission to settle en masse in the remaining Ottoman territories.) Beginning in the 1870s, as nationalism began to develop and the Jewish settlement in Palestine began to pursue

37. F.M. (I), 36, 46.374/33, February 1, 1877.

political goals, mass immigration into Palestine was greatly restricted. Still, individuals were allowed to immigrate freely. (The pilgrimage to the Holy Land was never prohibited. Visas for a maximum of three months—which were extended repeatedly—were issued to practically all applicants.)

The effects of the freedom enjoyed by the Jews in the Ottoman state, and of the policy that allowed them to immigrate only as individuals, can be seen in the figures concerning Jewish migration out of and into the Ottoman territory. The United States Hebrew Charities recorded that the total number of Jews arriving in the United States (the country receiving the largest number of Jewish emigrants) in 1884–1903 was 622,124. Of these, only 1,534, or barely 0.24 per cent, came from Turkey. At the same time, the Jewish population of Palestine increased slowly. Since the early Jewish settlers in Palestine were old people, one may assume that until 1882, and shortly thereafter, most of the increase in the Jewish population can be attributed to immigration. The Jewish population of Palestine consisted of about 12,000–15,000 people in 1868. By 1882, this population had nearly doubled, to 23,000–27,000 (the number varies according to the source). This increase is probably a result of the free immigration policy adopted by the Ottoman government. During 1881–1900, that is, during the period of intensive Jewish emigration from Russia and insistent demands for settlement in Palestine, the total number of Jews in Palestine was never more than 60,000 people out of a total population of about 500,000.[38] In sum, the Ottoman policy of allowing individuals to immigrate and to settle, but prohibiting large groups from doing the same, was successful.

---

38. The figures in the conclusion are based on Margalith, *Le Baron de Rothschild;* Max Margolis and Alexander Marx; *History of the Jewish People* (New York: Atheneum, 1969); *Jewish Encyclopedia;* J. C. Hurewitz, *Diplomacy in the Near and Middle East,* 2 vols. (1956; reprint ed., New York: Octagon, 1972); and a variety of other sources.

André Dirlik

THE ALGERIAN RESPONSE TO SETTLEMENT

IN FEBRUARY, 1936, more than a century after the French conquest of Algeria was begun, the debate over Algerian nationality was opened.[1] The two major protagonists in this debate, Ferhat Abbas, the pharmacist from Setif and one-time president of the Algerian Students Union at the University of Algiers, and Shaykh Abdul Hamid Ibn Badis from Constantine, the president of the Association of Algerian Ulama, passionately argued for and against the French identity of the Algerian people. For the Westernist Algerians, Abbas contended that there had been little in the past of Algerians that could prevent them from embracing the French culture. For the neotraditionalist Algerians, Ibn Badis underlined the distinctive character of the Algerians, whose period of Islamic history had finally made them part and parcel of the Arab world.

In 1954, the newly founded Front de Libération Nationale (FLN) adopted Ibn Badis' slogan, Algeria Is My Country, Islam My Religion, and Arabic My Language, and called for an armed struggle for

---

1. The debate was initiated by Ferhat Abbas in an article entitled "La France c'est moi," published in the newspaper *La Defense*, February 28, 1936, p. 1. Ibn Badis replied in the April, 1936, issue of his *Al-Shihab*, pp. 42–43. Pertinent excerpts from this debate can be found in André Dirlik, "Abd al-Hamid ibn Badis (1889–1940): Ideologist of Islamic Reformism and Leader of Algerian Nationalism" (Ph.D. diss., Institute of Islamic Studies, McGill University, 1971).

independence from France.² Ibn Badis had been dead for fifteen years, but his disciples rallied to the cause of the new Algerian revolutionaries. Abbas himself, and all those who had worked so hard for assimilation to France, also espoused the cause of liberation. In 1962, at the Evian Agreement, France conceded Algerians the right to nationhood. Algerian leaders and the Algerian people submitted to the notion put forward earlier by Ibn Badis that Algeria was not France, that it could not be France, and that, furthermore, it did not want to be France simply because its folk was Muslim and their language Arabic.³

Algerian Nationalism

Students of Algerian nationalism are, more often than not, prone to attribute the will of Algerians to achieve independence to the Algerian identity.⁴ Furthermore, such identity is conceived as stemming from the past rather than as related to the very nature of the French presence on Algerian soil. It is evident that in pre-French times, the inhabitants of the so-called Ottoman beylics of North Africa had shown little evidence of Algerian identity. Abdul Qadir al-Jazairi, who led the rebellion against the Ottomans and their political successors, the French, was jazairi only inasmuch as he belonged geographically to that area.⁵ The political chaos at the beginning of the nineteenth century in the Maghreb was what allowed his rebellion to succeed. The ideological basis of his movement remained traditional in that it was his newly founded *tariqa*, the Qadiriyya, which induced Algerians either to support him or to support his enemies, Ottoman or French. The Qadiri state, which reminds the historian of the *medinese* state of the Prophet, catered to identities which were traditional and far from Algerian. Both the Westernists and the neotraditionalists could well accept that. They used this episode in history, however, to substantiate their respective positions, to prove either that one could not find evidence in the past of a distinct Algerian movement or, on the contrary, that this episode clearly

---

2. See D. Gordon, *The Passing of French Algeria* (London: Oxford University Press, 1960), pp. 107-8.

3. This refers specifically to Ibn Badis' article in *Al-Shihab*. In the plebiscite of July 1, 1962, the Algerians overwhelmingly voted against assimilation and for independence.

4. See A. Nouschi, *La Naissance du nationalisme algérien, 1914–1954* (Paris: Les Editions de Minuit, 1962).

5. See J. Abun-Nasr, *The Tijaniyya, A Sufi Order in the Modern World* (London: Oxford University Press, 1965).

pointed to the consistent aspirations of the Algerians to reject alien rule.

The Abbas–Ibn Badis debate came a few years after the celebrations throughout Algeria of one hundred years of French rule. In preparation for the French Algerian centenary, French historians at the University of Algiers had gone to great lengths to prove that there had been no civilization to speak of in the beylics prior to the French conquest.[6] This, of course, denied the Algerians their right to nationhood. While Abbas agreed with this view, Ibn Badis could not. The year of the debate, the president of an association of Algerian workers in France, the Etoile Nord-Africaine, and a worker himself, Messali Hajj, put his weight behind Ibn Badis. Hajj, who once claimed to be a Marxist, was now converted to nationalism. He called for the immediate independence of Algeria.

No Algerian before Messali Hajj had gone so far in making political demands. He pointed to the exploitative nature of French Algeria and saw no alternative for the Algerians other than to expel all Europeans from their country and to break all relations with France. But Hajj lacked the historical arguments and the ideas to make his views understandable to everyone. His feelings were those of an Algerian worker who had discovered his identity upon emigrating to France. He was introduced to the struggle against colonialism by the French Left. Upon his return to Algeria, he became convinced that assimilation was an illusion. He found in Ibn Badis' writings the theoretical basis for Algerian independence. If such independence was to be achieved, now was the time to do it; according to Hajj, the French were not in Algeria to help civilize the Algerians, nor would they concede to reforms that would gradually bring equality between the Europeans in Algeria and the Algerians themselves.[7] The peculiar character of French Algeria, where a policy of settlement had brought nearly one million immigrants from Europe to live among four million Algerians, perpetuated the exploitation of the land and the people by France.

Hajj's arguments were revolutionary to Algeria's thinkers. Abbas and Ibn Badis, and their respective followers, were not prepared to accept them, and their initial reaction was to reject Hajj's movement. The revolutionary forces in Algeria are not to be found in the debate over Algerian identity, although this debate did, in time, provide the necessary arguments for Arabism in Algeria.

---

6. Most outspoken among them was Prof. E. Gautier. He made his views public in "L'Evolution de l'Algérie de 1830 à 1930," *Cahiers du centenaire*, Vol. III.

7. See Gordon, *Passing of French Algeria*, p. 28.

The French Policy of Settlement

French Algeria had come into being as a result of new strategical thinking within the French army. Prior to the time of General Bugeaud, the military in France continued to conceive of warfare as a confrontation between forces, each of which aimed to destroy the other. In the tradition of Napoleon, they concentrated upon organization, armaments, maneuverability, and the swift application of might to the enemy's weakest parts.[8] During the conquest of Algeria, in the first half of the nineteenth century, General Bourmont successfully defeated the army of the dey and stormed his cities. But when the French moved inland, they encountered, for the first time, the forces of tribal society. Their strategy and their tactics invariably failed until Bugeaud took over the command of the French Expeditionary Force. He concluded not only that the French should improve their mobility to beat the enemy at his own game, but also that, because of the conquerors' limited manpower, the occupied territory should be settled by Frenchmen if the French had any hope of retaining it.

The French policy of settlement in Algeria was less than successful until Napoleon III assumed power in France (1852). The instauration of the Second Empire coincided with the coming of age of French capitalism. As soon as the French entrepreneurs turned their attention toward Algeria as a close, safe, and profitable area of investment, the services of the state were made available for its development in an unprecedented manner. The early settlement of Algeria had consisted in the demobilization of troops or in the transportation of workers and farmers, often against their will, and in awarding them lands which had been confiscated from dissident tribes. Between 1844 and 1863, major legislation was passed which granted each tribesman the right of private ownership to land.[9] As had been anticipated by those who enacted French Algeria's land laws, lands which had once been collectively owned and tilled became the property of large French companies. The twofold objective which the French government had set for itself—to disintegrate traditional society and thereby check the military threat which tribalism always posed for France in Algeria, and to create a

---

8. See J. Gottmann, "Bugeaud, Galliéni, Lyautey: The Development of French Colonial Warfare," in *Makers of Modern Strategy*, ed. E. M. Earle (Princeton: Princeton University Press, 1952), pp. 235–38.

9. See P. Bourdieu, *The Algerians*, trans. A. Ross (Boston, 1962), pp. 120–21; Charles A. Julien, *Histoire de l'Algérie contemporaine, la conquête et les débuts de la colonisation (1827–1871)* (Paris: PUF, 1964), p. 427.

salaried Algerian working class which would become available to French employers—had been achieved. The rapid development of French Algeria now followed, unimpeded.

The major French banks extended their activities to Algeria. The Customs Law of 1851 had made Algeria an annex to France. That same year, 1,700 tons of mineral were exported to France. In 1857, the value of French imports from Algeria amounted to almost 67 million francs.[10] The growing opportunities which capital investments afforded attracted Europeans in ever greater numbers, to the satisfaction of the French state, which had never abandoned its policy of settlement in spite of the many difficulties it had encountered. In 1866, 252,000 Europeans were settled in the cities and on the land of Algeria, an increase of 100,000 over the 1851 figure.[11] They came from France, Corsica, Malta, Italy, Spain, Germany, and Switzerland. They were distinct, in values and in mores, from the indigenous Algerians. Their role in the economic life of French Algeria would give this initial distinction new meaning, and would precipitate the Algerian revolution.

NATIONALS AND SETTLERS

The Algerian revolution arose from the contradictions which French Algeria brought about for all those concerned. The immediate contradictions concerned the military, the settlers, and French capital. The new role which General Galliéni and General Lyautey, both disciples of Bugeaud, devised for the French officer aimed to bring him into the political field of colonization.[12] The Bureaux Arabes, for instance, which had been instituted in Algeria under Bugeaud, sought to ally all traditional leaders to the military.[13] The avowed aim of the French officers to support their newly formed friends among the Algerians often brought them into open conflict with the fortune-seeking and opportunistic settlers, whose goals in Algeria amounted to spoliation of the natives' valuables. French capitalism, on the other hand, although it needed the military to secure its investments and the settlers to manage

10. See Julien, *Histoire de l'Algérie*, pp. 381–82.
11. See T. Opperman, *Le Problème algérien, données historiques, juridiques, politiques* (Paris: Maspéro, 1961), p. 43.
12. See Gottmann, "Bugeaud, Galliéni, Lyautey," pp. 240–46.
13. See Y. Yacono, *Les Bureaux arabes et l'évolution des genres de vie dans l'ouest du Tell algérois* (Paris: Larose, 1953).

them, regretted the overprotectiveness of the military toward the Algerians and feared the independent ambitions of the settlers. It is interesting, however, that the moment Algerian nationalism made itself felt, the two major European interest groups in Algeria, the military and the settlers, united to confront and destroy it.

During 1936, the First Algerian Muslim Congress met. Algerians of all walks of life, spokesmen for the unofficial reform-minded Ulama, French-educated évolués, merchants, veterans of the First World War, members of various trade-unions and the association of Algerian workers in France, the Etoile Nord-Africaine, claimed for the first time their right to speak for the Algerians.[14] They refused to be represented any longer by those indigenous leaders, heads of mystical brotherhoods, tribal chieftains, and village elders, who spoke for a decreasing number of Algerians, the traditional society which had long been encroached upon by the money economy of the French and which was on the verge of disappearing altogether. The representatives of the new Algeria, the Algeria that could not ignore European settlement and development or be shielded from it, demanded reforms which would uplift their followers economically and culturally. They had faith in the new Front Populaire government and in its prime minister, socialist Léon Blum.

The events which followed the First Algerian Muslim Congress made it clear that the nature of French Algeria could not be transformed by way of reforms. The entire structure of the French Algerian state had been designed to establish a workable yet formal relationship between the two races. In fact, both the *évolués,* who were in favor of greater assimilation to France, and the neotraditionalists, who demanded the necessary means for greater cultural freedom, challenged the very status of the indigenous population in the French Algerian set-up. They demanded that the legal, the economic, and the social barriers which kept all Algerians subservient to the settlers be gradually lifted.[15] Their trust in the liberal institutions of France made them believe, naïvely, that they could achieve their aims within the existing set-up. It is therefore natural that the early Algerian political activists shunned violence. Messali Hajj, who advocated radical solutions, was ostracized, and the *évolués* and the Association of Algerian Ulama, long at odds with each other, were drawn closer together.[16]

---

14. See *Al-Shihab,* July, 1936, pp. 203–4, 210–11. The entire issue of this journal was dedicated to the Algerian Muslim Congress, attended by 3,000 delegates.
15. *Ibid.*
16. *Ibid.,* p. 210.

The End of the Settler State in Algeria

The French should have taken advantage of Algerian liberalism. When General de Gaulle assumed power for a second time, in 1961, he blamed those who had brought him to the Elysée for having not done precisely that. He arranged for a plebiscite in which Algerians could choose to become French citizens; but by that time the majority of the Algerian people had opted for independence. In the words of some naïve *évolués,* the Gaullist offer had come too late.

The last days of French Algerian history read otherwise. The only guarantee for the settlers against the gradual erosion of their economic privileges in Algeria had been, and remained, the preservation of the racial line which distinguished European from Arab.[17] In the hearts of Frenchmen and settlers alike, the roots of discrimination were deep. Islam and Christiandom had, after all, been at loggerheads ever since the Desert Religion had emerged as a major challenge to the Christian states. The Arabs, moreover, had threatened France more than once: at Poitiers in 732, and in Algeria the moment that Algerians identified with the Arab world. The settlers advocated the repression of Algerian nationalism, and this included Algerian liberals as well as Algerian revolutionaries. They found in the military, who could no longer support the defense of traditionalism, their most natural ally. After the Second World War, the *raison d'être* of the French army was the preservation of France's overseas empire. The less successful they proved to be in this goal, the more determined they became. French repression hardened the freedom fighters in their will to liberate Algeria and helped to convert undecided Algerians. When French capitalism realized that it cost more to remain in Algeria than to abandon it, it applied pressures on the government in Paris, which eventually caused France to abandon to their fate those it had worked so hard to settle in Algeria.

The question arises as to whether the fate of Algeria's European settlers could have been otherwise. They were forced to leave behind their belongings and to suffer the pains of resettlement away from a land which had become theirs by rights of birth and work. Those who least understand the nature of the settler state in Algeria believe that de Gaulle's offer was genuine. They fail to see that the land policies of France in Algeria, which deprived the old social structures of their economic basis, had opened the way for social change among the Algerians. The Arab tag which was placed on them by the settlers only eased the work of the Islamic reformists and the Association of

---

17. See Julien, *Histoire de l'Algérie,* pp. 405–6.

Algerian Ulama, and promoted their ideas that the distinction between a decadent civilization and no civilization at all should be made in Algeria. The Algerians achieved civilization the moment they embraced Islam and were Arabized. Furthermore, they were at that time undergoing a renaissance which would sharpen even more the distinction between themselves and the settlers. Their exploitation thwarted their natural development.

It was impossible to bring an end to the settler state without bringing an end to French Algeria. Otherwise, the settlers could choose to dissociate themselves totally from the Algerians. They could push them into the desert or into neighboring states. Better yet, they could exterminate them all. Those settlers who considered such possibilities were denying the very object of European settlement in Algeria: to hold that conquered territory for France and, at the same time, to exploit its cheap labor resources. The history of French Algeria is over. But similar histories are being written in Africa, Asia, and Latin America.

Adnan Abu-Ghazaleh

THE PALESTINIAN RESPONSE TO ZIONIST SETTLEMENT: A CULTURAL DIMENSION

IT IS GENERALLY STRESSED that Arab opposition to Jewish settlement in Palestine began with the First World War. While the Palestinian Arab response to Zionist ambitions assumed increasing proportions with the British promise of sovereignty to the Jews, awareness of the Zionist plans and opposition to them can be traced to the last two decades of the nineteenth century. The period between 1880 and 1914 is of vital importance in the story of the Arab opposition to Jewish settlement. This period witnessed the growth to maturity of those Arabs who led the opposition to Zionist plans in the 1920s and the 1930s. And in these leaders and in their actions and utterances lie the roots and patterns of later Arab sentiment. This paper, therefore, will first endeavor to examine the Palestinian Arab intellectual response to Jewish settlement in Palestine in the early stages of the Zionist movement. This will be a necessary prelude to the examination of the Palestinian response during the British Mandate, when the nature of the Zionist threat became more apparent and the opposition of the Palestinian Arabs, both political and intellectual, became more intense.

THE RESPONSE TO ZIONISM FROM 1880 TO 1914

Prior to the First World War, Jewish settlement in Palestine was theoretically prohibited. The regulations governing the movement of Jews within the Ottoman Empire were established in 1882. Early in that year individual Jews, including some members of the Lovers of Zion, in the wake of the first major series of pogroms in Russia, applied to the Ottoman consul general in Odessa for entry visas so that they could settle in Palestine. The consul general, due to the large number involved, sought instructions and on April 28, 1882, received regulations that were to govern Jewish immigration to the Ottoman Empire until 1917. According to the regulations, immigrant Jews were welcome anywhere in the Ottoman Empire except in Palestine. Moreover, they were to settle in small groups, relinquish their foreign nationality, and abide by the laws of the empire.[1] Nevertheless, Jewish immigrants did enter and settle in Palestine. Occasional relaxation of restrictions and bribes for port officials accounted for most of the entries.

The Arabs were aware of the Zionist movement almost from its inception, and it began to figure prominently in the press in the late 1890s. In 1898 *Al-Muqtataf* claimed, wrongly, that all Jews settling in Palestine were capitalists who had been dominant in trade and commerce, and that success for Zionism was far off and would not be easy: for one thing, land purchase and the transfer of poor Jews would be extremely difficult; for another, the Ottoman authorities opposed the idea.[2] A few weeks later, Rashid Rida, the Islamic reformer, reprinted the article in his journal, *Al-Manar*. Rida was both indignant at and inspired by the national revival of the Jews, and was critical of the indifference and disunity of his compatriots. At this stage, the national revival of the Jews was, to Rida, more a model than a menace.[3]

Zionist ambitions were taken more seriously by Yusuf Diya al-Khalidi, a former president of the Municipal Council of Jerusalem and that city's deputy to "Midhat's Parliament." In a letter to Zadoc Kahn, the chief rabbi of France and an intimate of Theodor Herzl, Khalidi expressed sympathy for Zionist ideas but went on to explain that Palestine was inhabited by Arabs, and that choosing it as a Jewish home would trigger a popular movement against the Jews which could not be quelled. He therefore suggested that another territory, preferably an uninhabited one, be chosen.

After the turn of the century, with increased incidents of anti-Semitism

---

1. Neville Mandel, "Turks, Arabs and Jewish Immigration into Palestine, 1882–1914," in *Middle Eastern Affairs*, no. 4, ed. Albert Hourani, St. Anthony's Papers, no. 17 (New York: Oxford University Press, 1965), p. 80.
2. *Al-Muqtataf*, XXII, no. 4 (1898), 310–11.
3. *Al-Manar*, I, no. 6 (1898), 108; *ibid.*, IV, no. 21 (1902), 801–9.

in Russia and Rumania, more and more Jewish emigrants reached Palestine, and land-purchase activities by the Zionist organizations multiplied. In 1903 the Anglo-Palestine Company, a bank set up to purchase land, opened a branch in Jaffa. In 1904 Ahmad Resid Bey, who openly supported Jewish immigration, was appointed mutasarrif of Jerusalem. Complaints from local Arabs forced his removal and the appointment of Ali Ekrem, who strictly enforced the restrictions against Jewish immigration.

The complaints that began to be heard from the Arab population showed some signs of a developing national consciousness. Najib Azoury, a Jerusalemite residing in Paris, issued his manifesto, *Les Pays Arabes aux Arabes,* at the end of 1904, and it was translated into Arabic in January, 1905. Both versions circulated in Palestine. The Ottoman authorities considered the pamphlets suspicious, and a number of Arab notables in Jerusalem and Jaffa had their houses searched and were themselves imprisoned for possessing the literature.[4] The ideas of nationalism were more strongly stressed in Azoury's book, *Le Reveil de la nation arabe,* which was published in Paris in 1905. The ideas expressed in this book were the outcome of Azoury's residence in France but also were definitely influenced by his experiences as an Ottoman official in Jerusalem around the turn of the century. In the introduction to the book he stated that two most important phenomena affect events in Asiatic Turkey: the revival of the Arab nation and the attempt of the Jews to restore the old monarchy of Israel. These two forces, he maintained, will continue to oppose one another in a way not unlike that in nationalist movements in other parts of the world.[5]

The Young Turk revolution had an important impact on the progress of events. Zionists began to clamor for representation in the Ottoman Parliament so that they might state their case for autonomy in Palestine. *Al-Asmai,* an Arabic newspaper which appeared in Jaffa at the time, attacked Zionists as foreign exploiters and called for an effort by Arab leaders to help improve the peasants' standard of living and strengthen their national consciousness lest they fall prey to Zionist designs.[6] In Haifa, Najib Nassar edited *Al-Karmel* with the objective of opposing Zionism and Jewish settlement. In Paris the Arab nationalist paper, *Nahdat al-Arab,* accused the Committee of Union and Progress (CUP) of complicity with the Zionists and even suggested that the 1908 revolution was engineered by the Zionists to destroy the empire and

---

4. See Mandel, "Turks, Arabs and Jewish Immigration into Palestine," p. 91.
5. Azoury, *Le Reveil de la nation arabe* (Paris, 1905), p. v.
6. *Al-Asmai,* I (1908), 14–15.

to establish a Jewish state on its ruins.[7]

In the meantime, the Zionist campaign to purchase land was continuing. The Anglo-Palestine Company became more active. In the autumn of 1910, Elias Sursuq of Beirut sold the company 2,400 acres situated between Nazareth and Jenin. Shukri Bey al-Asali, the district officer of Nazareth, who had jurisdiction over the area of the sale, tried, without success, to block the deal. In 1911 Asali became a deputy to the Ottoman Parliament, where he frequently raised the Palestine issue.

Zionism and its dangers began to elicit more of a response from the Palestinian Arabs. A telegram protesting leniency toward Zionism was sent from Jaffa, with 150 signatures, to Ottoman authorities.[8] Najib Nassar published a series of articles which he later combined in a book.[9]

In the three years preceding the First World War, the Ottoman government followed a policy toward Jewish immigration that wavered from strict prohibition to leniency. In 1912, for example, the disastrous defeats in the Balkan and North African wars left the treasury empty, and the *entente liberale* government modified its anti-Zionist stand and solicited financial help from the Zionists.[10] In 1913 that government fell, and the CUP was restored to power. The new government proposed "an Islamic-Jewish alliance" with the intention of relaxing restrictions on Jewish immigration but doing so through a prior agreement between the Zionist leaders and the Palestinian Arabs.[11]

To combat this trend in Ottoman policy, nationalist societies were formed in several cities, notably in Beirut, Damascus, Jerusalem, and Jaffa. The Decentralization party in Cairo also showed immense interest in the issue. Da'ud Barakat, the editor of *Al-Ahram* and a member of the party, advocated cooperation between the Arabs and the Zionists and cautioned the latter that they needed the friendship of the Arabs more than that of the Turks.[12] Nevertheless, an entente was reached between the Zionists and the Decentralization party. The existence of such an understanding became clear during the Arab Congress held in Paris in the summer of 1913. In the opening address Ahmad Tabbarah made only one ambiguous reference to Zionism: he saw no objection

---

7. Bernard Lewis, *The Emergence of Modern Turkey* (London, 1961), pp. 207 ff.

8. See Mandel, "Turks, Arabs and Jewish Immigration into Palestine," p. 96.

9. Nassar, *Al-Sahyuniyyah: Tarikhuha, Aghraduha, wa Ahamiyyatuha* [Zionism: Its history, aim, and importance] (Haifa, 1911).

10. Great Britain, Foreign Office, 371/1794, file 16925, no. 218.

11. See Mandel, "Turks, Arabs and Jewish Immigration into Palestine," p. 99.

12. *Al-Ahram*, February 19, 1913.

to the immigration of Jews provided it had *nizam khass* (a special form of organization).[13] Moreover, the congress adopted no resolution to deal with the Zionist problem.

This attitude had immediate repercussions in all of Syria, especially in Palestine. *Falastin* ran an editorial on July 9, 1913, attacking the congress' approach to the problem of Jewish immigration. Najib Nassar called for another congress to be held in Nablus to discuss the Zionist problem and the means for dealing with it.[14]

Meanwhile the CUP government, still hoping for Jewish financial aid, made more concessions to the Zionists: a Zionist society was allowed to open in Constantinople; three of the anti-Zionist Arab newspapers, *Al-Muqtataf* in Damascus, *Al-Karmel* in Haifa, and *Falastin* in Jaffa, were temporarily closed; and transfer of land in Palestine to Zionists was quietly authorized.[15] The concessions did not go unnoticed. Public criticism of Ottoman policies became more frequent. Attacks on Jewish settlers became more common, particularly in the north of Palestine and in the Jerusalem area.[16] When elections were held for a new Ottoman Parliament in 1914, many Syrian Arabs campaigned against Zionism. Rajib al-Nashashibi, the head of an important family in Jerusalem and a candidate for the representation of that city, proclaimed that, if elected, he would dedicate all his strength to removing the danger of Zionism and Zionists from Palestine.[17] In the summer of 1914 anti-Zionist societies were founded in Jerusalem, Jaffa, Haifa, and Nablus, and also in Cairo, Beirut, and Constantinople. The program of one of these societies indicates the nature of their activities. On July 19 a manifesto appeared in a local paper in Cairo describing the objectives of the Society for the Opposition to the Zionists. The society endeavored to oppose Zionists by awakening the public to the danger that Jewish immigration posed to the Arab world in general and to Syria and Palestine in particular. It aimed to give economic aid to the farmers and peasants of the threatened areas so that they could withstand the pressure from Zionist agents. Finally, it intended to found branches of the society in all the towns and villages in Palestine in order to achieve its purposes.[18]

Before 1914 the number of Palestinian Arabs who participated in

---

13. *Al-Mu'tamar al-Arabi al-Awwal* [The First Arab Congress] (Cairo, 1913), p. 93.

14. *Al-Karmel*, August 18, 1913.

15. Great Britain, Foreign Office, 195/2452, file 1254, no. 67; see also *Falastin*, November 16, 1913 (after it was reopened).

16. *Al-Manar*, XVII, no. 1 (1914), 320.

17. *Al-Iqdam* (Cairo), March 12, 1914.

18. *Ibid.*, July 19, 1914.

Ottoman political affairs was small: the heads of a few leading families, some intellectuals living in larger towns, and some officials and students residing in Constantinople. Most of them, broadly representing the most politically conscious elements in Palestine at the time, were conversant with the aims and activities of the Zionists. This political leadership was unanimous in its opposition to Zionist ambitions and Jewish immigration; it was aware of the danger of Zionism to the Arab nature of Palestine. Palestinian opposition to Zionism was to become more sustained and more serious when the realization of Zionist ambitions became nearer.

The Response to Zionism during the Mandate

Confronted with the British occupation of Palestine after the First World War and the establishment of the mandate, with its commitment to Zionist political ambitions, nationalist writing within Palestine developed a specifically Palestinian orientation. There arose during the mandate, basically in response to the Zionist threat, a body of Palestinian Arab literature—creative, political, and historical—which integrated national themes in such a way as to impress national consciousness on those who were exposed to it.

Creative Writing

The maturity of some of the Palestinians who had been members of the different literary clubs in the decade before the First World War, and the return of the few students from foreign universities where they had received a thorough education in the humanities, provided Palestine with a number of creative writers of varied viewpoints and interests. The economic development of the country and the growth of the number of schools and literary clubs simultaneously provided a sizable audience for the work of these writers.

Palestinian writers expressed themselves in a variety of literary forms. Some used the short story, while others used the novel and others used poetry. Their works were products of a nascent national revival, and nationalist themes often predominated over literary considerations.

Although the short stories of Najati Sidqi and Abdul Hamid Yasin reflect their concern over Zionism, their main interest is the social, economic, and cultural transformation of the Palestinian community.[19]

---

19. See Sidqi, *Al-Akhawat al-Hazinat* [The grieving sisters] (Jerusalem, 1928); Hamid Yasin, *Aqasis* [Stories] (Jaffa, 1946).

The response of Palestinian novelists to Zionist plans and ambitions was more direct. Representative of these novels is *Al-Malak wa al-Simsar* [The angel and the land-broker] by Izzat Darwazah, *Mudhakkirat Dajajah* [The diaries of a hen] by Ishaq Musa al-Husayni, and *Fatah min Falastin* [A girl from Palestine] by Abdul Halim Abbas.[20] *Al-Malak wa al-Simsar* is the story of a Palestinian Arab who is enticed into selling his land to a Zionist organization. Although stories about unscrupulous moneylenders hoodwinking farmers exist in almost every language, Darwazah tried to localize the tale by identifying Zionism as the principal source of misfortune and the Arabs as its innocent victims. His chief practical aim becomes very clear toward the end of the story, when he elaborately describes the way in which other villages decide to create a fund for saving lands threatened by Zionist buyers. *Mudhakkirat Dajajah*, on the other hand, is a parable employing the ancient device of depicting through the eyes of an animal a reality which human beings are unable to confront.

As the political situation changed, so did the setting and themes of the Palestinian novel. While the novels of Darwazah and Husayni are based on conditions in Palestine during the first two decades of the mandate, *Fatah min Falastin* is set against the background of the war between the Arabs and the Zionists in the last year of the mandate. The author, Abdul Halim Abbas, a participant in the events of 1948, has the novel begin in 1947 and end with the signing of the armistice agreements between Israel and the Arab states in 1949. In addition to picturing the hardships which the refugee Arab family underwent immediately after departure from Palestine, the novel indicates the concerns and the later political trends among the Palestinians. The novel abounds with nationalistic sentiment: it reveals the strong appeal of Arab nationalism to the Palestinian Arab youth and their devotion to restoring the occupied homeland to its owners.

Arab novelists faced special problems because they were adopting a Western European literary form. Poets, however, did not face the same problems, since there existed a body of classical Arabic poetry. This poetry exercised a strong influence on Ibrahim Tuqan and Burhan al-Din al-Abboushi, who are representative of the many Palestinian poets who expressed nationalist feelings during the mandate. In their poetry, both continued to look backward: they used the meters of classical poetry and acknowledged their indebtedness to past masters. But instead of addressing some wealthy patron, as was the custom in the past, they wrote for the general public, in books, magazines, and newspapers.

---

20. (Nablus, 1934); (Cairo, 1943); (Amman, 1949).

By stressing the heroic, Tuqan and Abboushi, like other poets of the period, figured as spokesmen for national loyalties and aspirations. Their nationalism became more intense in response to local and national events that stirred public opinion.

Tuqan's poetry was primarily concerned with national considerations; it was a call to his compatriots to rebel against the British authorities and to liberate their homeland from foreign rulers and the Zionists. Some of his poems solicited material help from Arabs everywhere. The inflammatory influence that he had on his fellow countrymen caused the mandatory authorities to order his arrest. He sought refuge in Iraq for three years and returned to his native town, Nablus, shortly before the outbreak of the Second World War. He died in 1939, at the age of forty. By then, biographies of him had been published, his works had been anthologized, and his poetry was known across the Arab world.[21]

Abboushi, a native of Jenin, a small town in central Palestine, was born into a well-to-do family of land-owners. He received a Western-style education. Although he was less productive than Tuqan, his writing reflected the influence that nationalist sentiment had on him. An example of his nationalist poetry is his play, *Watan al-Shahid* [The homeland of the martyr].[22] In the introduction to that play, he sums up his reasons for writing it:

> This play of mine is, to my knowledge, the first of its kind to be written on the Palestine problem. I have discussed in it, in verse, the designs of our enemies and their plots against our beloved country, Palestine. . . . This work of mine is dedicated, in the first place, to the commoner to lay off his slumber.[23]

Although Abboushi called what he wrote a play, this work has none of the characteristics of that form of literature in the drawing of the characters or the treatment of the plot. What Abboushi attempted to do was to arouse the patriotic feelings of his readers by stressing what their forefathers had done and by calling on his readers to try to

---

21. Among the most important books about him are: Fadwa Tuqan, *Akhi Ibrahim* [My brother Ibrahim] (Beirut, 1955); Zaki al-Mahasini, *Ibrahim Tuqan, Shair al-Watan al-Maghsub* [Ibrahim Tuqan, The poet of the usurped homeland] (Cairo, 1956); Yaqub al-Odat, *Ibrahim Tuqan fi Wataniyyatihi wa Wijdaniyyatihi* [The national and emotional poetry of Ibrahim Tuqan] (Amman, 1964).

22. (Jerusalem, 1947).

23. *Ibid.*, p. 1 (my translation).

imitate them. Earlier foreign invasions (the Crusades) had been frustrated. He urged the Arabs to defeat this new attempt at taking away from them a part of their land.

Political Writing

The nationalist themes that were found in creative writing were also expressed in a flood of political publications examining the reaction of the Palestinians to Zionism and the British Mandate in general. In these publications, which ranged from polemical tracts and booklets to more sophisticated articles and essays, Palestinian writers tried to acquaint their fellow countrymen with the history of the problem and to explain to other Arabs its implications. The origins, aims, designs, and techniques of Zionism were described, analyzed, and condemned. In some cases precautionary measures were also suggested for dealing with the situation.

Palestinian Arab writers treated Arab national issues somewhat differently than writers in other Arab countries did. Contemporary Arab writing paid great attention to the Arab nationalist movement and the form that Arab unity should finally assume. Palestinian Arab writers were interested in the Arab national movement, but they were also concerned with Zionism and imperialism. While other Arab countries fought for national independence, the Palestinians were fighting for their national existence. This view was elaborated by Bulos Abbud, a Christian lawyer from Jaffa, in the first year of the mandate. He warned that the establishment of a Jewish national home in the country would not only undermine the national character of the Holy Land but would also interrupt the peace that had reigned in the Holy City, because the Arab population was bound to oppose by force a plan that would make them a minority in their own homeland.[24]

Some writers adopted the theme of Arab unity as a solution to the new danger. Muhammad Izzat Darwazah, who had been influenced by his participation in the Arab nationalist movement in its early stages, tried to link the development of the movement to the future of Palestine. His writing was directed not merely to Palestinians but to Arabs in general. He maintained that the Palestine problem should serve as a unifying force among the Arabs. Moreover, while the other Arab countries were on the way to achieving some form of independence, the future of Palestine was still in jeopardy. He wanted to make it

---

24. Abbud, *Al-Ard al-Muqaddasah wa al-Sahyuniyyah* [The Holy Land and Zionism] (Jaffa, 1920).

clear that its loss would be a severe blow to the Arab nationalist movement.[25]

The bulk of this writing, however, concentrated on the situation that existed in Palestine as a result of the First World War. One of the most important tracts was written by Muhammad Yunis al-Husayni, whose family was known for its participation in the national movement. Husayni tried to discredit the legal and ethical basis of the Balfour Declaration.[26] After examining its alleged motives, Husayni maintained that since the declaration had no authority in international law because it had been issued in the form of a letter, the British government was not bound by its stipulations. He then argued that the British government had neither the legal nor the moral right to issue such a declaration. Lord Balfour, by his statement, was notifying the world that the British government was giving away a country to which England had no legal claim, and was disposing of a homeland that already belonged to another nation.[27]

The impact of Zionism on Palestine constituted the subject of two other books written by Palestinian Arabs during the 1930s. Emphasizing current hardships as well as legal claims was a work by Sidqi al-Dajani on the situation in Palestine during the 1920s and early 1930s. He gave an account of the unstable condition of the country and of the expulsion of Arab peasants from lands which they and their forefathers had occupied for centuries. He concluded by stating that although the Jews had suffered, it was unjust to try to alleviate the misfortunes of some human beings at the expense of others.[28]

A work on which Amin Aql, Ibrahim Najm, and Umar Abu-al-Nasr collaborated examines the efforts of Palestinian Arabs to frustrate the ambitions of the Zionists and the British rulers. The book looks at the various Palestinian revolts during the 1920s and 1930s, and pays special attention to that of 1936.[29]

The writing that appeared in Palestine after 1939 manifested a change in stress. With the promulgation of the White Paper of that year, with the start of the Second World War and the increase in the number

25. Darwazah, *Falastin wa al-Urubah* [Palestine and Arabism] (Jerusalem, 1929), pp. 4, 5.

26. Husayni, *Tahlil wad Balfour* [An analysis of the Balfour Declaration] (Jerusalem, 1933), pp. i, ii.

27. *Ibid.*, pp. 161–64.

28. Dajani, *Tafsir Zulamatu Falastin* [An explanation of the Palestine injustice] (Jerusalem, 1936), pp. i, iii.

29. Aql, Najm, and Nasr, *Jihad Falastin al-Arabiyyah* [The holy war of Arab Palestine] (Beirut, 1939), pp. ii, iii.

of British troops in the country, armed clashes between the Arabs and the British ceased. Arab moderates in Palestine as well as in the Arab states accepted the stipulations of the White Paper. Extreme nationalists were either in exile or in detention. Moreover, many of the intelligentsia, in view of the promise of independence in the near future, began to feel that the Arab character of the country had become secure since the Arabs would constitute a majority in the proposed state. They consequently began to address themselves to the Arab nationalist movement and the place that Palestine would take within that movement.

The Writing of History

Response to Zionism was noticeable on another level, in the work of Palestinian historians. History books written during the British Mandate covered a wide range of subjects dealing with Islam, Muslim institutions and civilization, local history, Arab nationalism, and European history. They were similar to the writings of other Arab historians in their diffusion of national consciousness through the glorification of past heroes and accomplishments. Sati al-Husri, one of the best-known Arab historians, rightly maintained that they were all led by national consciousness "to a sharing of pride in the glories of the past and a collective sorrow over present misfortunes."[30] Most Palestinian historians, too, were Arabists who tried to inculcate in their readers a love of past generations and to stimulate them to build a new Arab world in the image of the old one.

Some of the Palestinian historians emphasized the intellectual and cultural accomplishments of Arab civilization at its zenith. Representative of those is Qadri Tuqan, who reflected the pride which the Arab felt in the immense contribution of his ancestors to the scientific knowledge of present-day Europe. This was the subject of his *Turath al-Arab al-Ilmi* [The scientific heritage of the Arabs].[31] The high quality of the work and the demand for it led the cultural division of the League of Arab States to sponsor its republication in 1954 and 1963. Most of Tuqan's work, however, was a call to Arab intellectuals to make the Arab cultural heritage a moving force toward progress, toward improving present conditions and building a better future. Tuqan was not interested in history and biographies for their own sake; he always stressed those events and data which helped to give a spiritual picture of the period

---

30. Husri, *Ara' wa Ahadith fi al-Wataniyyah wa al-Urubah* [Views and addresses on nationalism and Arabism] (Cairo, 1944), p. 20 (my translation).

31. (Cairo, 1941).

with which he was dealing. Sometimes he even touched up his heroes to make them more attractive.

Two major trends are discernible in Palestinian accounts of Arab history. On the one hand there is the traditional and purely Islamic tendency to emphasize the bright side of Islamic history and to assert a strong belief in the regenerative power of Islam. On the other hand, and emerging more strongly in Palestinian historiography, there is the Pan-Arab tendency to see the history of the Arab world as one and indivisible throughout the ages, and to treat the pre-Islamic period and the Islamic period as a continuous one. Both approaches are discernible in the writings of Muhammad Izzat Darwazah, who began as an exponent of the first trend but shifted to the second under the impact of growing secular nationalism.

Zionism had a more direct influence on the writing of local history. The most important contribution in this field was Arif al-Arif's *Tarikh al-Quds* [The history of Jerusalem]. In the introduction to the book, the author sums up his motives for writing it:

> My acquaintance with the line of argument used by Zionist writers to assert the Jews' historical links with Palestine makes it my duty to try to refute their claims by examining the history of Jerusalem, the Jews' link with which the Zionists have stressed most, and to make it clear that the history of the Holy City reveals its Arab character, the tolerance of its people toward Christians and Jews, and the peaceful relations that have characterized the life of its inhabitants during the last ten centuries.[32]

Arif examines the origins of Jerusalem, pointing out that the city was built centuries before the ancient Israelites arrived in Palestine. He concentrates on the history of the city since the Middle Ages, because the records for that period are most complete and trustworthy. He stresses the humane and tolerant attitudes of the Arab conquerors of Jerusalem and its peaceful existence under Muslim rule, noting that this tranquility had been broken twice by incursions—at the time of the Crusades and at the present time.

Arif understood that the basic requirement of all historical scholarship was to verify statements of facts, and the importance he attached to this cannot be overestimated. His work contains a variety of historical material, including copies of letters and proclamations, selections from Islamic sources, lists of names, statistics compiled from various sources,

---

32. Arif, *Tarikh al-Quds* [The history of Jerusalem] (Cairo, 1947), pp. ii–iii (my translation).

and topographical observations. And Arif is always careful to note the source.

This cultural response to Zionist ambitions was to exert considerable influence on Palestinian national development. The number of Palestinian Arabs who were immersed in the cultural nationalist climate was small in comparison with the total population; but Arab society was in the process of change, and the educated sector of society was increasing. Because this sector was an economically and socially dominant group, its views influenced the outlook of large segments of society. Awareness of Zionist ambitions and the threat that they posed to the character of the country finally reached the population at large.

James J. Zogby

THE PALESTINIAN REVOLT OF THE 1930s

THE RESPONSE in the 1930s of the Arabs of Palestine to the combined forces of Zionist colonialism and British imperialism must be seen as a localized manifestation of the general movement toward national liberation that has occupied the whole of the Arab world from at least the turn of this century until the present time. In addition, the internal transformations that the British Mandate imposed on Palestinian society were such that the Palestinians' antisettler struggle coincided with an antifeudal popular democratic movement. The result was that the significant events of the 1930s in the struggle of the population of Palestine against the alien forces represent a key stage in the Palestinians development as a self-conscious nation dedicated to the establishment of a popular democratic state in their region.

In general the history of the Arab East from the nineteenth century to the present has been marked by the movement of its people from tribal and sectarian-based society toward unified national organization and consciousness.[1] The movement found its first concrete expression in the "great Arab revolt" of World War I. In 1915, with the "imperialist war" underway, Britain was eager to secure Arab support for the purposes of dividing the Ottoman Empire and opening a southern front in its war against the Central Powers. Sharif Hussein of Mecca,

---

1. George Antonius, *The Arab Awakening* (New York, 1965). This is a general survey of the development of the Arab national movement. Also see V. Lutsky, *Modern History of the Arab Countries* (Moscow, 1969); Ahmad al-Kodsy, "Nationalism and Class Struggles in the Arab World," *Monthly Review*, VII, no. 8 (1970), 11, 16–17.

responding both to British overtures and to Arab dissatisfaction with Ottoman policy, issued, in June, 1916, a call to the Arab people to revolt against Turkish rule and to fight on the side of the British and the French. Eight months earlier he had secured a pledge from the British government that if the Arabs revolted, Great Britain was

> prepared to recognize and uphold the independence of the Arabs in all regions [with some noted modifications] lying in the frontiers proposed by the Sharif of Mecca.[2]

But the aspirations of the Arab people for united nationhood and independence which had led them to this revolt were frustrated in the postwar period. For, regardless of its wartime pledge, Britain had designs of its own on the Arab land.

THE BRITISH DESIGNS

In the century and one-half that preceded this period, Great Britain had seized control of enormous areas of the world. It was driven in this by the need for raw materials to feed its ever growing industrial complex; the need for foreign "spheres of influence" to insure markets for British goods; and the need to protect these raw-material sources and markets from imperialist rivals on the European continent. As part of its imperial design, Britain needed Palestine to protect the northeastern flank of its all-important sea route to India and the East—the Suez Canal. In addition, control of Palestine and the Fertile Crescent would make possible a land route across Asia, which would guarantee contact with India in the event of loss of the Suez.[3] The British, knowing of French and German designs on this area, sought to frustrate them both. With the wartime pledge to their new "client," Sharif Hussein, they hoped to preclude any postwar French claim to "liberated" territory. The Arabs, then, were merely temporary allies; and the pledge to the Arabs, merely a wartime tactic.

Before long, Britain turned to a more permanent and safer client—the Zionist movement. Founded and directed by Theodor Herzl, Zionism

---

2. Antonius, *Arab Awakening*, p. 413. *Palestine Royal Commission Report (Peel Report)* (London, 1937), pp. 17–18.

3. See Herbert Sidebotham, "British Interests in Palestine, 1917," in *From Haven to Conquest*, ed. Walid Khalidi (Beirut, 1971), pp. 125–142; Ernest Main, "British Imperial Communications," in *ibid.*, pp. 317–20.

was by definition a servant of imperialism. It was a colonial movement in search of a patron, and it therefore courted a number of imperialist powers. In the prewar period, Herzl and his organization actively engaged the Ottoman sultan and the German government in hopes of selling them the plan for a Jewish state in Palestine.[4] An alliance between the British Empire and Zionism had been proposed, in both quarters, for some time. In 1876 Lord Shaftesbury, prominent member of Parliament, speaking on this subject, said:

> Syria and Palestine will before long become very important. . . . The country wants capital and population. The Jews can give it both. And has not England a special interest in promoting such restoration? It would be a blow to England if either of her two rivals should get hold of Syria, . . . Does not policy there . . . exhort England to foster the nationality of the Jews and aid them to return? . . . To England then, naturally, belongs the role of favouring the settlement of Jews in Palestine.[5]

Such affection was returned to Great Britain by the Zionists, including Herzl, who, in his address to the Fourth Zionist Congress, indicated his special feelings for Britain: "England the great, England the free, England with her eyes roaming all over the seas, will understand us and our aims."[6] Finally, with a promise to the Jews to found for them a "national home in Palestine," Great Britain hit upon the perfect answer to whatever postwar territorial claim to the area that its rivals might make.[7]

A few years after concluding the agreement with Sharif Hussein, Britain had, with total disregard for the rights of the Arabic-speaking population of the Middle East, concluded two additional pacts designed

---

4. See Neville Mandel, "Turks, Arabs and Jewish Immigration into Palestine, 1882–1914," in *Middle Eastern Affairs*, no. 4, ed. Albert Hourani, St. Anthony's Papers, no. 17 (London, 1965), pp. 77–108; Arie Bober, ed., *The Other Israel* (New York, 1972), p. 37.

5. Quoted in N. Sokolow, *The History of Zionism*, 2 vols. in 1, rev. ed. (New York: KTAV, 1969). Twentieth-century Zionist leader Max Nordau said, "If Zionism had not existed, Great Britain would have had to invent it." See Yuri Ivanov, *Caution Zionism* (Moscow, 1970), p. 33.

6. For this and other examples of the relationship between Zionists and Great Britain, see George Jabbour, *Settler Colonialism in South Africa and the Middle East* (Beirut, 1970), p. 26.

7. Prime Minister Herbert Asquith wrote: "The only other partisan of this proposal is Lloyd George, who I need not say does not give a damn about the Jews or their past or their future, but thinks it will be an outrage to let the Holy Places pass into

to solidify British hegemony over the area. With the French and the Russians, in May, 1916, they were party to the Sykes-Picot Agreement, which arranged for the partitioning of Ottoman holdings in the Middle East, and for European control of much of the area.[8] Equally insidious to Arab national aspirations was the declaration made by the British foreign minister in November, 1917.

> His Majesty's Government view with favour the establishment in Palestine of a national home for the Jewish people, and will use their best endeavours to facilitate the achievement of this object. . . .[9]

In the postwar period, as a result of these pacts, the Arab East, instead of attaining independence, was humiliated by British and French occupation. And instead of being united as one nation, the region was unnaturally divided into five sections (Lebanon, Syria, Iraq, Transjordan, and Palestine), with only the Hejaz being given independence.

THE ARAB NATION RESPONDS

In 1919, after years of Turkish rule, the fear of French and British domination, together with the declared Zionist intent to take over a part of their homeland, led Arab nationalists to convene the General Syrian Congress in Damascus, at which Arab delegates from the entire East expressed their desires for unity and independent nationhood (in a document that was forwarded to the King-Crane Commission).[10] Dr. Anis Sayegh, in his nationalist statement, *Palestine and Arab Nationalism*, refers to this congress as "the first comprehensive national congress

---

the possession of, or under the protection of . . . 'atheistic France.'" Ivanov, *Caution Zionism*, p. 33.

8. The Sykes-Picot arrangement is discussed in Zeine Zeine, *The Struggle for Arab Independence* (Beirut, 1960), pp. 1–24. The text of the agreement is in Antonius, *Arab Awakening*, pp. 428–30.

9. An example of the absolute disregard for the rights of the native community can be seen in the following statement by Lord Balfour, written in 1919: "In Palestine we do not propose ever to go through the form of consulting the wishes of the present inhabitants. . . . Zionism is of far greater importance than the desires and prejudices of the 700,000 Arabs who now inhabit the land." See "Memorandum," in *From Haven to Conquest*, ed. Khalidi, pp. 201–12.

10. The document is reprinted in full in Antonius, *Arab Awakening*, pp. 440–42.

of representatives of all the Syrian regions."[11] The congress consciously comprised delegates from all three zones of Syria—south, east, and west—as well as delegates representing all of the Muslim, Christian, and Jewish communities of the area. As expressed in the resolutions of the congress, the delegates met to "define the aspirations of the people who have chosen us—the Arabic-speaking people of Syria." They adopted, in their own words, "unanimously," resolutions which expressed the following: a demand for "full and absolute political independence for Syria," and a rejection of any dismemberment of it; a desire for the establishment of "a constitutional monarchy based on principles of democratic and broadly decentralized rule which shall safeguard the rights of minorities"; disapproval of "the tutelage of a mandatory power"; and a rejection of "the claims of the Zionists for the establishment of a Jewish commonwealth in that part of southern Syria which is known as Palestine." In a closing statement the congress said:

> We would not have risen against Turkish rule under which we enjoyed civic and political privileges, as well as rights of representation, had it not been that the Turks denied us our right to a national existence.

That same year the American King-Crane Commission, which had been sent on a fact-finding mission to the Middle East by President Wilson, published its findings.[12] It was clear to the commission that in reaction to Turkish rule and impending French and British rule, a new nation—one with widespread popular support—had been formed. It was, as they called it, an Arab state, and it was based on common factors—language, territory, history, and tradition—which molded its personality. The desires of this nation for unity and independence were clear. Further, it was clear that the people of Palestine (the coastal region of southwestern Syria) saw themselves as part of this Arab nation, and that their compatriots identified Palestine as an integral part of their nation.

The recommendations of the King-Crane Commission were rejected, the will of the Arabic-speaking people of the Levant was ignored, and the divisions of the French and British mandates were proclaimed at the San Remo Conference of 1919. As the foreign troops entered each of the mandated territories, the Arab response was immediate and sustained. From 1919 onward, riots, mass demonstrations, prolonged

---

11. Sayegh, *Palestine and Arab Nationalism* (Beirut, 1970), p. 29.
12. *Editors and Publishers* (New York), December 2, 1922, p. 1.

nationwide strikes, and armed insurrection were commonplace throughout the Levant.[13]

The struggles that emerged in each of the mandated regions were not unrelated. Aside from the peculiarities that marked these antimandate actions as they developed in reaction to the particular circumstances in each area, their united and Pan-Arab character was affirmed on many levels. For example, continued and increased Zionist claims to Palestine touched off reactions throughout the Arab world. In all the Arab capitals—Baghdad, Damascus, Beirut, and Amman—the Arab people established committees for the defense of Palestine to aid their compatriots materially and morally.[14] Izz ad-Din al-Qassem, a leader of the armed insurrection movement that developed in rural Palestine in 1935, and who became the organizer and martyred hero of the Palestinian peasant resistance, was a Muslim sheikh from the French mandated area of Syria.[15] Another of these "Syrians" was the commander of the Palestinian forces in the revolution of 1936–39, Fawzi ad-Din al-Kawakji. He had been military adviser to King Ibn Saud and later was a commissioned officer in the Iraqi army. In addition to these leaders, many volunteers from throughout the Arab world entered British mandated Palestine during this period to aid their fellow Arabs in their fight for independence.[16] The Muslim Brotherhood, which made support of the 1936–39 strike and revolt one of its major concerns, raised funds, sent supplies and equipment, and propagandized the Palestine issue in letters and telegrams to responsible authorities.[17]

One of the initial retaliatory acts of the British, in response to the outbreak of national resistance in 1936, was to cut communication wires between Palestine and the other Arab regions.[18] By 1938 this Pan-Arab support had become so pronounced that

> Jewish laborers were employed by the Government at the cost of 100,000 Pounds Sterling to build a barbed-wire fence around the northern and north-eastern frontier of Palestine. This fence was intended to separate the Arabs of Palestine from the Arabs of Lebanon and Syria.[19]

13. See Antonius, *Arab Awakening*, pp. 350–412.
14. John Marlowe, *The Seat of Pilate* (London, 1959), p. 139.
15. Robert John and Sami Hadawi, *The Palestine Diary* (Beirut, 1970), I, 251.
16. Marlowe, *Seat of Pilate*, p. 139.
17. Richard Mitchell, *The Society of the Muslim Brothers* (London, 1969), pp. 16–18, 55–58.
18. Barbara Kalkas, "The Revolt of 1936: A Chronicle of Events," in *The Transformation of Palestine*, ed. Ibrahim Abu-Lughod (Evanston, Ill., 1971), p. 244.
19. Neville Barbour, *Nisi Dominus* (Beirut, 1969), p. 192.

Aid came on other levels, too. In 1936 the Peel Commission reported that the attainment of national independence by Iraq, Jordan, Egypt, and Syria and Lebanon contributed to the motivation of the Arabs to intensify their revolt in 1936.[20] The commission stated that at the time of the pro-independence upsurges in Egypt, a Palestinian paper called on its readers to follow the Egyptian example: "Rise to rid yourself from Jewish and British slavery. . . . The leaders in Egypt have awakened. Where are our leaders hiding?" The Commission report continued:

> Again, a little later, the students of Palestine were urged to awake like their brothers. "The time is near and the situation is grave. Unify yourselves. Demand your violated rights and stolen freedom. Advance. God is with you." The opening of the Franco-Syrian negotiations similarly evoked the strongest expressions of sympathy with "our heroic brothers in the Northern part of this oppressed Arab country.[21]

But while these Pan-Arab developments were significant, the setting of the struggle for independence in Palestine was also the result of internal forces peculiar to the mandated area. Even though this struggle of the Palestinian Arabs was an extension of the thrust for general Arab national liberation begun with the "great revolt," and even though their continuing struggle was organically related to that of the Arabs of the other mandated regions, the might of the British occupation and the intensity of Zionist ambitions sought to isolate Palestine from the rest of the Arab world. And, in a real sense, after 1920 the "Palestinian Arabs found themselves, for the first time in history, a distinct political unit," shut off from their Arab brothers.[22]

Palestine Takes Form

Attention shall now be directed to developments within the mandated region of Palestine. It must be noted that from the very outset of the implementation of the Zionist land-purchase and colonization scheme, there were repeated instances of popular resistance. Neville Mandel's article on premandate Arab-Jewish relations in Palestine is

---

20. *Palestine Royal Commission Report*, p. 111.
21. *Ibid.*, pp. 93–94.
22. Barbour, *Nisi Dominus*, p. 94.

very clear on this point.[23] In most cases the indigenous population expressed their hostility to the foreign intruders with periodic attacks on their settlements. In addition, from the very beginning of the Zionist penetration into Palestine, there were warnings issued regularly by journalists, popular poets, and other intellectuals. The frequency and intensity of all of these indicate that even before the Balfour Declaration and the San Remo Conference, the indigenous community had clearly expressed its antipathy for the European Zionists' scheme in Palestine.

Until 1919, however, there was not an organized "Palestinian" response, on a leadership level, to this Zionist threat. Prior to that time, Muslim and Christian leaders within the Palestinian region formed associations whose initial purpose was to protest the dismemberment of the mandated area. In 1919 representatives of these associations met with their Arab compatriots at the first two meetings of the General Syrian Congress in Damascus. Facing the reality of the conditions that existed in Palestine after the mandate had been imposed, these same leaders, representing a temporary united front of rival familial and religious factions, convened the Third Palestine Arab Congress in Haifa in December, 1920.[24] This meeting was, in fact, the first independent Palestinian political event. The resolutions of this conference reflected the tactical shift of the traditional leadership of the now-occupied Arabic-speaking population. The separation from Syria and the Arab East was a fact for the time being. And the demands of the congress were now for "Palestinian independence."[25]

As a result of this congress the first Palestinian organization, the Arab Executive, which consisted of twenty-four Muslim and Christian leaders, was formed. The executive was, in effect, a temporary alliance of not only the sects but also the major tribal factions of the indigenous community.[26] The leadership of the executive—in fact, the major force behind its organization—was the powerful feudalist Husayni family. The Palestine Arab Congress did represent an emerging nationalist sentiment and did serve as a forum for issuing nationalist demands; however, neither the congress nor the Arab Executive were truly nationalist organizations, since they represented and drew their support

---

23. Mandel, "Turks, Arabs and Jewish Immigration into Palestine."

24. *Palestine: A Study of Jewish, Arab and British Policies* (New Haven, Conn., 1947), pp. 473-74.

25. Full text of these resolutions can be found in M. E. T. Mogannam, *The Arab Woman and the Palestine Problem* (London, 1937), pp. 125-27.

26. David Waines, "The Failure of the Nationalist Resistance," in *The Transformation of Palestine*, ed. Abu-Lughod, pp. 220-21.

from a tribal-religious sectarian, and not a national, social order.

There is a contradiction that should be noted here, one that runs through the history of Palestine under the mandate. The system of social organization that ordered the lives of the Arabs of Palestine was a feudal one, with a few powerful land-owning families (Muslim and Christian) controlling much of the wealth and the power. It was from these families, with their kinship or client ties to the rest of the population, that the leadership of the Arab community came. Since this was the only existing organized leadership, it was only through it that the indigenous population was able to respond politically to the mandate and the Zionist scheme. Even though some of these large land-owners, especially the absentees, sold their land to the Zionists, and in so doing displaced tens of thousands of peasants who had been working on that land, the majority of this class moved, albeit hesitantly, in a nationalist direction.[27] They were in a tremendous bind. It was not in their interest, as they saw it, to surrender totally to the British and the Zionists—even though tremendous profits might be made by selling their lands. At the same time they could not support a true popular revolution. In speaking of this problem Ghassan Kanafani noted:

> In brief, we can say that the Palestinian leadership was compelled, so as not to lose its privileges and positions of prominence, to borrow and trade with the slogans of the masses, but in order that those slogans should not be implemented to an extent where they would come to threaten their interests, they emptied those slogans of their content.[28]

This describes perfectly the role of this traditional leadership during the mandate. They met often and made fierce-sounding demands; but when the time came to translate those demands into action, they hesitated. And when, in the 1930s, the masses seized the revolutionary initiative from them, they sought to reassert themselves, to regain their monopoly of power, and to slow the masses down. And in the end it was this class, unable as it was to escape this contradiction, that led the masses to surrender and defeat.

This contradiction was the result of a set of forces that had been unleashed by the mandate. With the end of the Ottoman administration and the entrance of Great Britain and the Zionists, a process was begun

---

27. Ghassan Kanafani, "The Palestinian Revolt, 1936–1939," in *Shu'un Falastin* (Beirut), no. 6 (1972). See also Kanafani, "Palestinian Resistance: Experiments and Lessons" (Lecture given at the Al Istiklal Club in Kuwait, PFLP Information Department, 1970).

28. Kanafani, "The Palestinian Revolt," p. 21.

which was to transform the dominant form of economic and political relationships in the area from feudalist to capitalist. The feudalists of the Arab community were able neither to control nor to understand this process. Within fifteen years of the institution of the mandate, Jewish capital had seized the economic initiative from this class. Tremendous amounts of imported capital, coupled with the exclusivist (i.e., racist and repressive) practices of the Zionist national and labor organizations, left the Arab economic order in ruin. A fledgling Arab bourgeoisie could not compete with the much better financed and more modern Zionist enterprises. In the years 1933–36 an average of 20 per cent of the total number of Jewish immigrants were listed as "capitalists"—a total of over 14,600.[29] This appellation was used to describe those immigrants who brought with them enough capital to begin a modest enterprise (at least £1,000). In addition, the funds available to Jewish immigrants were quite plentiful. The Peel Commission reported that Jewish sources had raised over £77,000,000 and had set it aside for the exclusive development of the Jewish economy in Palestine.[30]

The smothering of an indigenous bourgeoisie was not the only effect of Zionist penetration into Palestine. The working class and peasants were, in fact, the groups most critically affected. During the 1930s, as a result of increased anti-Semitic activities in Europe, there was a flood of legal Jewish immigration into Palestine, reaching a yearly high of 72,000 in 1935.[31] In the three-year period, 1932–35, the Jewish population doubled, to 355,000, under the protection of the mandate. For a small underdeveloped nation of 1.2 million, this tremendous influx caused considerable pressure and great economic dislocation. But it was not so much the number of Jewish immigrants as the practices of the Jewish national and labor organizations that caused the indigenous population so much distress.

From the outset, leaders of the Zionist movement in Palestine recognized that to fulfill the ambition of constructing an exclusively Jewish state, the Arab population would have to be evacuated. R. Weitz, who for many years was the head of the Jewish Agency's colonization department, summed up this attitude in a 1940 diary notation:

> Between ourselves it must be clear that there is no room for both peoples together in this country. . . . We shall not achieve our goal of being

29. Waines, "Failure of the Nationalist Resistance," p. 225; Barbour, *Nisi Dominus*, p. 234.
30. *Palestine Royal Commission Report*, p. 212.
31. Khalidi, ed., *From Haven to Conquest*, pp. 841–44.

an independent people with the Arabs in this small country. The only solution is a Palestine . . . without Arabs. . . . And there is no other way than to transfer the Arabs from here to the neighboring countries, to transfer all of them: *Not one village, not one tribe should be left.* . . . Only after this transfer will the country be able to absorb millions of our brethren. There is no other way out.[32]

Such a perspective was reflected in the policy and practice of the Jewish National Fund (Keren Kayemet) and the Zionist Labor party, both designed for the specific purpose of insuring exclusive Jewish development at the expense of the indigenous community. The constitution of the Jewish Agency, for example, states that "land is to be acquired as Jewish property and . . . held as the inalienable property of the Jewish people." The constitution goes on to declare that as a matter of principle, Jewish labor shall be employed on Jewish lands. The provisions regarding Jewish National Fund lands were even more extreme, demanding that only Jewish labor be employed, and setting fines for violators who hired non-Jewish workers.[33] If one violated this order three times, the fund reserved the right to take his land away, with no compensation. David Hacoben, a leader of the Israel Workers party (Mapai), in discussing the role played by Zionist socialists during this period, notes how he refused Arabs membership in the Histadrut, stood guard at orchards to prevent Arab workers from getting jobs there, poured kerosene on tomatoes grown by Arabs, and attacked Jewish women who bought goods in the Arab markets.[34]

The purpose of all of this was simply to foster the development of an independent Jewish economy at the expense of the Palestinian Arabs. These exclusivist policies spelled trouble for the Arab working people: not only were there no jobs available to them in the Arab sector, since its development was blocked, but they were also forced out of the Jewish sector. As a result of this policy, there were large numbers of unemployed Arabs in the cities.[35]

Another problem confronting the Arab urban population was a deteriorating standard of living. The large sums of Jewish capital flowing into the country provided higher pay for Jewish workers and, at the same time, brought about inflation. In 1936, in identical job categories, the salaries for Jewish workers averaged 140 per cent higher than

32. Quoted in Bober, ed., *Other Israel*, p. 13.
33. John and Hadawi, *Palestine Diary*, pp. 224–25.
34. Bober, ed., *Other Israel*, p. 12.
35. Kanafani, "The Palestinian Revolt," p. 76.

those for their Arab counterparts. In some trades the salaries for Jewish workers were 433 per cent higher than those for Arab workers. In the rural regions of the area, the differential was 5:1.[36]

All of these problems were compounded by the large numbers of peasants who were being forced off their lands by absentee feudalist landholders who were selling this land out from under the residents. The amount of land involved in these sales to the Zionists should not be exaggerated, since at no time before 1948 did the Zionists own more than 7 per cent of the land of Palestine;[37] but these purchases were made in areas that sustained large numbers of peasants. For example, when the Sursocks sold 240,000 dunams to the Zionists, 8,730 peasants were dislocated. By 1931, 20,000 peasant families had been uprooted in this way; and by 1941, 30 per cent of all the Arab families employed in agriculture (119,000 families) were landless.[38] In addition, 50 per cent of the rest did not own enough land to sustain themselves. Many of the landless peasants flocked into the cities looking for work, while the rest were absorbed into other rural areas.

Together, all of these factors bring into focus the absolute economic ruin brought upon the indigenous population by the mandate. In testimony before the Peel Commission in 1937, George Mansour, secretary of the Arab Workers' Association, stated:

> In 1935, 1,000 workers in Jaffa were unemployed; . . . at the end of 1935 the number of unemployed in Jaffa reached 2,270. In 1937, the number of unemployed in Jaffa reached 4,000; in Haifa, 4,500; in Qalqilia and six neighbouring villages, 1,300; and in the Bethlehem and Nazareth areas about 74% of the labor force was unemployed.[39]

In continuing testimony, Mansour summed up the causes for this deterioration in the economic status of the Arab people. They were: (1) unchecked immigration, (2) dislocated peasants flocking to the cities, (3) the policy of Jewish labor replacing Arab labor, (4) the general instability of the economic situation, and (5) the despicable government mandate which sided with the Zionists.

---

36. *Ibid.*, p. 47; Waines, "Failure of the Nationalist Resistance," p. 225. See also Naji Aloush, *The Arab Resistance in Palestine* (Beirut, 1970), pp. 27–28.

37. Khalidi, ed., *From Haven to Conquest*, pp. 841–44.

38. Kanafani, "The Palestinian Revolt," pp. 51, 52: For the size of a dunam, see above, pp. 43 n. 1, 61 n. 9.

39. *Collection of Arab Testimony in Palestine before the British Royal Commission* (Damascus, 1938), p. 55.

With the disintegration of the peasantry and the rapid movement toward urbanization, the economic underpinnings of the feudal order were being destroyed, and the old leadership was losing its traditional base. The major problem of the period, as we shall see, was that since the possibilities for natural economic and political development had been thwarted by the "protected" Zionist enterprise, no new leadership was able to develop to lead the Palestinian Arab community, and so the decayed traditional leadership remained.[40]

THE PALESTINIANS RESPOND

In 1929 it became clear what the result of this absence of representative leadership would be. In 1928 the traditional leadership had convened the Seventh Arab Congress and had reissued its nationalist demands to the British: (1) immediate cessation of Jewish immigration, (2) prohibition of the transference of property to Jews, and (3) establishment of a democratic government with the largest proportion of representation to the Arabs in accordance with their numbers.[41]

Beyond this, and similar pronouncements, the congress did not move to respond to the growing political and economic chaos that had gripped the country. The masses, however, provoked not only by their deteriorating economic condition but also by repeated Zionist threats and harassment concerning Arab rights at one of the holiest of their religious places, struck hard against the Zionists.[42] In August, 1929, the Arab population was involved in a number of attacks on Jewish settlements, killing and wounding hundreds of the colonists and burning many of their synagogues and other symbols of their presence.[43] On the second day of disturbances, the Arab Executive issued an appeal to the masses, asking them to

> quell the riot, avoid blood shed and save life . . . to return to quiet and peace, to endeavor to assist in the restoration of order. . . .

---

40. Kanafani, "The Palestinian Revolt," pp. 48, 64; Nathan Weinstock, "The Impact of Zionist Colonization on Palestinian Society before 1948," *Journal of Palestine Studies*, II, no. 2 (Winter, 1972), 59–61.

41. Waines, "Failure of the Nationalist Resistance," pp. 225–26.

42. The best report of the events leading up to the 1929 revolt is the eye-witness account of Vincent Sheean printed in *From Haven to Conquest*, ed. Khalidi, pp. 273–302.

43. *Ibid.*; Richard N. Verdery, "Arab 'Disturbances' and the Commissions of Inquiry," in *The Transformation of Palestine*, ed. Abu-Lughod, pp. 287–88.

Be confident that we are making every effort to realize your demands and national aspirations by peaceful methods.[44]

In the aftermath of the 1929 insurrection the gap between the traditional leadership and the masses of Palestinians became clear. The traditional leadership, in the form of the Arab Executive, had proved unable to accomplish its political goal of ending the mandate and gaining independence for Palestine. At the same time, and in large part due to this failure, it was losing its ability to direct or control the indigenous population. This was principally due to the fact that, out of fear of losing privilege, and with no understanding of what forces were at play, the traditional leadership, in varying degrees, refused to join the masses in a revolt.[45] It pinned all of its hopes on working out a compromise with imperialism in an attempt to replace the Zionists as the imperialists' number one client.

One of the positive effects of the 1929 insurrection was that a process of independent politicization was begun. There was a rapid mobilization of different sectors of the Arab community. Women, students, young people, workers, and farmers formed organizations which began to provide, at least in urban areas, some opportunity for the Arabs to express their needs and defend their interests outside of the decayed traditional framework.[46]

In 1933, the Arab Executive did spring into action momentarily, with a call for a national strike and a boycott of British and Jewish goods. The effort was short-lived and unsuccessful, and the deterioration of the indigenous community's status continued. By the mid-1930s the

---

44. Mogannam, *The Arab Woman and the Palestine Problem*, pp. 174–75.

45. For example, in 1933 and again in July, 1937, disagreement over this very question caused a rupture between elements of the feudalists. In both instances the Nashashibi faction of the traditional leadership rejected the policy of militant confrontation with the British (the policy that was espoused by the Husayni faction) and moved in a moderate direction urging compromise with the mandatory government. But it should not be concluded that one faction was by nature more opposed to cooperation with imperialism than another. This divergence might better be explained as the result of different positions taken by opposing factions as they jockeyed for leadership of the Palestinian community. The Husayni faction worked with imperialism when it appeared to be in its own interests to do so. See Ann Mosely Lesch, "The Palestinian Arab Nationalist Movement under the Mandate," *The Politics of Palestinian Nationalism* (Los Angeles, 1973), pp. 14–40; ESCO Foundation, *Palestine* (New Haven, Conn., 1947), pp. 768–98; Mogannam, *The Arab Woman and the Palestine Problem*.

46. Lesch, "The Palestinian Arab Nationalist Movement under the Mandate," p. 31; Mogannam, *The Arab Woman and the Palestine Problem*, pp. 67 ff.

situation had grown critical. The traditional leadership, which had split up into competitive tribal groupings after the failure of 1933, was unable to respond. However, in the hills of Galilee there was taking shape a new development which was to determine the future of Palestine. Shaykh Izz ad-Din al-Qassem had come into Palestine to organize the peasants to fight for independence against the British. Qassem had made overtures to Haj Amin al-Husayni, the mufti, leader of the Arab Executive, to support this effort, but he had been turned down.[47] Nevertheless, he proceeded with his work, organizing the people of the countryside into guerrilla bands. Qassem was killed in his first battle with the British, in the winter of 1935. His work had earned him great respect from the masses of Palestinians, and his funeral in Haifa turned out to be a massive political demonstration.[48] Qassem was gone, but his peasant-based movement lived on. Its importance is that it provided for the majority of the people, creating in rural areas an independent organizing thrust, which in a remarkably short time would make possible the first broad-based Palestinian national organization—unrelated to the traditional leadership.

On April 15, 1936, Qassemite armed bands began their offensive against the British and the Zionist colonists. The Jews rose in protest, and Tel Aviv was filled with violent anti-Arab demonstrators who, in addition to attacking and wounding many Arabs, demanded the formation of an all-Jewish army. This outraged the Arab community, and its response was immediate. On April 19, Jaffa was the scene of a popular uprising. Arab antigovernment demonstrations spread to other cities. These efforts were complemented in the rural areas by the activities of the Qassemites. Spurred by the independent organizational thrust provided by the unions and congresses formed in 1933, and by the Qassemite movement, national committees (independent of the traditional leadership) were set up in almost every city and village. These were organized in rapid-fire succession from April 19 to April 21, with each community forming a committee, issuing a set of nationalist demands, and calling for a nationwide strike.

By April 25, in an effort to salvage their leadership, the feudalist parties reunited and merged with representatives of the local strike committees to form the Arab Higher Committee (AHC). The AHC

---

47. Leila Kadi, ed., *The Basic Political Documents of the Armed Palestinian Resistance* (Beirut, 1929), p. 11. On Qassem and the Qassemite movement, see Kanafani, "The Palestinian Revolt," pp. 61 ff.; Abdul Wahad al-Kayali, *Modern History of Palestine* (Beirut, 1970), pp. 291 ff.

48. John and Hadawi, *Palestine Diary*, p. 251.

met on May 7, with over 150 representatives of the national committees present, and agreed unanimously:

(1) to continue the national strike until the British government introduced a basic change in its present policy which will manifest itself in the stoppage of Jewish immigration;
(2) that the Arab nation should refuse to pay taxes from May 15, 1935, should the British government fail to introduce a fundamental change in its policy which will manifest itself in the stoppage of Jewish immigration.[49]

In addition, the AHC restated the three nationalist demands of the Arab Executive, including the demand to establish a democratic representative government in Palestine. Mayors of most Arab cities, the Arab National Guard, the Arab police, 137 Arab senior officials in the mandate government, and 1,200 other Arab officials in the government all publicly supported the demands and the strike. By mid-1936, the Palestinian Arabs were operating as a truly unified national organization.

The British became ruthless in their efforts to crush this revolt. By means of mass arrests, forced openings of businesses closed by the strike, collective fines or confiscations issued against villages suspected of harboring guerrillas, and widespread demolition, the British hoped to intimidate the Arab population into submission.[50] By June 19, 2,600 strikers had been arrested. On that day the destruction of Jaffa took place: the Hourani Quarter and most of the Old City were leveled.[51] By the fifth month of the strike the British had increased their army of occupation to 20,000 men. Through all of this, the strike and armed revolt continued.

The British discovered a more lethal weapon when they enlisted the aid of their "client kings," Abdullah, Ghazi, and Ibn Saud.[52] In July, Abdullah contacted the AHC and offered to mediate with Great Britain on their behalf on the condition that they call off the strike. Many members of the AHC who had been uneasy about militant action

---

49. Kalkas, "The Revolt of 1936," pp. 247–48. This article is a major source to be referred to concerning the following events.

50. Yehuda Bauer, "The Arab Revolt of 1936," *New Outlook*, IX, no. 7 (1966), 26; Kodsy and Lobel, *The Arab World and Israel* (New York, 1970), p. 69.

51. Kalkas, "The Revolt of 1936," pp. 252–53. See also "The 'Town Planning of Jaffa, 1936.' Judgments by M. F. J. McDonell and R. J. Manning," in *From Haven to Conquest*, ed. Khalidi, pp. 343–52.

52. Kalkas, "The Revolt of 1936," pp. 258–59. See Kanafani, "Palestinian Resistance."

to begin with saw this as an excellent out. But popular reaction was violently opposed to any surrender, and those newspapers which even printed Abdullah's offer were publicly burned. Then came Nuri al-Said, King Ghazi's foreign minister. Nuri also offered to mediate, but this time on the condition that the violence be stopped. The AHC found this offer more acceptable since it permitted them to continue the strike. This compromise, they were certain, would be more acceptable to the militants. Nuri's effort failed; but the first crack had been made in the national leadership and its will to win. By the fifth month, increased British repression began to take its toll on the strikers. Many members of the AHC panicked and reverted to their traditional stance of pushing a negotiated settlement with their "good ally Britain" as the only possible solution. With the leadership publicly expressing its demoralization, the will of the Arab community to sustain this struggle was severely weakened.

When, on October 8, all three Arab kings made a new appeal to end the strike, it was accepted. The appeal read:

> To our Sons the Arabs—we have been greatly pained by the prevailing situation in Palestine. We call upon you to resort to quietness in order to prevent bloodshed, confident in the good intentions of our good friend, the British Government, which has declared its desire to administer justice. Rest assured that we shall continue our efforts for the purpose of assisting you.[53]

The AHC called a national meeting of local strike committee representatives to discuss the appeal; on October 11, 1936, it was accepted, and the longest national strike on record came to an end.

One month later, a communique signed by Fawzi ad-Din al-Kawakji, who had taken command of the armed Palestinian revolt, was circulated around the countryside. In it Kawakji

> called for the complete halting of all acts of violence, the refraining from incitement to anything which would upset the atmosphere of negotiations from which the Arab nation hopes to benefit and secure the country's rights in full.[54]

As its part of the deal concocted with the "kings," Britain sent a commission to Palestine to study the Arab grievances, to report on

---

53. Kanafani, "Palestinian Resistance," p. 13.
54. *Ibid.*, p. 12.

the causes of the revolt, and to make recommendations that might solve the problems. From the Arab point of view the Peel Commission was an absolute failure. The mandate and "national home" policies were reaffirmed; and, instead of a representative democratic government, the commission suggested a partitioned, racially divided state.[55]

In the wake of this betrayal, the guerrillas resumed activities in Galilee in September, 1937. Britain's initial response was to outlaw the AHC and the national committees, and to arrest or exile the Arab leadership. But the rural revolt gained momentum. By mid-1938 the rebels were in control of 80 per cent of the countryside. One report says that

> British administration had become a fiction. The rebel forces levied taxes, administered justice, and provided civilian administrative services in the vast territories under their control.[56]

Britain exploded and unleashed its full fury on the Palestinian revolutionary forces. In addition to the 20,000-man occupation force, the RAF was now used, and hundreds of Jewish settlers were armed and organized into "night squads" to attack Arab villages.[57] The Arab toll was terrific. Walid Khalidi estimates that there were over 19,000 casualties. In addition to those who lost their lives, there were 5,600 Arab detainees. Property loss was also great. Hundreds of homes, orchards, and vineyards were destroyed, and the livestock of whole villages were confiscated or slaughtered as part of the policy of collective fines.[58]

In the end, the British accomplished what they had set out to do in 1917. The natives were disarmed, and their ability to resist was checked. At the same time, the Jewish colonists were armed, organized, and protected. The stage was set for 1948.

In spite of this defeat, something positive had also happened. The Arab population had been molded, in these years of struggle, into a national movement. This series of events left a legacy which, though it was to lie dormant for many years, has been resurrected. It is a legacy of victories which can be imitated, and which inspire those who are struggling today for the right of the Palestinian Arabs to self-determination in their homeland. It is also a legacy of errors of a decayed

55. Verdery, "Arab 'Disturbances,'" pp. 298–300.
56. Marlowe, *Seat of Pilate*, p. 151; Bauer, "The Arab Revolt of 1936," p. 24.
57. See "Orde Wingate," in *From Haven to Conquest*, ed. Khalidi, pp. 375–88.
58. *Ibid.*, pp. 357–65, 846–49.

leadership which lacked the understanding, ability, and desire to lead the masses to victory. And this legacy must not be repeated.

The Character of the Palestinian Response

The character and legacy of the Palestinian national revolt, as it evolved during this period, was remarkably progressive in spite of the native community's inability to develop a permanent progressive leadership. As expressed by both the traditional elements and the popular forces, the revolt was (1) anti-imperialist, (2) anti-Zionist, (3) democratic and popular-based, and (4) Pan-Arab.

From the outset of the mandate's imposition, it was clear that the Arab population, in all the regions, felt betrayed, and that they rejected the foreign occupation. This resentment was expressed repeatedly in demonstrations, political resolutions, and armed attacks. When the popular forces developed in Palestine in the 1930s, their prime target was the British government. In fact, one of the essential differences between the popular forces and the traditional leadership concerned the manner in which to deal with imperialism. It should not be thought that the Arab Executive, for example, accepted the mandate. They did not. They rejected it repeatedly, in resolution after resolution; and this fact caused the British great concern. The problem, however, was that this element of Palestinian society, did not understand the nature of British imperialism in Palestine and therefore never stopped seeing Britain as a potential ally. In one instance the traditional leadership even referred to Britain as the "cat's paw of Zionism."[59] And in a military communique of 1936, the same confusion is manifested:

> It is indeed regrettable that Britain should lose such a number of casualties in a sacred part of the homeland in the service of Zionism, while they were our allies and are so today.[60]

The popular independent leadership displayed no such confusion about the innocence of imperialism. George Mansour, in a continuation of the testimony cited above, said in answer to Lord Peel:

> MANSOUR: We consider the fault to lie entirely with the British Government.

59. Verdery, "Arab 'Disturbances,'" p. 295.
60. Quoted in Kanafani, "Palestinian Resistance," p. 12.

PEEL: And none with the Jews.
MANSOUR: No.
PEEL: And the Jewish garrisons, are they the British Government?
MANSOUR: They grew out of the British Government's policy.

From the beginning of the 1936–39 revolt, the popular forces had insisted on a no-compromise position vis-à-vis the British. It was they who insisted on the national strike and the boycott on paying taxes,[61] and it was from their ranks that the armed resistance was formed to fight both Zionism and imperialism.[62]

From the earliest days of Zionist penetration into Palestine, that movement was rejected by the indigenous population. It should be made clear that their opposition was not based on racism or anti-Semitism. The entire Arab East was divided into sectarian religious communities, as well as into familial groupings. The competitiveness and other forms of division that such tribalism and sectarianism breed cannot be equated with such aspects of contemporary class society as racism or anti-Semitism. The small numbers of Arabic-speaking Jews who had lived in Palestine before the turn of the century lived there in relative peace. Shortly after Zionist penetration into Palestine had begun, however, these native Jews were outnumbered—and the whole complexion of the relationship between the communities had changed. To the native of Palestine, Zionism and Judaism became one. The Zionist made it so. The relationship was no longer tribal or sectarian. In this period it was the indigenous population, seeking self-determination, versus the European colonists, seeking domination.

The Star of David and the Wailing Wall no longer were simply religious symbols: in the riots at the Wailing Wall in 1929 this became especially clear.[63] The Zionist made traditional Jewish symbols the symbols of his movement. To the indigenous population these became symbols of conquest—symbols of a movement which openly declared its intent to seize their land. The Palestinians, then, were from the beginning anti-Zionist and not anti-Semitic. Any attempt to identify their response to these foreign invaders with the Nazi slaughter of European Jewry is historical nonsense, serving only to obscure the Palestinians' just struggle for self-determination.

It must be pointed out that there was no mention, at this time, of pushing the Jews into the sea. The demands of the native population

61. Kalkas, "The Revolt of 1936," pp. 246–47.
62. Barbour, *Nisi Dominus*, p. 191.
63. See Sheean's account in *From Haven to Conquest*, ed. Khalidi, pp. 273–302.

vis-à-vis the colonists were to stop immigration, to outlaw the racist and exclusivist practices of the Jewish national and labor organizations, and to achieve independence with representative government. All of these are essentially democratic demands. It was the British and Zionists who were, from the outset, opposed to a democratic solution. The British, in their usual "fair-minded" way, offered a "representative government" on many occasions—but always with the proviso that the "mandate" remain and the British government retain veto power over all matters. The Zionists, on the other hand, wanted democracy but rejected representative government: they wanted a democratic state for Jews. A clear example of these positions can be seen in the responses to the 1935 proposal, made by the British high commissioner, for representative government in Palestine.[64] There was to be a representative legislative council of twenty-eight members—eleven Muslims, seven Jews, and three Christians (the remainder were to be appointed by the high commissioner to prevent a "biased majority"). The Zionist leadership rejected it "categorically," since "an advance toward real self-government meant an advance toward subjugation of the National Home to an Arab majority." Although the Arab press criticized this proposal, no Arab party rejected it, and public opinion was generally favorable. What the Arabs objected to was the fact that the proposal did not go far enough toward democratic self-government, that it maintained the mandate rule.

The imperialist powers hoped that the mandate would squash the nascent Arab national movement. As we have seen, this effort failed. From the first day of the mandate, central to each of the individual struggles for national liberation—and either vocalized by the leaders or put into effect by the masses—was a desire to re-create the lost Arab unity. By the 1930s each of these struggles for local independence had, to a point, been successful. Bending to continued resistance, the mandate authorities established independent but "friendly" governments in each of the areas—except Palestine.

The sustained struggle of the Palestinians during the last half of the 1930s was their response to this situation. As has been shown, they received popular Pan-Arab support in their effort. But not only did the popular masses rally in support of the Palestinian revolt; the forces of Arab reaction rallied in opposition to it, in an attempt to diffuse it, and in an attempt to reassert their control over the Arab masses. And while the popular Arab support was great, the intervention of the reactionary pro-imperialist monarchs finally cost the Arabs the

---

64. *Palestine Royal Commission Report*, pp. 90–91.

victory they had fought so hard to win. One of the profound effects of the 1936–39 revolt of the Palestinians was that from then on Palestine and the popular democratic struggle of the Palestinian masses became fixed as the focal point and the "great divide" in the continuing Arab struggle for unity and national self-determination against the combined forces of imperialism, Zionism, and Arab reaction.

PART III: SETTLERS AND NATIONALS: ALIENATION AND LIBERATION

Fawaz Turki

ALIENATION OF THE PALESTINIAN IN THE ARAB WORLD

THE ROLE THAT ARABISM has played in the evolution of the national psyche of the Palestinian people must, first of all, be demystified. The refugee from Palestine did not move from one part of the Arab world to another with the ease of a commuter moving from the city to the suburbs. Before his eviction from Palestine, in 1948, the Palestinian's essential repertoire of consciousness, the props of his daily life as a peasant, a professional, a tradesman, or an artist, were derived from the country of his birth. Palestine was the land from which he drew his myths, his metaphor, his laughter, and his ethos. The exquisite nexus that binds man to his nature, the intangible realities with which man identifies himself as a spiritual being, were to be found, for the Palestinian, in the village or the city in which he had grown up. The half-century-long struggle against the machinations of British imperialism and international Zionism, in which the Palestinian people drew on their optimal resources and endured acute trials and tribulations, was, in fact, a struggle that was waged to protect the reciprocal link between Palestinians and Palestine. But, above all, what crystallized this relationship was the series of events leading up to 1948, when the Zionist dreams were fulfilled at the expense of Palestinians.

The Palestinian became a refugee, disinherited of his homeland, inhabiting a world of nothingness in the surrounding countries of Lebanon, Syria, and Jordan. The alienation that he felt as a consequence is reflected in his art and literature, often replete with references to the anguish of being away from the homeland and to the hardship of living in the *ghourba*, or diaspora.[1]

It is this alienation and this hardship that I wish to discuss. People often find it all but impossible to understand what the Palestinians have had to endure in the Arab world for the last twenty-five years. For after all, they argue, are the Palestinians not Arabs? Do they not share with their Arab brothers their culture, their traditions, their language, and their struggle for liberation? How can an Arab from Palestine be an alien in, and become alienated from, the Arab world?

I have spent twenty-five years of my life—and that is virtually all of it—trying to identify my status, and the status of my generation of Palestinians, in the Arab world, trying to identify that delicate correlation between my political reality and my subjective experience. As I was growing up, I saw how the one was mutilated while the other was degraded, how the politics of alienation and existential discontent is the politics of the Palestinian experience.

There was time in the Arab world, soon after the emergence of Nasserism, when the Palestinians, leaderless and fragmented, looked to the Arab rulers to right the wrongs committed against them. The petty bourgeois nationalist movement of that time, which had toppled some of the feudal regimes and reactionary monarchies and, indeed, had challenged the ramparts of imperialism and its oligarchic agents in the Arab world, came to be known as the "new revolutionism." Its authority to introduce and dispense social justice and freedom was to be derived from the wishes of the masses. The Arab peoples, we were told, were to be galvanized, revolutionized, and unified. There was a consensus in ideology between the ruling classes and the intellectual elite. It was not long, however, before the Arab peoples and this elite got over their optimism. But the Palestinians looked to this movement to bring them succor and return them to their homeland.

Arab leaders made pronouncements and promises about the noble battle and the rights of the Palestinians, but the noble battle and the rights of the Palestinians were at the bottom of these leaders' lists of priorities. To have been part of that period, to have joined that movement, was to have participated in an exhilirating dance sequence, one which required extraordinary energy and which suggested an uninhibited climax, but one in which the dancers and their motions were lost in all the noise and all the music.

---

1. An excellent study of this was made by A. L. Tibawi in a paper titled "Visions of the Return: The Palestinian Refugees in Arabic Literature and Art," *Middle East Journal* (Autumn, 1963).

In the midst of all the rhetoric and all the mendacities, members of my father's generation of Palestinians could only mumble hopeful incoherencies as they waited for the day when they would regain their sense of worth and live again in their homeland. Those of us from the refugee camps, who were growing up on the streets of Beirut, Amman, and Damascus, and who were becoming wise from our street education, suspected that Arab leaders had spoken lies. Why did the Arab rulers, who proclaimed to have our interests at heart, continue to stand with their backs to us, and to hinder—indeed, block—our attempts to have a meaningful existence and a meaningful expression of our political aspirations? Why did we continue to be the subject of abuse and not the subject of compassion? And why was it that whenever a Palestinian lifted his head, it was hit?

As my generation was growing up, the link that bound it to the social, political, and emotional reality around it was weakening. My generation seemed to go its own way, to create its own ethos, to form its own identity. This metamorphosis in the psyche of the average Palestinian came about not only because of the void between the present and the past and because of the campaign of harassment, persecution, and torture in Jordan, economic and social restriction in Lebanon, and neglect everywhere else. It occurred because the Palestinian is, first of all, human and, only secondarily, a member of a national group. He has everyday needs to fill. He must eat, work, acquire an education, travel. He must feel free to enjoy privileges that others take for granted. Above all, he must share his humanity with those around him. But the Arab world was blissfully unaware that Palestinians were denied the chance to gratify even these basic needs, and that Palestinians, as a consequence of the ruthless obstacles placed in their way (Jordan and Lebanon come to mind), would have to exert additional energy and acumen to achieve what others consider a natural extension of their social reality.

Here is an example. A Palestinian wants to travel abroad to study. He goes to the aliens department at the ministry of the interior, where he gets in line to be issued his stateless travel document. He stands and he waits. American tourists go through. French businessmen go through. Italian nuns go through. Israeli spies go through. And the whole foreign community in Lebanon goes through. Only *he* has to wait interminably, as he clutches his UNRWA permit, his work permit, his residential permit, and his other wretched documents. And he does this for the simple privilege of traveling, a privilege that others in the Arab world consider their birthright.

When this same Palestinian returns to Beirut with a degree, he is not allowed to seek employment; for, as an alien, he does not possess the right to work without a work permit. To apply for a work permit, he must have a job. He is not allowed to vote. He is not represented in government, nor is there an authority for him to appeal to in a moment of crisis. He nervously and perpetually feels in his pockets for the card that identifies him as the refugee that he is. On impulse, he wishes to go to a neigboring Arab country to visit a relative or to seek a better way of life. Everyone can, on impulse, visit a neighboring country. But he, as a Palestinian, must wait for his papers to be processed. He goes to the refugee camp where he once lived, and sits by the water pump where he played as a child in the dust of the summers and the mud of the winters. Suddenly he realizes that he has a past of his own. Suddenly he cannot endure the pain of contemplating his people's aloneness, destitution, and suffering, the pain of thinking that his people might be trapped forever as insignificant fossils on the edge of history. Suddenly he realizes that the Arab world never cared. He looks at himself in the mirror of his Arab history, and the mirror is cracked. The image that he sees is blurred, the image of an outsider. And he can see the anxious, bewildered faces of his fellow Palestinians, scattered around the Middle East, treated as third-class citizens in Israel, terrorized under occupation in the West Bank and Gaza, and alienated in the Arab world.

Left with no privilege except the right to have an identity crisis (a right that, I can assure you, we have in one form or another exercised to the full), the young Palestinian of my generation turned inward, and away from his Arab brother. He turned to Palestine, which was to him not just a geographical entity, his homeland, but a state of mind, a kind of mystical reflection, a symbol of his mutilated reality in the diaspora. The more he was excluded from the mainstream of events governing the average Arab's daily life, the greater was his estrangement. The more he was reminded, in his everyday encounters, that he was a Palestinian and, by implication, a lesser being than others around him, the more he realized that he belonged to a group that had its own way of seeing and reacting and interpreting reality.

This atmosphere is one that leads to creativity, but also to madness. Palestinians have the highest literacy rate in the Middle East. Among them are found some of the best writers, poets, artists, and theoreticians who have created a revolutionary vision of the future. But Palestinians also have the highest rate of psychosomatic ailments in the Arab world. And among them the crisis of identity and disconnectiveness manifests itself in the most acute form.

Alienation, although it breeds a sense of frenzied recklessness, devastating rootlessness, and pain, is also a challenge. In his study of the philosophy of history, Arnold Toynbee discusses the role of challenge and response in the genesis of nations. A nation (or, microcosmically, an individual) is presented a challenge to which it responds. Professor Toynbee expounds the hypothesis that difficult rather than easy conditions in the historical continuum of a people are what produce achievements and propel men and women to strive harder and to overcome adversity.

A challenge can be too easy for a people who inhabit a lush environment, who, as it were, can pick the fruit off the trees, who are not threatened by the elements, and who do not feel called upon or stimulated to aspire to transcend their state. Conversely, a challenge can be too crushing, as in the case, say, of a people taken into slavery or a people whose reality becomes too mutilated to elicit a response. Finally, the attributes of a challenge can be such that people, though denied opportunities and privileges, are indeed galvanized into, as Toynbee says, "putting forth exceptional energy and showing exceptional capacity in such directions as are open to them—much as the blind develop exceptional sensitiveness of hearing."[2]

Whether we subscribe to this thesis or not, we cannot fail to find it remarkable that a people whose history had been deflected from its preordained course, and who had been relegated to a world of nonbeing, refused to vanish or to be subdued. Indeed, the continued existence of the Palestinian people has long since transcended politics and become an existential statement about man and his willingness to suffer, to endure, to survive, and to fight.

This has been the response so far. But this is not to say that the Palestinians will continue to survive regardless of how awesome the nature of their adversity may be. The challenge may intensify and become too crushing; and this will depend as much on the Palestinians as on the Arab world. This is where the destiny of the Palestinian people is so inextricably tied to the forces at play in the Arab world, and this is where the Arab masses can determine whether their Palestinian brothers will live or whether they must die.

The Palestinian's present source of alienation stems not only, as it did before, from his arbitrary exclusion from the spontaneous activities of the Arab world or from his being reduced to a fragment of a man. Since the Palestinian has commenced, in recent years, to use Marxist idiom and Marxist metaphor, he has discovered that he, his people, and his cause are now in the service of, and being sacrificed to, the

2. Quoted in *The Study of History* (New York: Dell, 1971), I, 654.

collaborative forces of mercenary Arab leaders (who profess solidarity with the struggle) on the one hand, and the reactionary monarchs and the bourgeoisie on the other.

The massacres in Jordan (in the West they are called the civil war) did not fail to leave their mark on the average Palestinian. The campaign of killing and harassment of Palestinians in Lebanon is not likely to be blurred and faded with time. Palestinian poets and leaders are gunned down by Zionist killers who are free to roam the streets of Arab capitals. And then Sadat and Franjeh send bouquets of roses and greeting cards assuring Palestinians of their continued moral support.

Some from the Arab world find it all but impossible to comprehend the alienation that a Palestinian feels when he looks into the face of his Arab brother and searches in vain for a reflection of his own suffering. Yasser Arafat (a man not noted for excessive alienation from the Arab leaders) stated at a meeting of Palestinians in Algiers in January, 1972: "Yes we suffered a defeat in Jordan, but the operation was not purely Jordanian. It was an Arab plot."[3] The organ of the Popular Democratic Front for the Liberation of Palestine, *Al-Hurriyah*, said much the same thing when it claimed that the Arab governments "waited to react until the resistance had been liquidated in a bloodbath, although they were aware of all the plots being hatched against the Palestinian people."[4] One cannot claim to speak for all the people in the Arab world who call themselves Palestinians. There is, however, a broad Palestinian experience that is strikingly cogent and that cuts across class lines: having recovered and reconstructed his identity and his relation to the past, the Palestinian now has a clear vision of the future; armed with this vision, he sees his complete return to himself as a social, human being.

---

3. *Africasia* (Paris), January 24, 1972 (my translation).
4. *Le Monde*, July 29, 1971 (my translation).

Eric Sellin

ALIENATION AND INTELLECTUAL INVISIBILITY OF ALGERIAN NATIONALS: THE WRITER'S VISION

THERE ARE TWO SETS of writers whose visions illuminate the relationship of nationals to settlers in Algeria and underline the alienation experienced by the indigenous Algerians. These two sets of writers represent two of the three categories of North African writers posited by the Tunisian Albert Memmi: (1) the *écrivains-touristes,* or tourist writers, like Flaubert, Gide, and Duhamel; (2) the colonialist, or settler, writers, like Camus, Jules Roy, and Emmanuel Roblès; and (3) the autochthonous writers, like Driss Chraïbi, Mohammed Dib, Kateb Yacine, Mohammed Khair-Eddine, Mouloud Feraoun, Mouloud Mammeri, Ahmed Sefrioui, Rachid Boudjedra, and Memmi himself. The first category—tourist writers—need not detain us, for these writers are neither nationals nor settlers. The last two categories are pertinent, however, and Memmi's elaboration is of note. He points out that the colonialist writer is only partially Maghrebine: if he were constrained to leave, say, Algeria, he would return to France and lose little or nothing of his identity. But if the autochthonous writer were forced to leave, he could go nowhere without significant trauma and loss of identity. It is in this spirit that Camus, when pressed to choose between his "mother" (France) and his "country" (Algeria), said that he would have to pick his mother, a choice which caused him to be rejected by many Algerian critics and intellectuals.[1] This distinction between colonialist and native writers, which can be extended to the general population, provides the basis for my understanding of the terms *settler* and *national*. In other words, I construe settlers as intruders unless they have been assimilated over the centuries, and nationals as those whose entire psyches are linked to the land in question, those for whom "mother" and "country" are one and the same. The French, regardless of their long-lasting cultural impact on the Algerian Arab-Berber population, have never become nationals since they could not share the full gamut of experiences entailed in the emergence and establishment of the Algerian nation. We are, rather, confronted with a situation of colonizer and colonized, and the one must suffer as the other rejoices.

Colonialism and Invisibility

In his *Invisible Man,* the American novelist Ralph Ellison analyzes the role forced upon the black man in the United States. The pervasive idea is that at the time Ellison wrote his novel—and the situation has changed due to the self-assertion of the repressed man—in the white man's view, the black man simply did not exist. If he was rejected, it was less a rejection of scorn or hate than a rejection because he was too petty and contemptible to notice.

The same invisibility occurs in the literature of European French writers of the Maghreb, where it is manifested in two ways. The Arab-Berber segment of the population either is not mentioned or is associated with exoticism. This latter form of invisibility, in which the indigenous culture appears solely in the service of the European individual's *Weltanschauung,* is worthy of existential analysis, but our scope here permits only limited discussion. Suffice it to say that when the nationals are mentioned or portrayed, even sympathetically, the portrait is generally fallacious and unauthentic since it emanates from the psyche of the colonizer or settler. Just as colonialism and settler regimes tend to exploit nationals for manpower, to pay them low wages, and to assign them menial tasks, the settler authors tend to reduce them to nothingness or to use them as items exportable to the metropole, like wine or oranges. A sad by-product of this state of affairs is that, just as those nationals seeking to become successful in the settler infrastructure had to adapt themselves to the settler mold, national

---

1. The only European writer to remain after the revolution and to opt for Algerian nationality was Jean Sénac.

authors wishing to succeed tended to adopt as their own the vision of the European writers. We have the irony of a few indigenous writers, especially in the early stages of the French-language literature, practicing exoticism since that was what they thought Paris wanted. As the Tunisian critic Mohamed Aziza said in a recent interview,

> There are, of course, some authors of the so-called colonial period, people like the Tunisian Hachemi Baccouche, like the Moroccan Sefrioui, the author of *Un Chapelet d'ambre;* those people are much less authentic [than the younger writers and the better earlier writers], I think, because they perceived the folkloric face of reality, a frozen image, an image to package and to present to tourists or for foreign consumption.[2]

Since any writer of consequence writes about what he knows intimately, it is but natural that the colonial writer and the indigenous writer should describe the inner feelings of his own people, and place his work in a familiar setting. To do otherwise would be to risk forfeiture of authenticity. It was appropriate that *pied-noir* novelist Emmanuel Roblès when told by the Kabyle Mouloud Feraoun that he should write a long novel about Kabyle society, replied, "You don't understand, then, that that is your job?"[3] The world which emerges from the authentic literature of both *colon* and *indigène* bespeaks an intimate truth. During the thirty-odd years of Francophonic Algerian literature and the century of French writing by Europeans who settled in Algeria or who, like Isabelle Eberhardt, adopted it as their homeland, we have a mutual separation based not only on mistrust but also on ignorance.

All the official rhetoric about France's "civilizing mission" and "policy of assimilation" is belied by the historical evidence of France's arrogant seizure of native land-tracts and the literary evidence of humiliation, separation, and subordination. There have been a few enlightened politicians, intellectuals, and literati, but in general the Algerian scene between 1830 and 1962 was typical of what we have come to recognize as the colonial adventure: a sequence of invasion, occupation, pacification, cultural and economic penetration, cultural and legal juxtaposition, and ultimately assimilation.[4] It has been at this last step that colonial

---

2. "Mohamed Aziza parle du théâtre et de l'Islam, Interview accordée à *L'Esprit Créateur* le 18 octobre 1972," *L'Esprit Créateur,* XII, no. 4 (Winter, 1972), 316 (all translations are my own).

3. Feraoun, *L'Anniversaire* (Paris: Seuil, 1972), p. 64.

4. For a straight-faced apologia of this sequence, see René Maunier, *Loi française et coutume indigène en Algérie* (Paris: Domat-Montchrestien, 1932), *passim,* esp. pp. 16–24. For a concise history of modern Algeria, see Charles-Robert Ageron, *Histoire de l'Algérie*

efforts in the twentieth century have failed, in Algeria and elsewhere. The failure of the assimilation policy is no doubt due to the fact that the requisite methods used to impose the desired goals in the earlier stages of occupation—pacification, penetration, and juxtaposition—are countereffective when it comes to assimilation.

In his essay entitled "Orphée noir," Jean-Paul Sartre said of the sub-Saharan African that "the white man created the black man," that the black man thought of himself simply as "man" until the European came along and told him that he was culturally inadequate. The self-hatred which, a number of political philosophers have suggested, is felt by all colonized people is the seed of rebellion; and, in the case of Sartre's African, it grew into a self-assertion variously called *Négritude,* the African personality, and Black Power. The very notion of a "civilizing mission" is humiliating; and the more effective such a mission is, the greater is the loss of self-esteem among the autochthonous people. The inverse of the Sartrean process of "creation" is decolonization. As Frantz Fanon aptly expressed it in 1959 in *L'An V de la révolution algérienne,* "The death of colonialism is at once the demise of the colonized man and the demise of the colonizer."[5]

The idea of being made aware of what one is through outside intervention—being "created," as Sartre put it—occurs in all colonial contexts, especially in those involving a marked social, racial, or cultural contrast. In *Cette haine qui ressemble à l'amour,* by *pied-noir* writer Jean Brune, an Algerian named Mohand Benallal is married to a French woman, Lucienne. The union is ill-fated, Lucienne having entered the marriage with a sense of charity and paternalism which mirrors the attitude of the colonial government. Lucienne thinks she has "helped" Benallal to become an *évolué*; when he decides one day to start wearing a fez, she castigates him, accusing him of being Europeanized when that seems to be the thing to do and of renouncing Europe when that seems propitious. But Benallal has forsaken his identity for the "synthesis of the two races." He wears European clothes, has a European education, and has adopted the French language. In the following segment of dialogue, we have a capsule rendition of the colonial process leading to rebellion, complete with Benallal's Sartrean contention that it is Lucienne and her people who have made him aware of his ethnicity and culture. Lucienne is addressing Benallal:

---

contemporaine (1830–1966) (Paris: PUF, 1966).

5. Fanon, *L'An V de la révolution algérienne* (1959); reprinted as *Sociologie d'une révolution* (Paris: Maspéro, 1968), p. 15.

"Haven't you always agreed that the misfortune of Africa lies in the fact that the people of this land have remained bogged down in a life-style which hasn't changed since biblical times? That one has to awaken them at any cost and invite them to take part in the great modern adventure? And that in order to achieve that end one has to drag them out of the contemplative metaphysics of the East and integrate them into the dynamism of the West? Isn't that why you set the example . . . why you dress and live as a Westerner?"

She added in a lower voice, "Wasn't it to help you in this effort that I consented to marry you?"

He exploded: "Consented . . . consented! Did you think that you were lowering yourself by marrying me? Did you think that you raised me up? Toward whom? Uh? Toward what? Did you think that through me you were raising the Arabs up toward the French? Uh? You were lifting up the Arabs! . . ."

"You know very well that you are not an Arab. Moreover, that has no importance, for the word *race* has no meaning for me!"

"It has for me," exclaimed Benallal. "It has for me, because your people revealed it to me!"[6]

THE FRENCH COLONIAL WRITERS

The colonial writers in Algeria were sufficient in number and talent to forge a significant literary group known as the School of Algiers, its most celebrated exponent being Albert Camus. This group of writers dates back to the turn of the century, when Isabelle Eberhardt, an adventuress who died in her mid-twenties, galloped across the desert, sending back newspaper dispatches and recording her experiences in a diary, in impassioned and sometimes florid prose. Other writers of this group are Emmanuel Roblès, Jules Roy, Max-Pol Fouchet, Jacques Berque, Marcel Moussy, Gabriel Audisio, Claude de Freminville, Robert Randau, and André Rosfelder. The work of these writers is deeply rooted in Algeria, but in an Algeria perceived within the context of the colonialist regime.

Colonial systems must, in order to achieve the penetration and juxtaposition deemed requisite to assimilation, send out or lure settlers to occupy and work the land in order to perennialize their claim to the soil. Sooner or later, the *colon* feels isolated from the metropole and seeks to become master of his fate. In the case of Algeria the sense of neglect and semi-exile felt by the *pieds-noirs* came to a head

---

6. Brune, *Cette haine qui ressemble à l'amour*, in *Anthologie des écrivains français du Maghreb*, ed. Albert Memmi et al. (Paris: Présence Africaine, 1969), p. 102.

in Algiers with the May 13, 1958, generals' insurrection. But this feeling of neglect and separation had prevailed in literature long before that date.

At the same time, the French colonial writers—indeed, the French people in general—were, by their sense of cultural superiority, completely cut off from the indigenous population. Their treatment of Arab, Berber, or Kabyle characters is generally of two kinds, as was mentioned before: local characters and customs are described in order to create an exotic effect, or they are described, if at all, in the most shallow, most stereotypical way. In 1957, in a brief article entitled "La Littérature algérienne," Mouloud Feraoun wrote as follows:

> If we are absent from the work of a Camus who continues nobly to proclaim the misery and grandeur of the human condition, if Moussy's Algerian [colon] characters, who could not be more authentic or close to us, continually rub elbows with us without seeing us, it is because neither Moussy nor Camus nor practically any of the others could get sufficiently close to us to know us.[7]

Feraoun surmises that it was this invisibility and neglect which finally led writers like himself, Mohammed Dib, Kateb Yacine, and Mouloud Mammeri to take up the pen and tell their side of the story.

The most celebrated example of invisibility is found in Camus's *La Peste*. Camus gives the reader a fairly detailed description of the city of Oran. The numerous characters who share the limelight with the protagonist, Dr. Bernard Rieux, are described in detail, with attention paid to peculiarities of clothing, diction, and behavior. We cannot accuse Camus of failing to be observant or of being a vague writer. And yet there is something about *La Peste* which makes it difficult to recall its episodes and easy to forget that we are in a hot, sunny Algerian city rather than in a gloomy metropolis like Metz, Strasbourg, or Lyon.

Some critics have said that Camus has achieved the effect of a universalized fable warning against the capricious appearance of fascism anywhere, at any time—generated spontaneously, like the plague. But after rereading *La Peste*, I believe that responsibility for the impression of vagueness can be placed elsewhere. Despite Camus's keen eye for detail, there are no Arabs in the novel. The only references to the true "nationals" of Oran and environs, or to Arabs in general, occur indirectly: for instance, there is a casual reference to the news item which inspired another Camus work, *L'Etranger*, in which a European

---

7. Feraoun, *L'Anniversaire*, p. 55.

kills an Arab; and one of the characters trapped in Oran by the plague is a French journalist sent to write a series of articles on hygiene among the Arabs. The thoughtful reader will wonder where this journalist is to find his material, since there seem to be no Arabs around. They simply do not cross the narrator's vision; or, if they do, he is impervious to their presence.

This flagrant omission could hardly have been intentional; it constitutes, rather, a psychologically revealing oversight. And it did not go unnoticed. Feraoun, despite the fact that he was a real *évolué* and was considered by some to be a handmaiden to the French "civilizing mission," did not mind pointing out the oversight to Camus himself.[8] Albert Memmi has also underlined the invisibility of the native population in Camus's book.[9]

In Camus's most famous novel, *L'Etranger,* the Arabs who exist are faithful to stereotypes forged by colonial disdain. They function on the fringe of reality and seem outside the story, even less real than less-important European figures. Their treatment constitutes an extension of invisibility, if you will; for the small-time characters of Camus's novel in no way resemble the small-time characters in a novel by a Kateb or a Dib.

The Autochthonous Writers

The major writers of the autochthonous school in Algeria are Kateb Yacine, Mohammed Dib, Rachid Boudjedra, Mouloud Feraoun, and Mouloud Mammeri. There are few European figures in their works. In the novels and poems there are portraits of soldiers, torturers, bosses, landlords, restaurateurs, and the like, but very few European characters whose lives are meaningfully intermingled with those of the protagonists or narrators. The major exception is the Frenchwoman, and even in this case the portrayal is usually somewhat lacking. The conquest of the Frenchwoman provided some writers with a symbolic form of counterdomination. In several novels by Feraoun, Boudjedra, and others, the protagonist marries or has an affair with a Frenchwoman. In his second novel, *La Terre et le sang,* Feraoun's protagonist brings a French wife home to his mountain birthplace, in rural Kabylia. Significant, I think, is the novelistic metamorphosis of Marie, referred to most frequently as "la Française" or "Madame." She appears in the

---

8. Feraoun, to Roblès, June 27, 1951, in *Lettres à ses amis* (Paris: Seuil, 1969), p. 54.

9. Memmi et al., eds., *Anthologie des écrivains français du Maghreb,* p. 15.

opening pages as a lady of dignified mien. When she first enters the village of Ighil-Nezman with her husband, Amer, she smiles at the Kabyles "like a condescending queen." We subsequently learn, through an introspective flashback, that this *belle dame* has a sordid sexual past from which she is fleeing. In the second half of the novel, the Frenchwoman slips into the background, supplanted in Amer's focus by several local characters, including a cousin's wife with whom he falls in love. It appears that Feraoun intended to investigate the effect of culture-shock on the psyche of the European woman, but found the subject too alien.

It should be mentioned at this point that, in general, the Kabyle novelists devote more space and more analysis to the European personality than do their Arab-Muslim brothers. Perhaps this is a result of the historic-cultural rivalry between Arab and Kabyle, which has made the French-language Kabyle author less zealous than his counterpart about the notion of Arabization. Furthermore, Kabyle literature is not written but oral, so the debate on whether to write in one's native language or in the borrowed one did not occur. When the Kabyle writer adopted the French language, he adopted with it the literary patrimony of the French; and his own traditions were gone, save for a few memories and some transliterated fragments of *isefra* by the great wandering bard, Si Mohand-ou-Mhand.

The notion that the Kabyle *évolué* is more aware of European culture is borne out in the work of another great Kabyle writer, Mouloud Mammeri. Mammeri's latest novel, *L'Opium et le bâton* (1965), is an ambitious fresco of the war years and, specifically, the liberation fighting in the rugged mountains of Algeria, from the Tell Atlas to the Aurès. The style is fragmented, not so much in the style of the new novel as in the journalistic ticker-tape style of Malraux's *L'Espoir*. The point of view constantly shifts from place to place and from person to person. At least a third of the narrative either is told from the viewpoint of the French army officers and noncoms or describes incidents in which they are intimately involved. The European characters, as revealed in their dialogue and thoughts, are convincingly portrayed, but the very action of the novel separates the colonizer and the colonized. The treatment of the two sets of characters is sufficiently stylized to make them clearly "good guys" and "bad guys." (It is no doubt this clear-cut distinction which caused the movie version of the novel to be, as Mammeri complained, a pastiche of an American western.) We are, in this novel, always on the side of the *fellagha* and exult in their amazing feats, such as eliminating fourteen soldiers with fourteen bullets during an ambush; and we seethe with anger at the cowardly and villainous behavior of the collaborator Tayeb. We never emotionally abandon Dr. Bachir Larzack and his fellow revolutionaries, despite shifts in point of view. Two sympathizers are mentioned: and in what is perhaps a structural weakness in the novel—but consistent with my present premise—the French guard who lets Ali escape and then deserts with him, and the French soldier of fortune named Hubert who suffers from an incorrigible Messiah complex, are both given considerable attention and then dropped like hot potatoes. Furthermore, Bachir's pregnant French girlfriend, Claude, promises to be a major character in the novel, judging from the opening pages, but she is methodically reduced from a lover, to a patient but weary fiancée, to almost a stranger. Midway in the novel, her place is taken by Itto, a Moroccan woman whom Bachir meets while he is recuperating from wounds. Itto, who reminds us a bit of Kateb's Nedjma and some of Dib's female characters, is an illusive and unabashedly erotic sylph, yet she seems more genuine an extension of the author's psyche than did Claude.

Sexuality forms the basis of the relationship between the protagonists and their French girlfriends in some of the works by younger novelists, notably in *Yahia, pas de chance,* by Nabile Farès, the misty evocation of a boy traumatized by the violence of the revolution, and in Rachid Boudjedra's *La Répudiation.* The opening section of this latter novel is a grotesque symphony to the physical attributes of Céline, the protagonist's French mistress. It is a brutal verbal dissection, and we feel that we are witnessing the counterhumiliation of the colonizer on a carnal plane.

Aside from these women and soldiers, there is only an occasional functionary, *toubib,* or whatever; and their relationship with the Algerian characters is often characterized by silence, a counterpart to invisibility. The most celebrated "resistance" novel published in French during World War II was Vercors's brief book *Le Silence de la mer,* which at first glance would appear to be anything but militant. There is no plot to speak of: a German officer is billeted in the home of a Frenchman and his daughter, the latter being a pianist. The German is well mannered, cultured, and considerate, and he addresses the girl when he enters or leaves the house. He speaks of the greatness of musical and literary masterpieces and of the relative merits of the French and Germanic cultural heritages. The description of the officer as so considerate and cultured could pass for something out of a collaborationist pamphlet. But the man and girl never speak to the officer. It is easy to combat an abstraction or a violent, overt enemy; it is difficult to remain steadfast in the face of civility. The weapon used by the French is absolute silence. With silence they maintain a solid front against the subtle political proselyting of the German officer.

Whereas Vercors's characters *chose* to remain silent, the silence which marks the relationship between colonizer and colonized is a by-product of the total misunderstanding or isolation inherent in the colonial process. This spontaneous silence, incidentally, is paralleled by a ritualistic, hieratic silence described in *L'Opium et le bâton* and several other books: the patriotic silence under interrogation and torture.

In those passages of *Nedjma* in which Kateb Yacine describes contact between the indigenous population and the French segment of the population, there is a silence laden with hostility. There are, in the opening section of the novel, three *pied-noir* characters of consequence: M. Ernest, a foreman at a work site; his daughter, Suzy; and M. Ricard, who runs a small but prosperous bus service. The chasm of isolation and silence between the Europeans and the Algerians is felt during the rides in Ricard's bus, when Ricard babbles on and ridicules the Muslim passengers, who remain mute; and the silence between the four workmen and the European boss, M. Ernest, is almost palpable. The tension is shattered only by violence, as when one of the workmen strikes M. Ernest, or when one of the passengers finally kills Ricard, or in the May 8, 1945, Sétif massacre, which Kateb saw and which he describes in this novel.

We might mention that there were two types of colonizer: the dynamic and energetic builder, and the undesirable who fled or was expelled from his homeland. The majority of the early settlers were—as was the case in Australia and America—adventurers, renegades, financial failures, unemployed workmen and farmers, and political undesirables, and were from Malta, Sicily, Naples, and the like, as well as from France. Some 15,000 Parisians alone were hustled out of France to Algeria in 1848.

The characters from the settler populace that are encountered in novels by indigenous Algerians tend to be of the second type. This is natural since the tripartite hierarchy of privilege and citizenship placed the two most wretchedly treated groups in social proximity: least privileged were the indigenous Muslims and Berbers, next came the non-French settlers, and at the top were the French settlers and overseas officials. The orgiastic wedding party of Ricard and Suzy described by Kateb Yacine depicts the European settlers as so base that the intervention of even a marginal person like Mourad—who enters and strikes Ricard fatally when he sees the latter whipping his maid across the eyes—seems just and noble.

Conclusion

Parallel to the invisibility of nationals in the works of colonial writers is the invisibility of settlers in the works of autochthonous writers. However, the indigenous writers adopted the imposed language, which came as a by-product of the unwanted cultural penetration and social juxtaposition. We have a contrived irony here, inasmuch as even when the colonialist characters are absent, their language—and, therefore, their impact—is present.

Those claiming to sponsor assimilation might have been expected to make a greater effort to achieve understanding than those upon whom assimilation was urged. The general invisibility of the indigenous population bespeaks an attitude, on the part of the colonizers, which provokes alienation, resentment, and rebellion. The colonialist wanted penetration without the consequent envelopment. The autochthonous people, including the writers, did not request the foreign penetration, which geographically and socially was by enclave only; and the invisibility of the settler in autochthonous writing is a mirror of reality. The autochthonous writer, with little access to the inner world of the conqueror, had ample justification for not describing it.

We can draw a rather simplistic conclusion from the literary evidence: the social and cultural segregation which obtained in colonial Algeria is faithfully mirrored in the writings of both the European and the Algerian authors. Authenticity is manifest only when each group deals with its own segment of society, ignoring the opposite society or treating it superficially.

Ruth B. Minter

EDUCATION OF FREEDOM FIGHTERS IN MOZAMBIQUE

MOZAMBIQUE, A SOUTHERN AFRICAN COUNTRY of 8.5 million people, is in its ninth year of armed struggle against its colonial oppressor, Portugal, which has claimed the country since the late fifteenth century. This struggle is being led by FRELIMO, the Front for the Liberation of Mozambique, which has armed militants active in five of the nine provinces of the country and is supporting underground organizing and political education in the remaining four. FRELIMO controls liberated areas in three of the provinces, where it is responsible for developmental efforts and administrative, economic, and judicial structures, as well as for military activity.

This paper considers what is involved in the transformation of a Mozambican under Portuguese colonial rule into a militant fighter for the independence of Mozambique and the development of its people. Oppressed persons must, first of all, recognize their own oppression and the suffering of their people. There are many personal accounts of the experience of oppression in Mozambique, two of which are cited below. The first describes life in an area of Mozambique before the beginning of the armed struggle:

> My name is Natacha Deolinda and I was born in Machanga, Manica e Sofala Province, on May 5th, 1945. My father drove a lorry transporting loads for a company: sacks of flour, sugar, rice. My mother worked in

the fields. There were five children. My father earned 300 escudos (i.e., $10) a month working every day and often at night as well, while the white lorry drivers earned at least 3000 escudos for the same work. My mother cultivated a very small field. All the land belonged to a Portuguese landowner who had taken all the land and left us practically nothing.

Life was difficult in our household: we ate a little maize, a little flour, sometimes a little rice, but it was very hard to buy meat; a very small piece would cost at least 15 escudos. . . . Our people suffered very much. . . .

. . . In our area we were forced to leave, abandoning our fields, and the Portuguese planted sugar cane everywhere. We were not allowed to use the wells we had dug; all the water was reserved for the cane. . . . They forced the people to work on the plantations, working from morning to evening for 2-1/2 escudos a day. The people had no clothes; they had nothing.[1]

The second account, from Tete province of Mozambique, describes events that took place after the beginning of the armed struggle. Conescence, the narrator, is the daughter of Aroni, one of those killed in the mass murders committed in the area of Mucumbura, Mozambique, in 1971.

The Portuguese came to the shamba where my father was cultivating, and by the time I took notice they had encircled him. They approached my mother and me and told us: "We are taking Aroni and he will not come back. You will never hear of him again." They tied my father's hands and took him away in a car. My mother tried to follow on foot but was left behind. Then she ran to the PIDE [secret police] office, but they refused to let her in and she came back home. Later we learned that my father had been killed. . . . The Portuguese gave my father a shovel and told him to dig a hole. He dug for a while and asked if it was enough. They told him to try to get into the hole. He got in. The Portuguese officer aimed at him but the gun got stuck. It fired on the second attempt. My father died immediately and they left him in the hole without burying him.

My mother went to the spot later. But when she was taking the body out of the hole the Portuguese soldiers saw her. She ran away to the bush where I joined her. Then we met some FRELIMO soldiers who took us to a base and took care of us. I decided to remain at the base and join the Women's Detachment.

My father was a peasant. He had a small plot of land, but in order

1. *Mozambique Revolution*, no. 35 (June–September, 1968), p. 12.

to pay taxes he had to work for the Portuguese for at least three months every year.

Besides my father, my uncle was also killed. He was beaten to death.[2]

Second, oppressed persons must recognize that the situation can be changed, and they must join movements seeking to bring about that change. Both of the young women whose stories were repeated above recognized the situation of their people as intolerable. Natacha Deolinda's people, deprived of land and sources of water, were forced to work for plantations. They were in no sense allowed to live their own lives. Natacha Deolinda chose to try to change the situation and sought out FRELIMO. Conescence had known of FRELIMO for some time but did not become a member until she witnessed Portuguese atrocities to her own family. She and a cousin then joined FRELIMO's Women's Detachment.

When FRELIMO receives new recruits, it faces three large educational tasks—the same tasks which it endeavors to carry out with regard to all people with whom it has contact. The first and most important task is political. Mozambicans in touch with FRELIMO are continually struggling to grow in political understanding of the meaning of the Mozambican experience for their daily decisions. Each person is involved in determining what life in liberated areas will be like. Each person has to understand who and what are enemy, who and what are also exploited by the Portuguese, and how the activities of each person contribute to advance the struggle—or hold it back. Each person needs to grow beyond his or her own regionalism or tribalism to a mature concept of a Mozambican people and a Mozambican nation. Each person needs to absorb deeply a sense of personal responsibility to the whole Mozambican people—to the whole struggle. FRELIMO's second educational task is to train as many as possible in specific skills needed in the revolution and in the development of the country. Natacha Deolinda, who already had a primary school education from a Protestant mission in southern Mozambique, was first put through a course on youth organization and a military training course. She was then sent out as a political organizer in the Cabo Delgado province of Mozambique. Finally, FRELIMO is anxious to expand the level of basic knowledge and understanding of its militants, generally raising the educational level of the people and in the process also producing persons able to handle more complex tasks of revolution and development.

From the beginning, education has been one of the major revolu-

2. *Ibid.*, no. 50 (January–March, 1972), pp. 9–10.

tionary tasks of FRELIMO. Under Portuguese colonialism, over 90 percent of the African population of Mozambique had no chance whatsoever to attend school. In 1961, when FRELIMO was organizing, less than two hundred African youths were attending academic secondary school courses (i.e., fifth year of school or higher) in Mozambique.

At first, FRELIMO tried to locate those with some education and assist them in getting more, often through foreign scholarships. Then FRELIMO began tutoring to help some students prepare for or succeed in the foreign schools. Finally, FRELIMO set up its own secondary school in neighboring Tanzania and established a constantly growing network of primary schools and literacy training programs in liberated areas of Mozambique. Continually changing short-term specialized courses are also taught—nurses' training, teachers' training, training in the management of a production cooperative, and others.

When a person is assigned to study, it is considered a revolutionary task and is to be pursued with the same intensity and discipline as any other task. Within the Mozambican struggle, study is in no way a superior task, nor does it lead to privilege for those who finish.

Eduardo Mondlane, the first president of FRELIMO, in a document written in 1967 primarily for Mozambican students then in secondary or university-level training, explained what was expected of students:

> The Student is part of the People, like any other group, and the same duties fall to him. . . . All students who leave Mozambique, before pursuing their studies, must participate during a certain period in specific tasks in the struggle for national liberation. From the beginning it was required that the student would by this participation acquire through practice initial revolutionary training and would fully participate in the struggle and aspirations of the masses; at the same time [the student would] be putting his knowledge acquired by study at the disposal of the national cause.[3]

Just as students have been expected to be involved in the revolution before and after being sent by FRELIMO on a foreign scholarship, so also involvement is expected of FRELIMO students at all levels. A militant with only a first-grade education may be teaching literacy to people of the villages where he or she has been sent. Students in primary school who are living at home are expected to teach other members of their family what they themselves have learned.

In the spring of 1973, an Afro-American visitor to the FRELIMO secondary school in Bagamoyo, Tanzania, found that many of the students had just returned from a three-month "vacation" which they

---

3. *African Historical Studies*, II, no. 2 (1969), 326.

had spent inside Mozambique as worker-fighters. The visitor asked a number of the secondary school students what they would do when they finished their course. Would they go on to higher education? He reported:

> Hands shot up. . . . The student answering told us the choice was not his and it would be selfish and individualistic to set himself above the people's daily struggle inside Mozambique. . . . "The important thing," he emphasized, "is to serve the people." The place, hazards, and tasks were unimportant to him.[4]

The response from students has not always been so clear. When FRELIMO began its educational efforts, there were two difficulties: many students, schooled partially under the Portuguese system, had learned the values and priorities of that system; and the higher-level students, even in FRELIMO's own secondary school, had had little political education or revolutionary experience.

At the beginning, students were chosen from among those with some education. Mozambique had a 98 per cent illiteracy rate at the time, so, numerically, the students were a tiny elite. But, more important, many had been educated in schools that encouraged a psychology of elitism. Many of the students believed that their role should rightfully include self-serving personal achievement. They believed educated people to be more valuable than others, with the corollary that more valuable people are to be exempted from dangerous tasks and are to be given more privileges in general, so that they will be available in the future free Mozambique to run the country.

At first, FRELIMO allowed many such persons simply to leave on foreign scholarships, since cadres with higher education and with specific skills were badly needed. Unfortunately, many of those who left never returned, especially those in the group of nearly sixty persons who were sent to the United States. For some, the initial experience with the struggle had been too small. They had little political understanding of the necessities of Mozambique. Once out of Africa, they lost touch with the developing struggle, and, especially in the United States, the effect of the culture and the schools was to reinforce their predisposition to work for individual success or security. They ignored the call of the Mozambican people for them to bring their education to the service of the revolution.

FRELIMO had a similar experience with its students in the first

---

4. *IFCO News*, IV, no. 4 (July–August, 1973).

years of its secondary school. Some started fifth grade already thinking of themselves as intellectuals and superior. The school was at that time in Dar es Salaam, a city with many international and nonrevolutionary influences. FRELIMO, preoccupied with political organizing and military activity five hundred miles away inside Mozambique, did not spend enough time impressing upon the students the realities of the struggle; and many of the students at the school were persuaded by counterrevolutionary persons to oppose FRELIMO policies. The secondary school was closed in 1968, and a majority of the students fled from FRELIMO jurisdiction, hoping for scholarships elsewhere.

When the FRELIMO secondary school reopened, it was in Bagamoyo, and it was closely integrated into the total FRELIMO program. Also, by then, many of the entering students had received all or part of their primary schooling in FRELIMO schools located in areas actively engaged in military struggle against Portuguese rule. They had lived and worked at the front. They had been schooled not only in formal classes but also in mass political meetings and in tasks of the revolution.

The new group of students understands more clearly the task of liberating and developing their country. They see study as a revolutionary duty to prepare them to perform whatever tasks they are assigned. If asked, most will be ready to abandon study at any level and take up other urgent tasks for advancing the struggle and helping their people.

FRELIMO experience showed clearly what can happen when people pursue knowledge without political understanding and without commitment as to how they will use that knowledge. It is a lesson that is important for all groups that are organizing efforts to transform societies.

Once the importance of political education for the socialization of a militant is understood, several other points also become clear. For one thing, education happens in all tasks of the revolution—not only in schools. Here is the saga of a FRELIMO militant full of understanding that could not be learned in schools.

> I think I am 53 years old. I was born in Marromeu, Province of Manica e Sofala. I suffered very much all my life under the Portuguese colonialists.
> I worked first in a British Company, the Sena Sugar Estates. They have big sugar plantations and big factories. Like most of the other workers, I had been arrested and given to the company to work. Every day we were given a certain amount of work, which we had to finish in time. Those who did not finish were beaten with palmatoria and did not get paid for the day. . . . The man who was responsible for furnishing the Sena Sugar Estates with workers was [the] administrator. . . .
> . . . Administrator Palhota had a friend, a farmer called Barreto. Barreto

wanted more land. Palhota then came with his policemen, arrested us and sent us out of our shambas. I myself had a piece of land where I grew pineapples, cashews and oranges. I lost everything. Our huts were burnt and the land given to Barreto. Some of us were absent, on forced labor in other regions. When we returned we did not find our homes, and we did not know the whereabouts of our families. It was the case with me. . . . When I returned . . . I was arrested by the Portuguese and sent to Morrumbala to work on building roads. I found my family there—all the people from the expropriated land had been sent there, to work in government projects—with absolutely no pay. For many years it was like this—constantly arrested and sent to work for government projects or in Company plantations for periods of six months to one year.

In 1959 I got a job as a waiter in the wagon-restaurant of the Nyassaland Railways that went between Beira and Malawi. . . . In October, 1962, I met on the train a comrade who told me about FRELIMO. I did not know anything; he explained to me that FRELIMO was fighting to bring freedom to our country. I met him several times after that—and each time he explained in more detail.

I decided to join FRELIMO. I was given two tasks: first, . . . to explain to other people about FRELIMO—its aims, the need for everybody to join the struggle; second, to help bring out those nationalists who were being persecuted and those who wanted to receive training in FRELIMO. I helped many people pass—some into Mozambique, those who were sent by FRELIMO for clandestine work. I also helped others out of Mozambique. I carried propaganda material for the FRELIMO militants in Mozambique.

I was arrested by PIDE on the 20th of May, 1964. The sister of one of those I helped escape could not stand the interrogation and denounced me. . . . I was badly beaten. The colonialists started by asking if I knew what FRELIMO was. I answered, "Yes, I know. FRELIMO is freedom." They insulted me. They said, "You are stupid, you don't even know how to write. What do you want independence for?" I answered, "We have those who know. They will teach us."

. . . Together with me, 14 people were arrested. We were all badly tortured. Comrade Joguente was suspended by his hands so long that the skin broke off. Agosto Pinto Jeremo was whipped with a whip with iron points, and a palmatoria with nails instead of the usual holes. . . . I was in prison from 1964 to 1971. I was never taken to any court, never tried.

. . . We were very well organized in all the prisons, we had meetings to discuss and solve our contradictions. We kept out discipline as FRELIMO militants. We had high morale. In our wards there were never fights: on the contrary in the criminal's wards they even fought with knives among themselves.

The colonialists tried to destroy our political consciousness using a combination of three weapons: tribalism, terror and corruption, and murder. Through tribalism they attempted to separate the Makondes from us. They started to give classes only for Makondes. But they failed.

Then they created a magazine called "Ressurgimento," where the prisoners were forced to write articles insulting FRELIMO, and eulogizing the PIDE. Those who refused were punished. A few of us betrayed from fear, but they were very few. We also began mobilizing the prisoners from the criminal wards. Some of them adhered to FRELIMO.

Aware of our strength in the prisons, the PIDE resorted to other tactics: they infiltrated agents provocateurs. . . . Those traitors succeeded in identifying 30 of our comrades, who were immediately isolated in special cells. They were never allowed to leave the cells. They were given food once a week—a cup of cooked beans. No water. 23 of them died before this regime ended. . . . I saw with my own eyes the bodies of 20 of the murdered comrades. These comrades are great heroes, none of them betrayed, none of them denounced who were the other militants of the FRELIMO clandestine network. In spite of their deaths, FRELIMO continued very much alive in the prison, in our hearts. We organized ourselves better, more carefully, in the wards and cells. We also collaborated with white and Asian prisoners who had been arrested for supporting FRELIMO, including some Portuguese soldiers.

I left prison in 1971, but many thousands of patriots still remain there. I am working with FRELIMO. For the first time in my life I feel free. We have to continue fighting to extend this freedom to all our people.[5]

The "vacations" that FRELIMO students spend working among the people within Mozambique are very important. In late 1971 Samora Machel, president of FRELIMO, referred to the relationship between study and practice:

We are in the habit of saying that it is in war that we learn war, which means, in fact, that it is by carrying out a revolution that we learn how to carry out a revolution better, that it is by fighting that we learn to fight better, and that it is by producing that we learn to produce better. We can study a lot, but what use is tons of knowledge if not taken to the masses, if we do not produce? If someone keeps maize seeds in a drawer, will he harvest ears of maize?

If someone learns a lot and never goes to the masses, is never involved in practice, he will remain a dead compendium, a mere recorder who is able to quote by heart many passages from scientific works, from revolutionary works, but who will live his whole life without writing a single new page, a single new line. His intelligence will remain sterile, like those seeds locked in the drawer. We need constant practice, we

---

5. *Mozambique Revolution*, no. 51 (April–June, 1972), pp. 10–11.

need to be immersed in the revolution and in production, to increase our knowledge and, in this way, to advance our revolutionary work, our productive work.

The seed of knowledge only grows when it is buried in the soil of production, of struggle. If we have already so greatly transformed our country, if we have won so many successes in production, education, health and combat, it is because we are always with the masses. We learn from them and pass on what we learn to them. We consistently apply what we know to production, correct our mistakes and enrich our knowledge. But we should not be satisfied.

Practice is not enough. One must also know, study. Without practice, without being combined with force, intelligence remains sterile. Without intelligence, without knowledge, force remains blind, a brute force.[6]

And so, within schools, the political and the practical are incorporated into all parts of the curriculum. History, geography, science, mathematics, reading—all are closely related to the real experiences, thoughts, and problems of the Mozambican people in their struggle against Portuguese colonialism and against poverty, injustice, ignorance, and disease.

The head of a pilot school in Tete province speaks of some of the ways his students—in the second and third years of school—are involved with the people and with ongoing tasks as they study:

> For the school every day begins at 4:30 A.M., before the sun is up. Then follows manual work or sport from 5 to 6, except for one group of students who spend this hour out on patrol looking for any signs of enemy infiltration. From 6 to 7 is cleaning hour—not only for personal hygiene; they clean their huts and the whole school. . . . At 7:30 classes begin, and go on for five hours. . . . At 12:30 everybody has lunch, followed by free time until 14:30. After the break, jobs are allocated for the afternoon—usually manual work on the land, or building and maintenance work on the huts and shelters. . . .
>
> Agriculture—learning how to use the land to produce food—is very much part of the education program. Everyone at the school takes part . . . in the cultivation of the fields. The center has three big shambas, two of maize and one of ground nuts. We are now going to introduce cassava and sweet potatoes—crops traditionally unknown in this province.
>
> Within their program, the students also go periodically to help the villagers in different jobs, such as agriculture, house building and cleaning. The people, in their turn, help the school. They give them food, lend

6. *Ibid.*, no. 49 (October–December, 1971), pp. 22–23.

hoes, axes, and pangas. Shortly we are going to organize a program to exchange experience and skills with the local people. The people will teach the students things like making mats, pottery and other handicrafts. And the students will teach them how to read and write.[7]

I would like to close with two poems written by Mozambicans in the midst of their struggle. The first is by Armando Guebuza, the first head of FRELIMO's Department of Education and Culture, and a member of the FRELIMO Central Committee:

If you ask me
who I am
with that face of yours
seared by marks of evil
and a sinister smile

I'll tell you nothing
I'll tell you nothing

I'll show you the scars of centuries
which furrow my black back
I'll look at you with eyes of hatred
shot red with blood, shed through the years
I'll show you my hut of grass
falling into disrepair
I'll take you to the plantations
where from dawn to dusk
I bend over the soil
as the tortuous work
racks my body

I'll take you to the fields full of people
breathing misery every hour

I'll tell you nothing
I'll just show you this

And then
I'll show you the fallen bodies of *my* people
treacherously gunned down
huts burned, by *your* people

---

7. *Ibid.*, no. 46 (January–April, 1971), pp. 4–7.

> I'll tell you nothing
> but you will know why I fight.[8]

The second poem expresses feelings that are made clear in almost all contact with FRELIMO militants, whether students or those involved in some other task. It is a presupposition, even if unstated. The author is unknown.

> i
> son of Mozambique nationalist and patriot
> in the name of those things most sacred to me
> my people and my country
> swear to devote all my energies to the service
> of the revolution
> i shall never vacillate
> until the liberation of my people
> my life belongs to the Revolution[9]

---

8. *Ibid.*, no. 43 (April–June, 1970), p. 15.
9. *Ibid.*, no. 35 (June–September, 1968), p. 13.

Yasumasa and Alice K. Kuroda

SOCIALIZATION OF FREEDOM FIGHTERS: THE PALESTINIAN EXPERIENCE

A YOUNG GRADUATE of Israeli prisons said to one of us in 1972, as we sat in a coffee shop in Beirut and began to discuss Palestinian problems, "I don't mind dying, but I surely do not want to be killed. I would rather choose the place and time of my death." An attitude such as this is not uncommon among those who have dedicated their lives to a cause. The classical warrior creed in Japan defines the way of *bushi* ("warrior") as to find the way to die.

What made this young Palestinian intellectual utter words reminiscent of the traditional warrior code of Japan? The answer can be found in his experiences, which have made him aware of the fragile nature of man's life. Those who have not faced death in any realistic situation would find it difficult to make this kind of statement. Warriors must always be ready to face death without any warning. And freedom fighters involved in one capacity or another in the active liberation of their homeland face the danger of death, even those who use nonviolent means.[1]

This paper will attempt to explain how Palestinians are socialized

---

1. For example, the case of Adel Wael Zuaiter. Although he was the official representative of El Fatah in Italy, he was admired by liberal Israelis in Rome for his passion for the arts and for culture. He was shot in the back with twelve bullets in October, 1972. For how at least some Israelis regarded him, see Livia Rokah's article in *New Outlook* (November–December, 1972).

into taking active political roles. The socialization experience of the Palestinians is discussed, and, Palestinian freedom fighters are described. Then, empirical evidence showing why some Palestinians become sufficiently politicized to take active roles in commando activities is presented. Concluding remarks indicate the significance of the socialization experience with regard to the protracted crisis in the Middle East.

SOCIALIZATION

By *socialization* we mean the process that begins at birth and in which a person acquires a particular set of values, beliefs, attitudes, and action patterns—the process of growing up in a society to become one of its members.[2] Traditional institutions, such as family, church, schools, pressure groups, peer groups, and others, are referred to as *agents of socialization*. In any study of socialization, the key questions are, Who teaches what values to whom, for what reasons, and with what results?

Any attempt to revolutionize an entire social system requires changes in the process of socialization, as can be observed in such revolutionary societies as China and Cuba. Social institutions responsible for the rearing of children must be changed so as to eliminate forces not favorable to a new regime. This is the theory behind the establishment of communes in China and Cuba and *kibbutzim* in Israel. An equivalent agent of socialization in Palestinian society is "Ashabl," designed to train the freedom fighters of tomorrow.

In a survey of 234 Palestinian tenth graders that we conducted in the late spring of 1970,[3] one question asked the respondents to check which of the following they considered most important in making them good Palestinians: my father (26 per cent), my mother (2 per cent), my parents (35 per cent), my teacher (21 per cent), my siblings (1

---

2. Socialization as a concept thus assumes that man is a *tabula rasa* when he is born. An implication here is that man is born neither good nor bad, but that his upbringing will shape his behavior. For a comprehensive review of socialization, see Edward Ziegler and Irvin L. Child, "Socialization," in *The Handbook of Social Psychology*, ed. Gardner Lindzey and Elliot Aronson (Reading, Mass.: Addison-Wesley, 1969), III, 450–689.

3. The survey was conducted in two schools in Jordan. For detailed reports, see Yasumasa Kuroda, "Young Palestinian Commandos in Political Socialization Perspective," *Middle East Journal*, XXXVII, no. 2 (June, 1972), 285–303; Yasumasa Kuroda and Alice K. Kuroda, "Personal Political Involvement of Palestinian Youths: A Study of Political Socialization in a Revolutionary Polity," *Middle East Forum*, XLVII (Summer, 1971), 51–65; Kuroda and Kuroda, "Palestinian and World Politics: A Social-Psychological Analysis," *Middle East Forum*, XLVIII (Spring, 1972), 45–57; Kuroda and Kuroda, *Palestinians without Palestine* (forthcoming).

per cent), my friends (3 per cent) and radio (1 per cent). Eleven per cent failed to make any check marks. The answers to this question definitely suggest the continuing influence of the family in the process of socialization among Palestinians. Civic awareness education or political socialization appears to be more in the father's domain than in the mother's, as far as this survey can ascertain, although more chose their parents rather than their father alone.

It should be noted here that a relatively high percentage of respondents chose their teacher as their strongest influence (21 per cent). Formal schooling constitutes an important aspect of the socialization process in any modern society, and Palestinian society is no exception.[4]

What do Palestinian children learn, and what are some characteristics of their socialization patterns? As assumed in the concept of socialization, they are neither commandos nor Zionists when they are born. They learn to identify themselves by their name, nationality, religion, and what have you. What makes it unique in the Palestine case is that they are socialized in exile. They learn to be Palestinians while residing in Jordan and other host countries. In our survey one question simply asked: Who are you? The answers were quite revealing: 52 per cent checked Palestinian; 12 per cent, Arab; 15 per cent, student; 7 per cent, commando; 12 per cent, not ascertainable (n.a.). A majority identified themselves as Palestinians. Some 15 per cent, consisting mostly of women, said they were students, followed in number by those who identified themselves simply as Arabs. What is striking is that a small number considered themselves commandos. Just as Jewish refugees during World War II consistently identified themselves as Jews from Palestine, today's Palestinians, no matter where they were born and reared, seem to learn to be Palestinians.

Although Palestinians have maintained their national identity for the past twenty-five years of life in exile, it was not until the 1967 war that they stopped thinking of themselves as refugees, or as Palestinian refugees. It was the advent of the Palestinian commando group, and the battle of Karameh, that gave them cause to be proud of being Palestinian. Long before such slogans as Black Is Beautiful became popular, Clark and Clark demonstrated that small black children, including some three years old, were convinced that being Negro, or black, was not desirable, as evidenced in their rejection of black dolls.[5]

---

4. For a recent and comprehensive review of formal schooling of Palestinians, see Ibrahim Abu-Lughod, "Educating a Community in Exile: The Palestinian Experience," *Journal of Palestine Studies*, II, no. 3 (Spring, 1973), 94–111.

5. Kenneth Clark and Mamie Clark, "Racial Identification and Preference in Negro Children," in *Readings in Social Psychology*, ed. Theodore M. Newcomb and L. Harley (New York: Holt, 1947), pp. 169–78.

Today, the situation is different. In this sense, it is significant to observe that today's young Palestinians identify themselves as Palestinians and as commandos. We may hypothesize here that the commandos act as an important agent of socialization, and that young Palestinians find a key source of pride in them.

The agents of socialization for Palestinian children are not limited to institutions such as the family and schools, but include events such as the death of someone close to them in the war against Israel. Young Palestinians respect *fedayeen* and consider them as their heroes; such an event may prompt them to join the commandos and to work toward the goal of liberating Palestine.

Freedom Fighters

In the summer of 1973, U.N. representatives met to discuss problems related to international terrorism. To those well-established nations in the West, international terrorists are troublemakers whose aim is to change the status quo. However, to Asian and African nations, they are patriots and freedom fighters. To Asians and Africans, the U.S. bombing in Cambodia or Israeli bombing in Lebanon is "state terrorism," terrorism carried out by governments, which is much more effective in destroying people and property than international terrorism is.

How can we define freedom fighters? They are those who fight for national, class, or ethnic liberation from oppressive forces. The concept as defined here is highly relative—for instance, President Thieu, of the Saigon regime, can be viewed either as a freedom fighter or as an oppressor, depending upon one's political perspective. While we realize that the purpose of liberation lies in providing equal opportunity for all those oppressed people not only to articulate their interests and desires but also to enjoy whatever there is offered in this world, it is at times difficult to make an empirical assessment of competing forces.

Empirical assessments can be made easier, however, if we limit ourselves to national liberation movements of those who are fighting against alien rule for the right of self-determination. The Palestinians certainly fall into this category, just as those who fought against the Soviet occupation of Czechoslovakia and those who fought against the Nazi occupation in Europe.

Methods employed by freedom fighters vary from the quiet reading of poems composed by Mahmoud Darwish to Leila Khalid's spectacular hijacking of a jumbo jet. Like French resistance to Nazi occupation, Palestinian resistance to foreign occupation is fought on all grounds.

What are the Palestinian freedom fighters like? How are they different from other Palestinians? Who among Palestinians are most likely to become freedom fighters?

Observers of Palestinian affairs generally agree that Arab inhabitants of the British Mandate of Palestine who left their homes in the 1948–49 war were refugees and showed little spirit other than to dream of recovering their land. They remained refugees for nearly twenty years. In the early 1960s they began to take concrete steps toward realizing their dreams. After the 1967 war, it became apparent, with the rise of commando groups, that the refugees were firm in their determination to initiate actions that might lead to the liberation of Palestine. In the words of Don Peretz, Palestinians became refugees, and then refugees became Palestinians again.[6]

We will restrict the category of freedom fighters to those who have been actively seeking to regain Palestine in the period after the 1967 war. The Palestinian commando activities reached what was perhaps their peak in the summer of 1970. With King Hussein's attempt to halt Palestinian commando activities in September, 1970, the commandos lost a secure place from which to wage guerrilla warfare against Israel. More recently, in 1973, Lebanon took measures to curb Palestinian commando activities. There is no longer the high spirit of nationalism and vigor that once characterized Jordan's Palestinian population. Hisham Sharabi reports: "Gone are the animated throngs of only such a short while before. Amman was again the town I had known in 1949 on the morrow of the first defeat—faceless, desolate, conquered."[7]

Fedayeen life consists largely of military training and some political education in addition to guerrilla activities. The more politicized the group to which the *fedayeen* belong, the more emphasis there is on political education. For example, political education may be kept at a minimum for El Fatah, while other more ideologically inclined groups, such as the Popular Democratic Front for the Liberation of Palestine, place more emphasis on political education. What unifies all these *fedayeen* groups is the desire to return home, although each group has its own preferred means to achieve this goal. Life is not easy for the *fedayeen*.

---

6. Peretz, "The Historical Background of Arab Nationalism in Palestine," in *A Palestine Entity?*, Special Study No. 1 (Washington, D.C.: Middle East Institute, 1970), pp. 1–57.

7. Sharabi, "Liberation or Settlement," *Journal of Palestine*, II, no. 2 (Winter, 1973), 33–48.

They often share what little food they have in order to promote an *esprit de corps*.[8]

As noted at the outset, a young Palestinian intellectual told one of us that he does not want to be killed, but that he does not mind dying if he can choose the time and place of his death. Bassam Abu Sharif, who lost one eye and three fingers in a letter bomb explosion, defines his life philosophically: "I can die; therefore I am."[9] These two young men seem to have reached a point of self-awareness unmatched by those who have never been exposed to the danger of being killed. Even though these young Palestinians are not actively engaged in violent activities that fill the front pages of newspapers, they are prepared to die, if necessary, for the cause that makes their lives meaningful.

A young boy about fourteen years of age in a red *kaffiyeh* responded to a reporter: "Revolution is my life." "Revolution against whom?" asked the reporter. "Against Israel? Against Jordan?" "Against the whole world," came the answer. This is the voice of those Palestinians who have slowly but surely discovered, to their dismay, that they cannot depend on anyone but themselves for the liberation of Palestine. What is significant is that the boy was so young; and he was already carrying a rifle with a fixed bayonet.[10]

A sixteen-year-old *fedai* by the name of Ibrahim Youssef tells of his life experience: "When I was twelve I wondered why I did not have a country. Is there anyone in the world without a country of his own?"[11] Khalid Ismaelis saw the Israelis kill his mother in Jaftalak refugee camp, near Jericho, when he was ten years old. He started to walk eastward. A commando found him tired and nearly dead. Two years later, after the 1967 war, he "threw a hand grenade on the El-Al office in Brussels and escaped."[12]

What is the attitude of Palestinian children toward these freedom fighters? This question can be at least partially answered by reviewing some of our survey findings. We asked our respondents to indicate,

---

8. There are several works that describe the life of freedom fighters, or *fedayeen:* see Gerard Chaliand, *The Palestinian Resistance* (Middlesex, England: Penguin Books, 1972); Hisham Sharabi, *Palestine Guerrillas: Their Credibility and Effectiveness* (Washington, D.C.: Georgetown University Press, 1970); Sakuji Yoshimura, *Arabu Gerira* [The Arab guerrilla] (Tokyo: R. Shuppan, 1972).

9. Quoted by Gavin Young, *Washington Post,* May 17, 1973, p. F 2.

10. Larry Henderson, *The Arab Middle East* (Camden, N.J.: Thomas Nelson, 1970), p. 148.

11. Chaliand, *Palestinian Resistance,* p. 14.

12. Mona Saudi, *In Time of War: Children Testify* (Beirut: Mawakef, 1970), p. 156.

on a list of people, the two to whom they would give prizes as the best in Palestine. The results are as follows: commando, 74 per cent; someone who teaches what is good for Palestine, 56 per cent; someone who works hard, 16 per cent; someone who obeys the law, 11 per cent; someone whom everybody likes, 4 per cent; someone who studies hard, 4 per cent; someone who helps other people, 4 per cent; someone who goes to church or to the mosque often, 3 per cent; and n.a., 30 per cent. (The total per cent for this answer comes to 202, because respondents were asked to check two categories.) Commandos are the undisputed national heroes of the respondents in our survey, followed by those who teach what is good for Palestine.

Another of the questions asked what three wishes they would like to see come true if they had an Aladdin's lamp. As their first wish, 29 per cent of them indicated the regaining of Palestine; 12 per cent, the liberation of Palestine. The first wish of 26 per cent was expressed in a variety of ways signifying a desire to destroy Zionism, to eliminate foreign domination, to win victory for the commandos, and to attain other nationalistic goals. The fall of traditional regimes in the Middle East was mentioned by 3 per cent. As their first wish, 10 per cent indicated a personal goal, such as success or getting married; 21 per cent failed to respond. Thus, 70 per cent considered the regaining or liberation of their homeland as their greatest dream, while 10 per cent expressed concern for personal matters. One may say that the Palestinian students in our survey are obsessed by a desire to regain their country. Thus, understandably, they have much respect for anyone who contributes toward that goal.

Several points can be made on the basis of the description of Palestinian commandos and our respondents' views of them. First, these *fedayeen,* or freedom fighters, are dependent upon no country. This position is based upon their experiences of the past twenty-five years; the anticipation that their neighbors and other friendly nations would help them has disappeared. The advent of the Palestinian commandos, in the 1960s, signified a new chapter in the Palestinian-Israeli conflict. In the words of a fourteen-year-old boy, the *fedayeen* are fighting the whole world, not just the Israelis and their allies.

Second, since there is no secure base in the Middle East for the Palestinian commandos to operate from, no Hanoi for the Palestinian Resistance Movement, the commandos have employed certain techniques that have not been used as extensively by freedom fighters in Ireland or in Viet Nam—for example, hijacking planes, assassination, and other limited guerrilla warfare techniques. Palestinian commandos have made extensive use of hijacking in recent years and have contributed at least in part to the sharp rise in hijacking activities in general.[13] This guerrilla technique, used by certain groups of Palestinian commandos, represents a sensational means of focusing world attention on the Palestinian problem. It has been one of the few means open to the commandos, operating on meager resources. Public opinion throughout the world on the matter of hijacking has not been favorable. But Palestinian commandos were not asking for the world's sympathy for their national problem; they were asking for, and have received, the world's attention. They seemed to prefer being disliked and feared to being forgotten. Two major groups that have employed this technique are the Popular Front for the Liberation of Palestine, headed by Dr. George Habash, and the Black September group. (It seems that the former of these has abandoned this activity.)

Third, the activities of the commandos affect domestic politics in Arab countries to a large extent, which, in turn, may draw the superpowers into the Middle East conflict. The increasing shortage of oil in the West and in Japan adds significance to the whole situation. These countries cannot remain disinterested.

Fourth, commando activities are definitely supported by young students of Palestinian origin in Jordan. Although the Western press reports would have us believe that Black September "terrorism" is the work of extremists, and that it is not supported by the masses, the evidence presented in this paper would suggest otherwise. Many Palestinians under occupation in Israel today, although they cannot publicly say so, may support the aims of such groups.

Mass media such as UPI reach the peak of irresponsibility when they refer to the attack on Lidda airport that was carried out by Okamoto and his colleagues as being an act of hired guns. They fail to mention how much these "terrorists" received for their lives. The Japanese government's apologetic posture, taken immediately following the incident, deserves the criticism that it received from the most important among moderate Arab rulers, King Faisal of Saudi Arabia.[14] Palestinian freedom fighters (of whatever nationality) are generally slurred by Western mass media. They are invariably referred to as "terrorists," while uniformed Israeli soldiers using U.S.-made jets to kill Palestinians in Lebanon are not. Nor are the activities of U.S. soldiers in Indochina labeled as terrorism. Palestinian commandos are to be blamed, at least in part, for this state of affairs. Their efforts to propagate their cause

---

13. See D. V. Segre and J. H. Adler, "The Ecology of Terrorism," *Encounter* (February, 1973), p. 18.

14. *Asahi Shinbun*, September 27, 1972.

in the United States leave much to be desired. These efforts certainly do not approach Israel's sophisticated "educational" programs, which have been effective in creating a favorable image of Israel in the West.

Young Palestinian Commandos in Jordan

What makes some young Palestinians commando members while others remain nonactive even if they are sympathetic to the cause? The findings to be presented here are based on the survey of Palestinian tenth graders that we have referred to throughout this paper. It should be pointed out that evidence gathered from the survey definitely indicates the popular support which the commandos enjoyed among Palestinian youths in 1970 prior to the Black September incident.

Being a commando member is not an isolated act but an integral part of being politically active. The results of a factor analysis revealed, among other things, that political aspiration ($-.709$), political interest ($-.627$), commando membership ($-.537$), and sex ($-.489$) together constitute what may be referred to as a "political activity" pattern among the youths. If one is a commando member, one is likely to be a male who is interested in politics now and who, it is expected, will be actively involved in political activities in the future. Being a commando is not the only way to be a freedom fighter; freedom fighters are politically active citizens who like politics and who are willing to take an active part in determining their future. Our decision to focus attention on commando membership was based on the assumption that it was the best indicator that we had included in our survey.

Demographic Variables

Commando membership, which requires not only mental ability but also physical skill, attracts more men than women, although there are commando heroines. Of those who were included in our survey, 50 per cent of the male students said that they belong to one unit or another of Palestinian commandos, whereas only 8 per cent of the female students so indicated. Freedom fighting in terms of commando membership is still the domain of men.

An interesting demographic variable which relates closely to commando membership is place of birth. Those students whose families were forced to move from their homes in the 1967 war are much more likely to become commandos than are those who were born and reared on the East Bank. Among the former, 54 per cent said they were commandos, while among the latter, only 19 per cent made that claim.

An implication here, of course, is that those who suffer more are more likely to take up arms against the enemy.

A father's occupation seems to have some bearing on his son's commando membership. We found that commando fathers were likely to have commando sons. Government employees and the unemployed produced the next largest number of commando sons. The father's social status, as measured by literacy, shows no appreciable effect on the son's commando membership. People of all social classes, both low and high, are equally represented among the commandos.

Religion is a key variable in spite of the fact that many Arab intellectuals and leaders do not consider it important today. Like Halim Barakat and Michael W. Suleiman in their empirical work, we also found that religious affiliation continues to be a factor in determining the attitudes of Palestinians.[15] The relationship that we found is in keeping with their findings that Muslims are more likely than Christians to take on active, militant attitudes toward the Palestinian-Israeli conflict. The tabulation of data demonstrated that 21 per cent of the Christian respondents, as opposed to 43 per cent of the Muslim respondents, were commando members. This partial relationship remained the same when the sex factor was held constant. Barakat reports that in all three universities in Beirut—i.e., American University of Beirut, St. Joseph University, and Lebanese University—Muslims showed stronger support for popular armed struggle than did Christians in a ratio of roughly two to one. That is the same ratio that our survey reported on this matter.

Political Variables

An identification is an important part of being politically active. Today, many Palestinians, no matter where they reside, identify themselves as being Palestinian. We asked our respondents to tell us where they were from. About 80 per cent of them said either Palestine or the name of some Palestinian town from which their parents had fled years ago. However, a small minority of the students said Jordan or gave some other name. We found that 45 per cent of those who identified themselves as being from Palestine were commando members, while only 14 per cent of those who did not identify themselves as Palestinians were.

---

15. See Barakat, "University Students in Lebanon and the Palestinian Resistance," *Journal of Palestine Studies*, I, no. 1 (Autumn, 1971), 87–112; Suleiman, "Attitudes of the Arab Elite toward Palestine and Israel," *American Political Science Review*, LXVII, no. 2 (June, 1973), 482–89.

Another variable which relates closely to commando membership is what we might refer to as political cynicism. We asked the students to tell us how the head of the community was performing his task. A number of them gave cynical replies, while others gave views in support of the community leadership. When these open-ended answers were coded into two categories, "cynical" and "trusting," and were run against the commando membership variable, we found that 34 per cent of the "trusting" and 59 per cent of the "cynical" were commandos. This would suggest that the more cynically the young Palestinian views politics, the more likely he is to become a freedom fighter.

This finding suggests another aspect of Palestinian political culture. It appears that politically active Palestinians are those who hold politics and political leaders in disrepute, a point which may be one of the factors motivating them to join forces for the liberation of their country. It seems that those elements among the Palestinians who are least satisfied are the ones who are becoming interested in participating in commando activities. In this sense the Palestinian political culture is revolutionary and dynamic.

Socialization Agency Variables

Who affects attitude-formation in young Palestinians? Does the answer to this question affect in any way their joining commando organizations? Our survey results reveal that parents continue to play the foremost role in the socialization process, although a minority (25 per cent) of the respondents said that their teacher, rather than a parent, is the one from whom they would seek advice. An interesting relationship was revealed when this variable was run against commando membership: among those who would look to their teachers for advice, 56 per cent were commandos, while among those who would look to their parents, 36 per cent were.

Those who have lost a close relative in the conflict are the most likely to join the commandos. This is particularly true among women. We found that 25 per cent of those women who had lost someone close to them were commandos, while none of those who had not were commandos. This finding, along with an earlier one which showed that those who had been uprooted in the 1967 war were more likely to join commando groups, suggests that the punishment techniques employed by Israeli forces to retaliate for commando activities, if their primary goal is to reduce commando activity, are not working. These actions simply induce more youngsters to take on active militant roles. If Harry N. Howard's estimate is correct, approximately two-thirds of the Palestinians are twenty-five years old or younger.[16] There will be no shortage of young men and women volunteers to join the Palestinian Resistance Movement. Increased activity against the Israelis may, in turn, help the Israelis receive increased aid from abroad. It appears that the war of nerves that is going on between Israelis and Palestinians represents a vicious circle of violence which most people would like to see broken. This situation represents our inability to solve problems through politics—a war fought without blood, as Chairman Mao put it.

Concluding Remarks

We have shown who teaches young Palestinians to be good Palestinians and commandos. What are some of the implications of what we have found? What are the consequences of young Palestinians' learning these values and behavioral patterns?

It may be helpful to look at the leaders of today's Palestinian freedom fighters and to note how they were socialized. They are yesterday's student activists; in the process of their socialization they learned to participate in politics by getting involved at the college level—in Cairo for Arafat and in Beirut for Habash and Hawatmeh. The role that the General Union of Palestinian Students (GUPS) has played in fostering political awareness among its members should not be underestimated.[17] The GUPS chapters extend beyond the Middle East to universities in the West; over twenty chapters exist in Germany, for example. It is this student activism that trained the leaders who emerged after the 1967 war.

For some reason, the top leaders among the commando groups are, for the most part, Palestinians who were educated in the Middle East or in Europe, not in the United States or the Soviet Union. Michael W. Suleiman reports that the longer Arab students stay in the United States, the more compromising their attitude toward the Middle East conflict becomes—which is not at all surprising, given the kind of political

---

16. Howard, "The Middle East Refugee Problem," in *Refugees: Background Papers*, The National Conference on World Refugee Problems, November 18–19, 1969, Washington, D.C., p. 33.

17. We wish to thank Mohamad Dajani, president of the Student Council at the American University of Beirut, and others with whom we talked in Beirut in September, 1972, for pointing this out and for offering other insights into the life of Palestinian student activists.

culture in which they are spending their college years.[18]

Organizations such as GUPS provide an opportunity for Palestinian college students to establish closer relationships with other Palestinians who are scattered all over the world. These contacts among young Palestinian intellectuals will provide important links for the political leadership of Palestine in years to come. Consequently, GUPS and other student organizations should also be considered as key agents of political socialization for these stateless Palestinians. Other Arab organizations composed of adult members of Arab communities also act as important agents of socialization affecting the future of Palestinians through such activities as scholarship programs.

The advent of *fedayeen* groups provided an opportunity for young Palestinians to learn skills necessary for combat. Freedom fighters learn not only to be politically aware but also to use guns and other weapons that were forbidden by King Hussein, for example, prior to the 1967 war. If a large number of young children learn these skills, they may be ready to take up arms if they are given an opportunity to fight in future years. (In Jordan, much of this activity has been halted.)

One probable consequence of Palestinians' learning to admire *fedayeen* and becoming *fedayeen* while still young is that the Palestinian-Israeli conflict will continue until the day of national liberation. Eventually the Israelis will find it necessary to recognize the existence of Palestinian commandos and will be forced to negotiate with them, as well as with other Arab countries, in solving the Middle East conflict. In the long run nothing can prevent the commandos' pursuit of national liberation.[19] As our survey results show, these young Palestinians are obsessed with the liberation of their country, and they place national liberation above personal desire.

A question that comes to those of us who would like to see tensions in the area eased is, What can be done to reduce the hatred among young Palestinian students? There are so many things young Palestinians find in their environment to remind them of their life in exile that unless they are given their own country, in which they can live in peace with their neighbors, they will find it impossible to start loving the other Semitic peoples. Gen. Moshe Dayan admitted the justifiable existence of Palestinian views when he said:

---

18. Suleiman, "Attitudes of the Arab Elite."

19. Who could have predicted the establishment of Israel when Zionists began their movement in Europe toward the end of the last century? Those who predicted it were probably labeled pro-Zionists or Zionists, even though their predictions may have been based upon objective criteria.

> It is not true that the Arabs hate the Jews for personal, religious or racial reasons. They consider us—and justly, from their point of view—as Westerners, foreigners, invaders who have seized an Arab country to turn it into a Jewish state.[20]

Unless these conditions which surround the Palestinians are remedied, no one can force them to be peaceful. In the words of a Palestinian in Bethlehem, as reported by Juan de Onis in the *New York Times* on May 18, 1973, the Palestinians will be peaceful after justice is restored:

> "They say shalom means peace," asserted a man in Bethlehem who works in a Palestinian textile factory, and who maintains that his land was taken without compensation. "They kick you out and take what you have and say 'shalom.' Let them give me back my house and land; then I will say 'shalom.'"

Israelis accuse Palestinians of teaching their children to hate them. But Palestinian children do not have to be encouraged by their parents and schoolteachers to hate Israelis; Israelis provide events and policies that make young Palestinians want to take up arms against Israel.

As for Americans, an approach suggested by I. F. Stone would help us to better understand the nature of the Palestinian-Israeli conflict. He suggests that we develop double vision in looking at the Middle East conflict. He urges us to equate Irgun, Hagana, and other Zionist extremist groups with Fatah and other Palestinian commando groups, for their purposes and tactics are similar.[21] This is definitely a step in the right direction in our view; and similar views have been expressed by Amos Kenan of *Yediot A'Haronoth* and Robert Pierpoint of CBS.[22]

Since it is difficult to apply pure logic and reasoning in order to reduce the aggressive behavior of individuals as well as nations, particu-

---

20. Quoted in *Le Monde*, July 9, 1969.

21. I. F. Stone, *I. F. Stone's Weekly*, XVII, no. 1 (January 13, 1969, 1–3. Naturally there are those who would disagree. Fatah and other Palestinian commando groups are different from Zionist extremist groups in a few important ways. First, the Palestinians have done no wrong to European Jews, who were the target of anti-Semitism in the West. Palestinians simply desire to return to the land they lost only a few years ago. Second, none of the commando groups demands the establishment of a racially exclusive state; they wish to establish a democratic state in which every religious group, including Jews, will be equally treated.

22. See Kenan, "Israel Today—A Colonial State?" *Los Angeles Times*, May 6, 1973, p. IX 4; Pierpoint, "CBS News Commentary," March 7, 1973, reported in *AAUG Newsletter*, VI, no. 2 (June, 1973), 2.

larly when there is perceived self-interest involved, we must seek other means to reduce the violence in the Middle East. The United Nations had its chance but failed. The technique of hoping that Palestinians would forget about their homes and country seemed to work for a while, but certainly not after the 1967 war and the subsequent rise of the Palestinian commandos. Unless the world can come up with an alternative to the Black September movement, we fear that the only hope for restoring peace with justice as far as Palestinians are concerned will be in the hands of the Palestinian commandos.

One of the ways that social psychologists suggest to reduce tension between individuals or groups is to create a situation in which the two parties involved become mutually interdependent for the purpose of achieving shared goals. There is, without a doubt, a need for economic and social development in Israel-Palestine. But how can these two Semitic peoples be made to work together?

Here we are reminded of one of the findings of our survey, which indicates that the overriding concern of these young Palestinians is not their own material well-being but rather the liberation of Palestine. No material comfort can satisfy the needs of young Palestinians aspiring to regain their homeland. This is more remarkable in view of the fact that these refugee children live under miserable conditions in Jordan. If we are to reduce tensions in the area, we must turn our attention toward these psychological needs, and not toward matters of material well-being.

PART IV: INTERNATIONAL IMPACT

Neville Rubin

THE IMPACT OF ZIONISM AND ISRAEL ON THE POLITICAL ORIENTATION AND BEHAVIOR OF SOUTH AFRICAN JEWS

There has been no comprehensive study of the political attitudes and behavior of South African Jews in recent years, though few commentators on contemporary South Africa have omitted mention of the subject. This paper does not purport to fill the gap by providing a systematic analysis of South African Jews and their political role. Its aim is more modest than that. It will merely point to some features of the political conduct of Jewish South Africans and will indicate the possible interconnections between their outlook in the era of apartheid, the existence of a powerful Zionist movement, and the existence of Israel.

Characteristics of the Jewish Population

There are some 130,000 Jews in South Africa. They make up somewhat less than 0.3 per cent of the total population of the country, and less than 4 per cent of the white population (of which they are regarded as a part). There have been Jews in South Africa since the earliest days of colonial settlement, in the seventeenth century, and several of them figured prominently in public life during the periods of Dutch and British rule. It was only during the period of industrial expansion, though, that they began to arrive in significant numbers. Persecution in imperial Russia and its satellites, coinciding with economic development of the mining industry and its offshoots, produced the first major wave of immigration.[1] Another group sought refuge approximately one generation later as a result of Nazi persecution in the 1930s. Despite considerable opposition to their arrival from pro-Nazi elements in South Africa (including leading members of the present South African government and its adherents),[2] members of this group added to the population at a time of further industrial expansion into secondary industry, during the Second World War and afterward. There has been little immigration of Jews in more recent times.

Several characteristics of the South African Jewish population are worth noting at this point because they may have a bearing on subjects to be considered later. First, a large portion of South African Jews were born in South Africa. The ratio of those born outside the country to those who have lived there all their lives has been, and is, declining steadily. This means that South African Jews have come to be a part of the settled white South African community.

Second, there has been no major move to emigrate on the part of South African Jews. A feeling of insecurity during periods of political uncertainty has caused some Jews to leave, and others have done so as a result of their distaste for apartheid or because there have been occasional demonstrations of open hostility to them as Jews. But this has not significantly reduced the size of the Jewish population or diminished its rate of growth.

Nor has emigration to Israel noticeably affected the numbers of South African Jews. Despite frequent appeals to move, first to Palestine and then to Israel, there has been no major efflux of Jews in this direction over the years. South African Jews have displayed a strong allegiance to Zionism, however, and many participate actively in Zionist activities, which have not decreased as a result of the disappearance from the scene of those Jews inspired by the early Zionist movements of Eastern Europe. Youth movements, newspapers, and frequent visits from Israeli political leaders and officials of the World Jewish Congress and its affiliates have kept alive a commitment to the movement. Constant appeals for greater participation in the economic expansion or military activities of Israel have produced a continuous, but not dramatic, response in terms of numbers of Jews leaving South Africa. There is a small but influential contingent of South African Jews in Israel,

---

1. On the origins of South African Jews and their early participation in South African life, see Louis Herrman, *The History of the Jews in South Africa* (Cape Town, 1930).

2. See Leo Marquard, *The Peoples and Policies of South Africa*, 3d ed. (Cape Town, 1966), pp. 250–51; Leslie Rubin, "Afrikaner Nationalism and the Jews," *Africa South*, I, no. 3 (April–June, 1957), pp. 28–34.

some of whom have held important positions in government, in the trade-union movement, as ambassadors abroad, and as functionaries of the Zionist movement itself.

On the whole, though, South African Jews have preferred to remain in South Africa, in comparative comfort, and have opted for monetary rather than human contributions to the growth of Israel. This is, in part, a function of the third feature of South African Jewry that is worth recording: its economic prosperity. Jews, like most South African whites, enjoy a high standard of living—absolutely and in relation to the black population. Only a small number of Jews have ever been among the poorest members of the privileged white sector of South African society. Far more have played prominent roles in the expansion of trade, commerce, industry, and finance, as well as in the professions. While it would be inaccurate to suggest that Jews dominate any facet of the South African economy, there are few economic activities in which they have not played a major part. They have, on the whole, been distinctly less involved in farming than in other branches of the economy; and their participation in the civil service has been confined to the more senior levels of professional and technical grades. In general, it would be true to say that most Jews are to be found in the middle, upper-middle, and upper income groups of white South Africans. In none of these strata do they predominate over, or are they more numerous than, other white South Africans. But they have a sizable stake in the South African economy, and a substantial interest in the prevailing economic structure of South African society. It is from this base that they have been able to make regular and increasing financial contributions to Israel. It is probably of more than passing political importance that their wish to preserve the opportunities to contribute to both the manpower and the material resources of Israel has been well understood; and this has, without a doubt, influenced relations between the Jewish community and the South African government.

Political Behavior of the Jewish Population

Individual Jews have participated actively in the political life of South Africa, though their position as a group has been deliberately ambiguous and difficult to define. There has been no period in South African history during the twentieth century in which Jews have not held elective office at national, provincial, or local levels. Despite their relatively small over-all numbers and their heavy concentration in urban areas, there is no identifiable "Jewish vote" in the country as a whole. Those

Jews who have been elected to office have depended on the support of non-Jews to an overwhelming degree. Most have represented white, urban constituencies at the national level. Where Jews have played a major part in securing the election of one of their own number to provincial or city councils—in the rare instances in which there have been sufficient Jewish voters, because of the smaller constituencies, to influence the result—they have invariably done so within the context of white politics, and as members of all-white political parties. There have been Jewish members of Parliament and senators, provincial and city councilors; but the overwhelming majority of them have been elected by white constituents as representatives of the United, Labour, and Progressive parties. During the period when blacks were allowed to be represented by whites in the country's national and provincial legislative organs, a number of Jewish members of the United, Communist, and Liberal parties were elected to represent them.

Jews, therefore, have been elected outside the ranks of the National party, though the overwhelming majority of those elected have stood for policies involving the continuation of white control over the affairs of the country. In this they have faithfully reflected the views of their white constituents and have also given voice to the attitudes of by far the greater portion of their Jewish compatriots.[3]

It is true that the tiny minority of whites who have been prepared to declare their total opposition to any form of white supremacy, and who have worked for its overthrow, has included Jews among its members. But their views are as peripheral to the main body of Jewish opinion as they are to that of the remainder of white society. They have certainly never received any significant support from Jews as a group; and participation has been confined to a few committed individuals who have never been identified with the principal organs of collective Jewish opinion. Just as there have been Jews who have been rendered silent or inactive by the government's security apparatus because they held minority views challenging the structure of South African society, so also have there been Jews who, as senior police officers, prosecutors, and judges, have been active in bringing about the enforcement of laws which have led to the disappearance of the first group from the political scene.

These exceptions should not be overemphasized. It would not be unfair to say that both categories are regarded with disapproval by

---

3. On the relative attitudes of Jews and other white South Africans to race, see I. D. Mac Crone, *Race Attitudes in South Africa* (London and Cape Town, 1937), chap. 11, esp. fig. 9 and p. 206.

most South African Jews, who prefer to remain in the safe center of white South African political opinion. The fact that their political activity involves support for, and leadership of, parties that vie with the National party for determining the manner in which white power can be maintained should also be seen in its proper perspective.

Jewish political behavior is, first of all, a reflection of the socioeconomic conditions of the Jewish population of South Africa. Jewish support for the parliamentary opposition is principally a function of the fact that the Jewish population is almost wholly (1) English-speaking, (2) concentrated in urban areas, and (3) concentrated in the upper income groups. It is from these groupings that the present opposition parties have traditionally drawn their support.

A second factor which undoubtedly has played a part is the explicit identification of the National party and its allies of the 1930s with anti-Semitism and Jew-baiting. It was this which galvanized the official organs of the Jewish community into political action, leading to open criticism of the National party and rather more covert support for its opponents. This was the only period during which organized Jewish political activity occurred. And it is worth noting that this activity was mainly related to protecting Jews from a perceptible threat—rather more forbidding than the social discrimination of a more amorphous variety which they had felt until then.[4] There was some questioning of race as a criterion for political discrimination, but this was largely confined to within the white community, although such debate occasionally did include more general considerations of the ethics of racial politics. The principal effect of this political activity was to bind the Jewish population more closely to the United party, led by General Smuts, and to create an abiding suspicion of an Afrikaner nationalism which had so easily espoused the ideology and the cause of Nazi Germany.[5]

During the period under consideration, Jews were not merely subjected to verbal abuse by the National party and its newspapers; they were barred from membership in the National party in the Transvaal (the province in which most South African Jews have always lived); and anti-Semitism was used as a means of winning votes among disgruntled members of the less-privileged urban white electorate. By contrast, an increased number of Jews were elected on the platform of the United party, which was swept into power during the Second

---

4. On social discrimination, see Marquard, *Peoples and Policies of South Africa*, p. 250.

5. See the examples quoted by Rubin in "Afrikaner Nationalism and the Jews" and in "South African Jewry and Apartheid," *Africa Report*, February, 1970, pp. 22–24.

World War; and the only Jewish cabinet minister in recent South African history held office during the Smuts administration, which was elected in 1943 and remained in power until the National party won the election of 1948.

Thus the basic allegiance of Jewish voters within the context of white politics was firmly established some three decades ago. It has changed little since then. The factors already mentioned have sustained the loyalty of most voters to the United party, with occasional minor deviations either toward the more liberal (but altogether powerless) Progressive party or, infrequently, but in equally insignificant numbers, toward the National party.

The National Party and the Jewish Population

Those who included anti-Semitism among their virulent racist views have held high offices within the National party, as well as lesser positions, as members of Parliament and senators, ever since the party came to power. None of them has ever disavowed his opinions. The leaders of the Jewish community have never called on them to do so. The National party has removed its ban on Jewish membership, but it has not gone out of its way to seek Jewish support. It has proved to its own satisfaction that it does not require this support, and, electorally, the stress on apartheid has paid far higher dividends than anti-Semitism. There have been gestures by individuals which have given some semblance of an atmosphere of détente: formerly anti-Semitic cabinet ministers have appeared at Jewish functions; and leaders within the Jewish community, including the chief rabbis, have been prepared to praise successive prime ministers and accord them other honors. The South African Jewish Board of Deputies has concentrated its attention on matters of exclusive concern to the Jewish community and has explicitly abjured any desire to influence the electorate or comment on the "pros and cons of the country's racial policies."[6]

The existence of Israel has proved useful—as a carrot and a stick—to the National party government in its relations with the Jewish community. It was able to acquire an early measure of kudos for its rapid recognition of the state shortly after the election of 1948; and it is thought to have turned a blind eye to the recruitment of Jewish reserve officers

---

6. G. Saron to Rubin, in *Africa Report*, February, 1970, p. 24.

who wished to join the Israeli forces at that time.[7] Since then, similar attitudes have been adopted toward those who wished to assist Israel by joining its army (in the 1956 Suez campaign) or by donating funds, even in times when strict exchange control measures have curtailed the expatriation of money. It could be argued that Israel has repaid the compliment by refraining from anything but muted criticism of South African policies; and South African prosperity, as well as the strategic value of the country to the West, has increased considerably since the Suez Canal was closed, in 1967.

But when Israel has been more outspoken in criticizing apartheid, the government has reminded Jews that they can enjoy a precarious tolerance only if they are prepared to demonstrate their primary loyalty to white South Africa and its policies. Even the Board of Deputies has been prepared to come off its carefully constructed fence in situations of this type, the most notable of which occurred in 1961. Israel had joined sixty-five other countries in censuring South Africa's foreign minister at the United Nations. Dr. Verwoerd, then the prime minister, successfully revived the old anti-Semitic flavor in his party's approach by linking the Israeli vote to alleged Jewish support for the Progressive party and to the fact that few Jews favored the National party. The Board of Deputies, which had remained faithful to its policy of "no comment" on the Sharpeville massacre, which the foreign minister had been seeking to defend, found it possible to issue a public rebuke to Israel for its vote.

This incident, and similar ones that followed, may have helped to bring home to South African Jews one of the major realities of their role in South Africa: they are dependent on the South African government, but it can do without them (except occasionally to use them as scapegoat when the old rallying cry of anti-Semitism proves useful in distracting attention from other issues or simply in putting a stop to any tendency that might fracture white solidarity).

There is indeed evidence to suggest that this reality is recognized by South African Jewry. In 1967, one commentator was able to report that

> South African Jews realise that their destiny is increasingly bound up with the rest of the White community, and are leaning as heavily as the rest on the Government which can and is providing order and security.[8]

---

7. Edward Feit, "Community in a Quandary: The South African Jewish Community and Apartheid," in *Race*, VIII, no. 4 (1967), 406.
8. *Ibid.*, p. 400.

Lest the last phrase be misunderstood, it must be recalled that this statement was made the same year in which the government passed the Terrorism Act, the most far-reaching measure to eliminate any form of protection for those expressing, or engaging in activities to further, views which the government regarded as threatening the prevailing order of South African society. This act elicited no official Jewish reaction. Instead, that year the Board of Deputies, in its annual report, was content to reveal its own priorities in the following description of the situation of South African Jews: "The Jewish community is well integrated and the Jewish citizen enjoys full opportunities in all spheres."

This remark was quoted with approval by a senior officer of the board three years later,[9] and there is no reason to believe that the position has changed in any material way since then. In the context of present-day South Africa, the statement may be taken to reflect an element of self-congratulation and to indicate a simple truth. On the one hand, the words testify to evident contentment with the absence of any suggestion of overt discrimination against Jews in South Africa. On the other hand, they illustrate cryptically—and with perhaps unintended irony in the curious choice of the words *well integrated*—the fact that South Africa is one of the few countries in the world in which Jews, by virtue of race, are legally placed in a position of privilege. The "full opportunities" are, of course, the preserve of the dominant one-fifth of South African society, of which the Jews are part. And the integration referred to relates only to the place of Jews in the white community and directs attention to the fact that they have become a complacent, if nervous and insecure, constituent of a white oligarchy.

South African Jews have no special claim to be considered differently from the remainder of the white community; and, what is more, they do not officially wish to be regarded in any other way. If Zionism has provided an alternative focus for their intellectual and political energy, it has not notably detracted from their ability to assimilate the attitudes of their fellow whites. If Israel provides a possible escape from persecution, South African Jews have chosen to play down their need to make use of it rather than play up their own faithful observance of the requirements of apartheid society. If Israel is still useful as an insurance policy to South African Jews, it is one for which most have been prepared to pay the premium in cash; but the price may also have to be calculated in terms of their easy accommodation to racial repression.

---

9. Letter from G. Saron, *Africa Report,* May, 1970, p. 42.

Richard P. Stevens

SMUTS AND WEIZMANN: A STUDY IN SOUTH AFRICAN-ZIONIST COOPERATION

Perhaps few personal friendships have so influenced the course of political events during the twentieth century as the remarkable relationship between Gen. Jan Christian Smuts, South Africa's celebrated prime minister, and Chaim Weizmann, the charismatic Zionist leader and Israel's first president. But the significance of this little-publicized relationship far transcends its personal elements as well as its contribution to Zionist success. A study of this friendship helps to place into perspective both the contradictions of Western liberalism and the psychological climate in which the dominant position of a white minority in South Africa and that of a new European settlement in Palestine were rationalized. It also underscores the crucial relationship between Zionism and South Africa, a relationship drawing its strength, first, from the Zionist character of the South African Jewish community, with its privileged economic position; second, from the very nature of the South African economic-political system; and, third, from the imperial factor as it affected South Africa's domestic and international situation. In short, the personal interaction between Smuts and Weizmann was but a microcosm of all the cultural, economic, political, and imperial factors converging in the triangular relationship of Zionism, Britain, and South Africa.[1]

---

1. The Smuts-Weizmann correspondence, consisting of approximately one hundred and forty items, is located in the South African government archives and the Weizmann

The importance of the Smuts-Weizmann friendship can be fully appreciated only if it is remembered that without Weizmann there would have been no Balfour Declaration, and without Smuts the Union brought forth in 1909 might well have foundered. Both men held much the same position in their respective "constituencies," and both represented in their "constituencies" the imperial factor in its economic, political, and strategic dimensions. On the personal level it must be noted that during the entire thirty-three years of this relationship, extending from 1917 to Smuts's death, in 1950, both men took for granted the moral legitimacy of the other's position. Thus, not a word is to be found in Weizmann's correspondence or writings questioning the racial basis of the South African state, on which Zionism was so dependent, or questioning Smuts's own role in upholding its racist system. In short, the subordinate position of the African majority in South Africa posed no difficulty for Weizmann, nor did it detract from the respect felt by the "New Moses," as Smuts called Weizmann, for the South African leader. Similarly, Smuts assumed without question "the right" of Jewish settlers to occupy Palestine without regard to the rights of the indigenous Palestinian Arabs. In both cases, Smuts and Weizmann projected at the highest level the capacity of Western civilization to rationalize domination and exploitation, conquest and control, as Christian civilizing mission or as ethnocentric Judeo-Christian fulfillment.

Scarely noticed by the Western press was a different image of General Smuts, an image that challenged his reputation as founding father of a new international moral order and as champion of civilized values. This image, evoked by Dr. W. E. B. DuBois, the father of the Pan-African movement, was conveyed in the Manifesto of the Fourth Pan-African Congress, which asked:

> What more paradoxical figure today confronts the world than the official head of a great South African State striving blindly to build peace and goodwill in Europe by standing on the necks and hearts of millions of Black Africans?[2]

Library in Rehovot, Israel. No attempt will be made in this paper to show Weizmann's reliance on Smuts or the role of Zionism in South African politics. I intend to demonstrate this in an article I am preparing for the *Journal of Palestine Studies* and, in much greater detail, in a book. At this time I will endeavor to do little more than set forth the background of the Smuts-Weizmann relationship.

2. Quoted in Colin Legum, *Pan-Africanism: A Short Political Guide* (New York, 1963), p. 30.

And just as this appeal on the part of a new generation of Africans, West Indians, and black Americans went unanswered, so would the objections of those Jews and Gentiles who, like Judge Mayer Sulzberger, would contend that

> democracy means that those who live in a country shall select their rulers and shall preserve their powers. Given these principles, a Convention of Zionists looking to the government of people who are in Palestine would be in contravention of the plainest principle of democracy. It can have no practical meaning unless its intent is to overslaugh the people who are in Palestine and to deprive them of the right of self-government by substituting the will of persons outside, who may or may not ever see Palestine.[3]

In a remarkable convergence of imperialistic design and liberal philosophy, the perpetuation of white domination over South Africa and the sanctioning of eventual Jewish control over Palestine would be effected in large part by the same handful of politicians—indeed, by some of the outstanding representatives of the British ruling class. Thus the South Africa Act of Union (1909) and the Balfour Declaration (1917) each owed their birth in large part to Lord Milner, Lord Selbourne, Lord Balfour, Joseph Chamberlain, and General Smuts. As for South Africa, the important thing for both Liberals and Conservatives was to hold the empire together, and this could be done only by placating the Boers and entrusting power to those who, in the words of Balfour, "think like us." Consequently, knowing full well that by passing the South Africa Act the British Parliament would be relinquishing its right to intervene on behalf of South Africa's nonwhite population, both parties proceeded to ratify the act and left the African majority to the mercy of the white rulers. In the final analysis it was the argument advanced by Balfour which carried the day: "You cannot," he declared, "give the natives in South Africa equal rights with the whites without threatening the whole fabric of white civilisation."[4]

With Palestine, also, imperial necessity and professed liberal philosophy would prevail. For "the Zionist movement was the favoured candidate in governing circles in Whitehall," said the British historian

---

3. Quoted in George Lenczowski, *The Middle East in World Affairs* (Ithaca, New York, 1956), p. 315.

4. Quoted in A. P. Thornton, *The Imperial Idea and Its Enemies* (New York, 1968), p. 159.

A. P. Thornton. "It was supposed," he said, as Theodor Herzl had proclaimed,

> that Jews when inserted into Palestine would perform the same function that was expected of those Greeks who it was also intended [would be] inserted into Asia Minor. They would act as injections of European culture and technology into a decaying Asiatic trunk.[5]

It was in June, 1917, in London, that Weizmann and Smuts were first introduced to each other. Weizmann contrasted the friendliness of this meeting with the coldness he had encountered from Lord Reading, an anti-Zionist Jew.[6] According to Weizmann, he was received by Smuts

> in the friendliest fashion, and given a most sympathetic hearing. A sort of warmth of understanding radiated from him, and he assured me heartily that something would be done in connection with Palestine and the Jewish people. He put many searching questions to me, and tried to find out how sincerely I believed in the actual possibilities. He treated the problem with eager interest, one might say with affection.[7]

Henceforth, as Weizmann testified, General Smuts would lend his unfailing assistance to Zionism, and at every crucial juncture his valuable advice and intercession would be available.

GENERAL SMUTS: BACKGROUND TO ZIONIST COOPERATION

Smuts's long championship of the Zionist cause grew naturally from his background, experience, and conception of Western civilization. On another level, it was related to the exigencies of political survival in South Africa. Born in 1870 at Malmesburg, in the Cape Colony, of Dutch (Boer) stock, Smuts was immersed at an early age in the classics and excelled academically. Having won a scholarship in 1891 to read law at Cambridge, he subsequently completed his studies with distinction. Returning to South Africa in 1895, he settled in Cape Town, where he became a supporter of Cecil Rhodes, the premier of the Cape Colony, founder of Southern Rhodesia, head of the De Beers and Chartered Company, and managing director of the Gold Fields

---

5. *Ibid.*, p. 175.
6. Leonard Stein, *The Balfour Declaration* (London, 1961), p. 480. This dating contradicts that assigned by Chaim Weizmann in *Trial and Error* (New York, 1966), p. 159.
7. Weizmann, *Trial and Error*, p. 159.

Company. But the Jameson Raid of 1895 into the Transvaal, an operation originally sanctioned by Rhodes to extend his own economic and political power under the British flag, caused Smuts to break with him and to move on to Johannesburg, where he was appointed state's attorney. With the outbreak of the Boer War, in October, 1899, Smuts joined Kruger's forces and was appointed a commandant general. Following the Boer defeat, in the spring of 1902, Smuts was named to the peace negotiating team. Thereafter he traveled on to England. Owing much to his persuasive power, the Transvaal and the Orange Free State, both of which had been defeated in the Boer War, were granted responsible self-government in 1907. In the first elections under self-government, the Het Volk party of General Botha and General Smuts took over the reins of government in the Transvaal, and Smuts himself became responsible for three ministries. As colonial secretary, Smuts set out to enforce rigidly the pass laws imposed upon Indians. Smuts convinced their leader, Mohandas Gandhi, that they should register voluntarily, promising that he would subsequently repeal the act. Gandhi registered only to discover that Smuts would not fulfill his promise.[8]

Although Smuts won considerable popularity at home for his handling of the Indian situation, it was his close identification with Rhodes's vision of an Anglo-Boer union within the British Empire that was to propel him into the inner circles of the imperial system. As one of the architects of the South Africa Act, ratified by the British Parliament in August, 1909, Smuts took his place alongside Prime Minister Botha, as minister of interior, mines, and defense, in the first Union cabinet.[9] In a cabinet reshuffle in February, 1912, he became minister of finance, but some months later he resumed responsibility for defense and held that position until 1919.

As minister of defense, Smuts acted vigorously to crush incipient rebellion in early 1914. Pledging continued loyalty to the empire after the outbreak of war in Europe, Botha and Smuts led South African forces into South-West Africa, where they routed the German army in July, 1915. Responding to a British appeal for assistance in German East Africa, Union forces landed there in February, 1916, under the leadership of General Smuts as British commander in chief. Toward the end of 1916, before this campaign could be completed, Smuts was delegated to represent Prime Minister Botha at the special war cabinet summoned by Prime Minister David Lloyd George. Thus it

8. Edward Roux, *Time Longer than Rope* (Madison, Wisconsin, 1964), pp. 105–6.
9. See Eric A. Walker, *A History of South Africa* (London, 1965), p. 532.

was in 1917 that Smuts found himself in London representing the Union at the war conference (March 21–April 27) and at the imperial war cabinet (March 20–May 2). Although he declined the command of British forces in Palestine, Smuts remained in London as "special delegate from South Africa" at the service of the British government and war cabinet. His position as a member of the British war cabinet was "something quite without precedent, for Smuts was not a British Minister, not even a British Member of Parliament." But in the words of Winston Churchill, if England did not use Smuts as he should be used, "she deserved to go under";[10] and apparently Lloyd George agreed. As Dorothy F. Wilson observed,

> Smuts was invaluable in the Cabinet. . . . Smuts was called "The Orator for the Empire." He also became "The Handyman of the Empire." Because of his detachment, because he was not tied to any department and had no personal axe to grind, Lloyd George used him for one important mission after another. He sent him on European diplomatic missions, sent him to settle strikes and labour disputes, he asked him for reports on the Army, Navy and Air, sent him hither and thither. . . . At his first War Cabinet meeting, Smuts found himself sitting next to Milner. The two men began this association with mutual respect and ended with fast friendship.[11]

The close identification of General Smuts with imperial decision-making not only was dramatic testimony to the importance Britain attached to South Africa but also indicated that the British factor continued to play a vital role in Union politics. "The special relationship . . . formed during the Botha-Smuts period," was then a two-sided arrangement involving gold and diamonds, trade and defense, emigration and investment; in short, it spoke to the very special way in which both parties interpreted dominion status and imperial security.[12] Together with Balfour, Churchill, and Milner, General Smuts would contribute to the development of a new imperial approach to the Middle East question. As the bearer of Rhodes's vision of the future of Africa, Smuts would throw himself wholeheartedly into those questions affecting the continent's security; and for Smuts, as for Rhodes, the continent clearly began at Suez.

Although there is no evidence that Smuts concerned himself with

---

10. Dorothy F. Wilson, *Smuts of South Africa* (London, 1946), p. 80.
11. *Ibid.*, p. 78.
12. Dennis Austin, *Britain and South Africa* (London, 1966), p. 120.

Zionism before 1916, it is important to understand his attitude toward Jews in general and South African Jewry in particular; at the same time, the special characteristics of South African Jewry must be taken into consideration. On one level Smuts's attitude toward Jewry was a necessary corollary to his belief in the dominant historical role of Western civilization and the role of Jewry in that context, all of which was underpinned by his Boer religion. On another level were the facts of South African political life and his association with a political party which essentially represented the interests of mining, banking, and industry. Smuts touched on some of these factors when he spoke on the future of southern and central Africa at the South African dinner held in his honor in London in May, 1917. In this speech, remarkable for its candor, Smuts confessed that there were many intelligent South Africans who doubted that they could ever succeed in making a white man's land of southern Africa. "Nevertheless," said Smuts, "we have started by creating a new white base in South Africa, and today we are in a position to move forward towards the North and the civilization of the African continent."[13] But this venture can succeed, he said, only by establishing "as an accepted axiom in our dealings with the natives that it is dishonourable to mix white and black blood." While strongly affirming the implementation of the Christian moral code as a condition for the salvation of Europe, he also called for a "Christian" approach "to the natives of Africa." In this "Christian" approach, Smuts said, it must be understood that "natives have the simplest minds, understand only the simplest ideas or ideals, and are almost animal-like in the simplicity of their minds and ways." Therefore, "political ideas which apply to our white civilization largely do not apply to the administration of native affairs,"[14]

In short, if the defense of civilization, which Smuts so insistently equated with "white civilization," required white unity, particularly in its South African base, it also meant the permanent subjection of the black race. As Smuts's admirer and biographer, Sarah Gertrude Millin, herself a South African Jew, observed, Smuts computed the worth of white civilization as sufficient reason to deny black liberty.[15] While it was true that Smuts occasionally spoke of "self-government for the native," this was to be in areas granted by whites and on white sufferance. Only in the context of racial separation could he speak of liberty—white man's liberty was distinct from black man's liberty. No sooner had

13. Jan C. Smuts, *War-Time Speeches* (London, 1917), p. 85.
14. *Ibid.*, pp. 86–87.
15. *Ibid.*, pp. 90–91.

Smuts and his colleague General Botha set about forming their Het Volk party after the Boer War than they declared that it was "open to all white men whether Boer, Jew or Briton."[16] Since it was only through white unity, according to Smuts, that white civilization could be preserved, anti-Semitism was rejected.

In a more personal vein, it has been suggested that Smuts's love of power and success was somehow related to his liking for Jews and to his own background. And according to his good friend Gertrude Millin, Smuts was convinced that the South African Jews, for the most part of Lithuanian extraction, "would be the Spinozas and Maimonideses of the future."[17] But Smuts's specific dedication to Zionism, according to a report in the *South African Zionist Record,* was effected during his recuperation at Irene in 1916, after his return from the East African campaign; Nathan Levi approached him and told him of a resolution unanimously adopted at the South African Jewish Congress held earlier in Johannesburg, in April, 1916. The resolution requested that the claim of the Jewish people to Palestine be recognized at the peace settlement following the war. Smuts related that when Dr. Weizmann approached him for support in 1917, he told Weizmann of the promise made at Irene and of his obligation to carry out that promise.

But to champion the Zionist cause—"to see the Jews great again"[18]—of necessity meant to oppose the Arab renaissance. "Justice apart, [Smuts] had natural sympathy with neither French nor Arabs."[19] In short, Smuts's attitude toward the Arabs was essentially racist. Whereas some Europeans might tolerate a romantic attitude toward the Arabs, Smuts, like most South Africans, could not be so inclined. As his biographer noted:

> As to Arabs, a Bedouin Arab quite naturally cannot seem so romantically strange to a South African as to a European, for the South African very well knows dark-skinned peoples; peoples resembling, indeed, the Arabs—and with reason, since Arab blood is in them. All his life the South African has been surrounded by millions of these dark peoples who, like the Bedouins, live in huts or wander over the land; are more courtly, courageous and poetic than he will admit; and (unless civilisation compels them), like the Bedouins again, do, make, grow, want and own nothing.

16. Sarah Gertrude Millin, *General Smuts* (London, 1936), II, 108.
17. *Ibid.*, p. 109.
18. *Ibid.*, p. 110.
19. *Ibid.*, p. 111.

Smuts thinks as a European rather than as a South African—yet dark-skinned people cannot seem exotic to him.[20]

Although Smuts's cultural and racial bias undoubtedly worked in favor of Jews, the fact remains that, from its inception, the party of Botha and Smuts—the South African party and its successor, the United party—was the party "that represented mine owners, industrialists and bankers,"[21] and in at least two of those categories Jews were well represented. While not the dominant economic force in South Africa, Jews clearly controlled certain industries such as the manufacture of clothing and, later, the cinema. Although few Jews were farmers, those who turned to agriculture were heavy investors in machinery, and both the "potato king" and the "maize king" were Jews.[22] The vast majority of the group, some 80 per cent, traced their origins to Lithuania, thus making for an unusual degree of homogeneity.[23] Despite their original poverty, Jewish immigrants, like all white immigrants to South Africa, quickly discovered that the racial inequalities of the country allowed for upward group mobility; the working-class element soon became a small minority. According to many observers, the South African Jewish community had become, by the end of the First World War, the wealthiest Jewish community in the world on a per capita basis.[24] The size of the Jewish community, as Rabbi Dr. Andre Ungar observed, was not a true reflection of its position in South African life:

> It would be a grievous mistake to underestimate the significance of the Jewish minority. Even purely numerically speaking, under the absurd rules of South African ethnic arithmetic, the size of the Jewish population constitutes a factor necessary to reckon with. . . . South Africa is the land *par excellence* where minorities can have a say—and a vast majority be deprived of it—quite without regard to what, in a democracy, their numbers would warrant. And in the two main cities, Johannesburg and

---

20. *Ibid.*, pp. 112–13.

21. J. H. Simons and R. E. Simons, *Class and Color in South Africa* (Baltimore, 1969), p. 288.

22. Bernard Sacks, "South Africa: Life on a Volcano, The Jewish Community in a Caste Society," *Commentary,* IX (June, 1950), 530.

23. Dan Jacobson, "The Jews of South Africa: Portrait of a Flourishing Community," *ibid.,* XXIII (January, 1957), 39.

24. *Ibid.*

Cape Town, the Jews constitute one-tenth of the citizens "that count": the Whites.[25]

Jewish institutions correspondingly reflected the Zionist priorities and interests of the community. The main organs of Jewish life were the South African Zionist Federation, founded in 1895, and the South African Jewish Board of Deputies, founded in 1912. These bodies were not mutually exclusive. Zionists not only "formed the majority of the Board of Deputies but also occupied the leading posts in the Jewish community."[26] Fully 99 per cent of South African Jews were Zionist-affiliated.[27] In short, Zionism was without question the primary cultural expression and group concern of South African Jewry.

With the small but influential South African Jewish community committed to Zionist philosophy, Smuts readily saw the political wisdom of embracing the Zionist vision. The fact that Zionism would fit in nicely with the imperial scheme of things was all the more reason to accept it wholeheartedly. And in what better way could Britain provide continental security, in the most economical manner, than to deliver Palestine, at the very crossroads of Africa and Asia, to the Jews. British politicians listened to the arguments advanced by Herzl and Weizmann linking the Zionist program to British imperial interests. In the thinking of such imperialists as Sir Mark Sykes, Balfour, and Lord Milner, Palestine would be an important strategic point in the British Empire, and it would be worthwhile to develop it after the war. But

> the only people with the money, energy, and the inclination to do that would be the Jews; both for the present crisis and for future needs, Zionism ought to be backed to the full. To Smuts also the idea appealed in every way. Rhodes had dreamed of an all-[British] Africa. Smuts dreamed the same dream. Palestine developed and made strong would be an auxiliary to that dream.[28]

Even Lloyd George's offer of the Palestine command, although declined, "brought home to me," said Smuts, "more than ever before, the

---

25. Ungar, "The Abdication of a Community," *Africa South*, III (January–March, 1959), 29–30.

26. Sacks, "South Africa," p. 533.

27. Sarah G. Millin, *The People of South Africa* (New York, 1954), p. 236.

28. H. C. Armstrong, *Grey Steel: J. C. Smuts, A Study in Arrogance* (London, 1937), pp. 300–301.

consideration of Palestine and of the Jewish question generally."[29] While declining to seek military glory in Palestine, Smuts recalled that he thought he "would probably be of more service and do more useful work at the center of things." So important was Zionism to the civilized world, Smuts would argue, that "one of the great objects for which we fight this war is to provide a national home for the Jewish people."[30] Smuts, like Lord Milner, was also much interested in Vladimir Jabotinsky's idea of a Jewish legion for service in Palestine. According to Leonard Stein, there was a fairly clear indication that "Smuts was thinking, as Milner was, of what the Zionists might be able to do to counter the pacifist propaganda which was driving Russia away from her allies."[31]

WEIZMANN: ZIONIST ADVOCATE AT THE IMPERIAL COURT

Weizmann first visited England in 1903, shortly after the Sixth Zionist Congress. The following year, as a refugee from tsarist oppression, he decided to settle in England. Although he accepted a lecturing position at the University of Manchester, Weizmann continued his Zionist activities and played an ever greater role in the Zionist leadership, which, since Herzl's death, in July, 1904, was centered in Berlin.

But Weizmann's relatively quiet academic years were suddenly changed by events precipitated by the outbreak of war in August, 1914. The entry of the Ottoman Empire into the conflict against Britain opened new possibilities for Zionist diplomacy. A British advance into the Middle East to safeguard oil supplies and communications, possibly paving the way for Jewish settlement in Palestine under British auspices, had long been expected. Now, with British forces in motion in the area, Weizmann saw the postwar possibilities. As he wrote to a friend in 1914:

> Don't you think that the chance for the Jewish people is now within the limits of discussion at last? I realize, of course, that we cannot "claim" anything, we are much too atomized for it; but we can reasonably say that should Palestine fall within the British sphere of influence, and should Britain encourage a Jewish settlement there, as a British dependency, we could have in twenty to thirty years a million Jews out there, perhaps

---

29. *South African Zionist Record*, September 22, 1950.
30. *Ibid.*
31. Stein, *Balfour Declaration*, p. 480.

more; they would develop the country, bring back civilization to it and form a very effective guard for the Suez Canal.[32]

But, as his biographer explained, Weizmann was made president of the English Zionist Federation in 1917 only for convenience' sake:

> He was not on the Zionist Executive, nor even an inner member of the Actions Committee. At what precise moment it was that Weizmann realized that Herzl's mantle of world Zionist leadership had descended on him is not easy to say. Perhaps one could say simply that through the sheer stature of his personality he took on this role and so moved Zionism from its Central European into its British phase.[33]

During the war, having already broken with the Berlin Zionist leadership, Weizmann was approached by a representative of the British branch of Nobel's, manufacturers of explosives, to assist in discovering a method of producing acetone.[34] Weizmann's outstanding success induced David Lloyd George, then the minister of munitions and later prime minister, to offer Weizmann some honor in recognition of his discoveries. While declining any personal recognition, Weizmann reportedly requested instead that Lloyd George do something for the Jewish people by assisting their repatriation to Palestine.[35] This explanation, while containing an element of truth, certainly does not sufficiently explain the British decision to endorse the Zionist program, nor does it convey anything of Weizmann's own extensive lobbying activity. As General Smuts said about the British war cabinet: "We were persuaded—but remember that it was Dr. Weizmann who persuaded us."[36]

Weizmann's efforts to convince British leaders of the soundness of the Zionist program were immensely facilitated by his accepting government employment in London. Here he was able to meet British statesmen and to pursue his diplomatic mission. Building upon the contacts that Herzl made in 1902 with Lord Rothschild, Joseph Chamberlain (colonial minister), and Lord Lansdowne (foreign secretary), Weizmann cultivated the friendship of Britain's highest political figures, including Lord Balfour, whom he had first met in 1906, Lord Selbourne, Lord Milner,

32. Weizmann, *Trial and Error*.
33. Meyer W. Weisgal and Joel Carmichael, *Chaim Weizmann* (New York, 1963), p. 147.
34. See Samuel Shikor, *Hollow Glory* (New York, 1960), p. 23.
35. *Ibid.*, p. 26.
36. Quoted in Weisgal and Carmichael, *Weizmann*, p. 143.

and General Smuts. At last, on November 2, 1917, Weizmann's efforts were rewarded with the famous Balfour Declaration.

Smuts and the Balfour Declaration

The background of the Balfour Declaration, destined to unleash one of the major conflicts of the century, has been the object of considerable discussion and research. While the names of Lloyd George, Lord Balfour, and Lord Milner have long been identified with it, the role of General Smuts has not received the same attention, despite the fact that by the general's own account he figured prominently in that decision.

Smuts's intriguing role in the Balfour Declaration has, however, occupied the historian of that document, Leonard Stein. Although Stein concluded that Weizmann must have met Smuts before September 21, 1917, the day recorded by Weizmann, he could not give the exact date of their first meeting. (There was probably at least one earlier meeting: on June 14, 1917, one of Weizmann's associates had advised that since Smuts was joining the war cabinet and not accepting command of the British forces in Palestine, "we must try to win him for our cause.")[37] While Weizmann, writing of their meeting in September, 1917, described the friendly reception accorded him by Smuts, he gave no details of their conversation. On September 25, Weizmann's correspondent, Sacher, expressed satisfaction that Weizmann had found Smuts so very understanding.[38] Concluding that "the part actually played by Smuts in helping to secure the approval of the Declaration is, however, difficult to assess," Stein nevertheless admitted that "he must rank among the architects of the Declaration," even though his contribution "was not of the same order as that of Balfour, Milner, or Lloyd George."[39]

Yet the whole story cannot be told. As Stein admits, Smuts, as was his custom, "exerted his influence in the background."[40] It is this "influence in the background," so amply demonstrated on Zionism's behalf over the next three decades, that concerns us. At the same time, it becomes quite evident that Smuts's involvement with Zionism was more than an emotional response stimulated by a Bible background or a visit to the Holy Land. Indeed, his visit to Palestine early in 1918 for consultations with Allenby, at the request of the war cabinet, "helped

---

37. Quoted in Stein, *Balfour Declaration*, p. 480.
38. *Ibid.*
39. *Ibid.*, p. 482.
40. *Ibid.*

to raise his interest in Zionism to a plane on which it reflected, not merely an intellectual conviction, but an emotional experience."[41] But the fact that he was a spokesman for imperial interests, for South African designs, and a skilled politician within an exploitive economic-political system, also accounted for Smuts's sustained support of the Zionist cause. It was precisely because of this multifaceted background that Smuts was able to use "influence" as few others could at the highest centers of power. And by Weizmann's own testimony in later years, Smuts's championship and support of the Zionist cause was one of the most vital factors in keeping the promise of the Balfour Declaration alive.

41. *Ibid.*, p. 483.

Peter Anyang'-Nyong'o

THE IMPACT OF THE MIDDLE EAST CONFLICT ON AFRICAN POLITICAL ORIENTATIONS AND BEHAVIOR

A COUNTRY USUALLY PARTICIPATES in international affairs and conflicts as a sovereign state or as a member of an alliance of such states. The extent to which a state can be effective in international politics is a function of its own power or the power that it derives from allying itself with other more powerful nations. Western nations—that is, Great Britain, France, the United States, West Germany, Portugal, etc.—belong to the North Atlantic Treaty Organization, which binds them to protect each other's interests in any international conflict. But this does not mean that the United States cannot enter an international conflict by itself, without the approval of other NATO members. Even within such alliances, countries that are more powerful can control the actions of those that are less powerful.[1] Thus Portugal cannot take part in any "international adventure"—for example, its colonial wars in Africa—without the blessings of the United States, West Germany, and Great Britain; but the United States can create havoc in Viet Nam no matter what Turkey may think.

1. In this paper we shall hold that power exists in any structural situation of asymmetrical relations, whether or not coercion is used. Thus, a system of international social and economic inequality, summarized as uneven development, implies a power structure in which the underdeveloped countries relate to the developed ones in an underdog-favorite syndrome, much to the disadvantage of the underdeveloped countries.

A nation's power—and therefore its position in international matters—is determined by its level of development and modernity. The United States, rich in resources and with a developed technology, has taken upon itself (with some consultation with the Soviet Union) the task of policing the world. The only thing that can counteract the actions of the United States is for other nations to modernize rapidly, to acquire a developed technology, and to convert the asymmetrical power relations to symmetrical ones. To some extent, the Soviet Union has done just this, and that is why certain analysts of international relations have advanced the theory that there is one "international system" characterized by the bipolarity of U.S.-U.S.S.R. relations. This bipolar system is the dominant one in the world today, and other systems—the *subsystems*—are subordinate to it in the sense that changes in the major system affect a minor system more than changes in the latter affect the former.[2] The Middle East and Africa, as subsystems in international politics, can remain where they are, subordinate to the dominant system; or they can change, and become autonomous actors themselves.

The Nature of the Conflict in the Middle East

At a very superficial level, the conflict in the Middle East is seen as one between the Arabs and the Israelis, each party having the backing of one of the two big powers: the United States and its allies supporting Israel, the Soviet Union and its allies supporting the Arab world. The Palestinians, although constituting a third group, are often thrown together with the Arabs.

Let us consider a basic question: Why should there be a conflict between the Arabs and the Israelis? From the point of view of the Arab states, it was the establishment of the state of Israel, with the military, economic, and political backing of the Western imperialist powers, that created the conflict. The Arab governments have refused to recognize the state of Israel, have sought from time to time to ostracize it from the international community, and have successfully isolated it in the Middle East. Israel, in turn, has armed itself to the teeth, has fought vicious wars against its Arab enemies, has mobilized world opinion to support the "ever persecuted Jews," and has continually sought to carry out acts of massive retaliation in response to the slightest

---

2. Leonard Binder, "The Middle East as a Subordinate International System," *World Politics*, X (April, 1958), 408–29.

provocation from the Arab nations. This passion for retaliation has even led Israeli Premier Golda Meir "to hold honorable" Israeli terrorists who forge passports and murder Palestinian civilians in cold blood. Comments Ali A. Mazrui:

> If British commandos were to enter the Irish Republic to try to root out and kill terrorists of the Irish Republican Army before any more sons of England were shot in the back in the streets of Belfast, both the Irish Republic and the world would be justifiably enraged. But the Israeli prime minister is capable of congratulating Israeli commandos who have moved into Beirut, carrying forged British passports, and who break into homes of Palestinians and kill them in their beds. The fact that the Palestinians carry out such terrorist activities is not an adequate reason for official brutality by a government.[3]

Caught in between this are the Palestinians. Neither the Arab governments nor the Israelis ever address themselves to the Palestinians' long-term interests: namely, getting back their land and re-establishing a Palestinian state. To the Zionist ruling class in Israel, the Palestinians are not a state to be negotiated with: they are, at worst, a bunch of "terrorists" to be annihilated for the good of both the Zionists and the Arab states, and, at best, an Arab people to be absorbed into the states where their "social types" are to be found. To the Arab bourgeois and feudal governments, the Palestinians are just one part of the Arab world. These governments have never made any commitment as to what will happen after they have "thrown the Israelis into the sea." Will there be a sovereign Palestinian state with Palestinians determining their own destiny, or will Palestine simply be part of an extended Arab state ruled by whatever ruling class happens to grab control?

The Nature of International Conflicts

We have to recognize that states and regions do not act. A "state" or a "region" is a concept, an analytical construct which we use in referring to a certain mode of political and social relations among people who are engaged in a process of production in a certain geopolitical environment and at a certain time in history, when their

---

3. Mazrui, "Nation-Building and Race-Building: Israel and Amin's Uganda as Racially Purist States" (Paper delivered at the Ninth World Congress of the International Political Science Association, Montreal, Canada; August, 1973).

productive forces are at a certain stage of development. The living and acting entities within a state, or among states as "international actors," are men and women, who, in the process of production, relate to each other as *classes*. As R. N. Berki has noted:

> Classes, and not nations or states, are the basic units in history, and the struggle between classes, instead of interstate conflict, occupies the center of attention. . . . The modern sovereign state, the supreme politico-legal authority over a certain part of the earth's territory and a certain number of the world's population, is itself the emanation of the class struggle in its capitalist phase. Internally, the state's function as the "managing committee of the ruling class" is to maintain the system of exploitation; externally, its main preoccupation is to facilitate the economic expansion of its own bourgeoisie.[4]

Before the era in which the capitalist mode of production became dominant in the world, feudal and semifeudal ruling classes engaged in conflicts as they sought to expand their empires and acquire more resources for themselves. But with the coming of capitalism, a dynamic and revolutionary ruling class called the bourgeoisie came into being in Western Europe. In their worldwide search for new resources and new markets, members of this class frequently found themselves in conflict with one another over who should control what resources and which markets in which parts of the world. They fought two imperial wars in the first half of the twentieth century, entered into an arms race that could lead to a third clash, and are still bickering among themselves and with the socialist countries, which now provide a formidable threat to their position of dominance.

In this era of capitalist domination, the nature of international conflicts can be understood by observing how such conflicts are perpetrated by bourgeois ruling classes that are out to control and exploit resources all over the world.[5] Sometimes they create conflicts merely to prevent other people from using their own resources fully and hence reaching the same level of development that they, the capitalists, have attained. In turn, those who are exploited as markets for capitalist production

---

4. Berki, "On Marxian Thought and the Problem of International Relations," *World Politics*, Vol. XXIV, no. 1 (October, 1971).

5. See "Battle over the Persian Gulf: Oil and Arms," *New Republic*, June 23, 1973; and "The U.S. Energy Crisis and the Middle East," *Military Review* (a professional journal of the U.S. Army), Vol. LIII, no. 3 (March, 1973). Both suggest that oil is the main interest of the Soviet Union and the United States in the Middle East.

begin, in the end, to fight back and seek national liberation. This merely escalates capitalist reaction and usually results in conflicts and wars such as those in Viet Nam, Mozambique, Guinea (Bissau), Angola, and the Middle East. The people who suffer most from this "dictatorship of capitalism" are those who have been directly subjugated, politically and economically, by the European imperialists, and those who were at such a low stage in the development of their productive forces when they entered into relations with the Europeans that they have rarely managed to bargain with them on equal terms in international conflicts. The ruling classes in these states become apologists for or acquiesce to Western imperialism. Some even agree to be middlemen for the West.

THE POSTCOLONIAL AFRICAN STATE IN INTERNATIONAL RELATIONS

The modern European state was created by an indigenous and innovative bourgeoisie, interested in consolidating its power by providing a legal framework and various institutions essential for the maintenance and development of capitalist relations of production. The colonial African state was essentially imposed by the metropolitan bourgeoisie on social forms which were at a stage of development very different from that in Europe. Thus the colonial state, a replica of the political superstructure which had autonomously developed in the metropole, was created merely as an apparatus by means of which the metropolitan bourgeoisie could exercise dominion over the indigenous social classes of the colony. Therefore, the "superstructure" in the colony is "overdeveloped" in relation to the "structure" in the colony, for its basis lies not in the colony but in the metropolitan structure, from which it is separated when the colony becomes independent.[6]

The colonial state is therefore equipped with instruments of political domination that do not arise from the needs and techniques of the indigenous peoples. Such a state assumes the right to settle conflicts which have arisen among the people. But these conflicts have nothing to do with the people in their relations of production; in fact, the state has created such conflicts by establishing a ruling class in the image of the metropolitan one. These ruling classes, without the command of the productive forces that propelled the European bourgeoisie to ascendancy, remain petty in the eyes of their masters but formidable in the eyes of those they rule, who, after independence,

---

6. Hamza Alavi, "The State in Post-colonial Societies," *New Left Review*, no. 74 (1972).

can rarely determine where these rulers get their power from.[7]

The "overdeveloped" postcolonial state easily acquires "super-sovereignty" over the indigenous peoples; and although the African national and comprador bourgeoisie classes masquerade as masters of this state, they cannot finance it, control it, or keep it going without an alliance with, and help from, their metropolitan masters.[8] Thus they enter into military agreements and defense treaties of all kinds with their former colonial masters—and with other imperialist clients, like the Zionist state of Israel—and then they must bleed their subject classes for taxes to pay for the second- and third-rate arms they have bought from the metropoles "for defense purposes."

It has been postulated that in affairs which do not concern them, the metropolitan ruling classes will let the ruling classes of other polities do as they wish, but that in affairs which are of interest to them, they will intervene with all their might. It is in the interest of the bourgeoisie and ruling classes in the metropoles that the national bourgeoisie and ruling classes in the underdeveloped and postcolonial states do not become autonomous classes. The nexus between the center and the periphery has to be maintained for the survival of imperialism. And this can be done by maintaining the present world culture, which keeps these states underdeveloped and weak but allows the metropoles to continue to develop and become even stronger.[9] For example, the African states have continued to maintain trade relations with the Western metropolitan countries, even though the African states are, in this relationship, the producers of raw materials and the consumers of manufactured goods. The few major factories and industries—and in certain states even the processing plants—are built and owned, not by the Africans, but by multinational corporations with headquarters in the metropolitan countries. Thus Zaire cannot be expected to take a stand against Israel, for Israel trains and equips Zaire's paratroopers. Nor can Zaire take a stand against Belgium, for 30 per cent of Zaire's import-export trade is with that country.

Through such alliances as the Commonwealth of Nations, the Organization of Malagasy and African States, and the "Entente" Powers, African

---

7. John Saul, "FRELIMO and the Mozambique Revolution," *Monthly Review*, Vol. XXIV, no. 10 (March, 1973).

8. For an analysis of the various categories of the bourgeoisie in postcolonial states, see Alec Gordon, "The Theory of the 'Progressive' National Bourgeoisie," *Journal of Contemporary Asia*, Vol. III, no. 2 (1973).

9. Walter Rodney, *How Europe Underdeveloped Africa* (Dar es Salaam: Tanzania Publishing House, 1972). See also Johan Galtung, "A Structural Theory of Imperialism," *African Review*, Vol. I, no. 4 (April, 1972).

postcolonial states maintain political subsystems on the international scene which in many ways subordinate their actions to those of their former masters.[10] The African ruling classes are only too ready to rationalize these relations in terms of "the national interests" of their own countries. Thus Kenya will justify having a close military relationship with Great Britain because Great Britain is a fellow member of the Commonwealth, and because, with next-door Somalia getting military aid from the Soviet Union, Kenya has to protect itself by getting equally equipped with weapons from a non-Communist power. In Ethiopia an archaic imperial rule is maintained, with the peasants and workers paying taxes to maintain a formidable army that justifies its existence by nothing other than the "Communist scare" from Somalia and Sudan.[11]

Somalia, Ethiopia, and Kenya could never fight a decisive war against any other of their neighbors without massive help from the metropolitan powers. In such a situation, these countries would deplete their meager resources by paying for arms manufactured and assembled in the metropolitan countries. The situation would be very different if they could at least manufacture their own arms, as South Africa is doing. But the capitalists would thereby lose their markets. Hence, the national or *lumpen* bourgeoisie, masquerading in Africa as the ruling class, must forever be buying weapons and fighting insignificant battles against its own peoples. Thus even Israel, a lackey and middleman of the imperialist powers, orients its aid to Africa along "military lines."

How Effective Have the African States Been in the Middle East Conflict?

With regard to the conflict in the Middle East, African states have, by and large, been ineffective. The line that most of the African countries have taken, through the resolutions and pronouncements of the OAU, has been to condemn the way in which the state of Israel came into being, but to recognize that the world community has stilled its conscience and has accepted the original act of aggression against the Arab people as a *fait accompli*. Israel's further acts of aggression against the Arabs have defied the civilized sympathy that it has received from well-meaning

---

10. See Veniamin Chirkin, "The Downfall of the Colonial System of Imperialism and the Liquidation of International Inequality" (Paper delivered at the Ninth World Congress of the International Political Science Association, Montreal, Canada; August, 1973).

11. See "Repression in Ethiopia" (Paper prepared by the Ethiopian Students' Union in North America, as an African Research Group Publication, no. 5, 1971).

African states which have taken a political stand on the Middle East crisis.[12] But without the power to enforce their will, the African states have had to suffer humiliation at the hands of as small a state as Israel.

Nonetheless, it is not military power that decides all international conflicts in the twentieth century. The ruling classes of the Western world do not have unlimited resources to pursue all that they want internationally at whatever cost. If they can achieve something without paying too dearly for it, so much the better. And they will use whatever avenue provides the least resistance. Moreover, within the metropolitan world, there are antagonisms among classes with different interests as to how the state machinery should be used at home and abroad. Hence, in rationalizing their actions, the ruling classes have to make some concessions to progressive elements within their societies on certain international issues. Thus, for example, the ruling class in the United States has had to tone down its imperialist aggression in Viet Nam because of political pressure from some more progressive elements in the United States and Western Europe. The NATO powers, on the whole, are also being pressured by progressive elements within each member state to stop dealing with Portugal. Recently the Tory government of Edward Heath, in Great Britain, met tremendous resistance from progressive elements when Heath decided to fraternize with Portugal's dictator, Caetano, only a few weeks after the chairman of the OAU, General Gowon, had paid a state visit to Britain.

African states have tried to use such avenues as the United Nations to put pressure on Israel and its imperialist backers to cease their aggression against the Arab peoples. This kind of pressure is of the same nature and in the same tradition as that which the Africans adopted in their "fight for independence." It appeals to the values and morals

---

12. See, for example, Tanzania Information and Tourism Minister Makame's policy speech in the National Assembly, July 3, 1967, in *Africa Diary*, VII (1967), 3531. The African stand is close to positions that the Palestinian liberation movements, particularly El Fatah, have taken. Yasser Arafat, for example, said in 1969: "We have not taken up arms to force two million Jews into the sea or to wage a religious or racial war. The Jews lived alongside the Arabs, including the Palestinians, for many years, and we have never proposed to expel the Jews from Palestine. We are carrying the war forward to expel from our country a military occupation force set up by international imperialism and led by the U.S. government, British imperialism, and international Zionism—which served as the instrument for carrying out imperialist policy in the creation of Israel. . . . We are a national liberation movement which is struggling just as the fighters of Vietnam, Bolivia, or any other people of the world" (quoted in Peter Buch, *Burning Issues of the Middle East* [New York: Path Printers Inc., 1973]).

that, the Western powers claim, govern their behavior, and it challenges these powers to live up to these standards in their international actions if they are going to demand the same values and morals from other peoples.

If these political pressures did not count, Israel would not have bothered to woo African countries to support its stand. Before the rise and success of nationalism in many parts of Africa, Israel had held a negligent attitude toward the Africans; it even sided openly with Africa's oppressors. Soon after the independence of Ghana, however, the Israelis started towing a new line. Thus, as early as April, 1958, when the Conference of Independent African States was held in Accra, Ghana, Israel was surprised at the "solidarity feeling" that Black Africa shared with Arab Africa. (It has always been the wish of imperialism to drive a wedge between sub-Saharan and Saharan Africa, as if all the historical and geopolitical connections of these African peoples are not relevant to the dynamics of the twentieth century.) Israel then proceeded to develop "a policy toward Africa," a policy meant to woo sub-Saharan Africa away from the Middle East conflict and to appease those African countries having Muslim populations (and, hence, which might tend to identify with the Muslim Maghreb) with "aid," making them sympathetic to Israeli propaganda.

At the founding conference of the OAU, in Addis Ababa in May–June, 1963, most "controversial issues," including the Middle East one, were excluded from the agenda. And from that time until the 1967 June War, Arab-Israeli conflicts were not directly mentioned at OAU meetings. But with the vicious war of June, 1967, and the threat posed to Africa when the Israelis demonstrated that they could strike so easily, and with such importunity, an African city as far from the theater of war as Cairo, most African countries began to see the Zionist "friend" in a new light. Meanwhile, Israel had been giving aid, and Israeli officials had been visiting African countries, making propaganda speeches.

In September, 1968, in Algiers, the OAU heads of state, at their Fifth Summit Meeting, passed a resolution which, among other things, reaffirmed OAU support for the U.A.R. and called for the withdrawal of foreign troops from all Arab territories occupied since June 5, 1967, such withdrawal to be in accordance with the United Nations Security Council resolution of November 22, 1967. Since this 1968 resolution, which was rather weak in both tone and content, the OAU has become progressively tougher with Israel, no doubt because of the duplicity that Israel has shown in dealing with some of its "friends" in Africa, and the limit to which Israel can go in trying to "bribe" its friends with aid.[13] A recent essay in *Africa Report* had the suggestive title, "Africa and the Middle East Crisis: Is the Romance with Israel Over?" The author noted the African countries that have broken diplomatic relations with Israel—Guinea, Uganda, Chad, Niger, Mali, and Congo—and suggested that the "Libyan factor" in inter-African politics has much to do with the rapidly deteriorating Israeli profile in Africa. Factors other than the Libyan one—which may account for the behavior of only Chad, Uganda, and Niger—have allowed Africans to see issues in fresher perspectives.[14] Thus almost all of the countries that have broken diplomatic relations with Israel, with the outstanding exception of Uganda, have sent top-level delegations to the People's Republic of China and have made trade and aid agreements much more suitable to their needs than what they could have expected from the Israelis.

It is difficult to speculate as to how far this anti-Israeli sentiment in Africa will spread. Libya was unwise to pose as the "most revolutionary state in Africa," calling upon the other regimes to break diplomatic relations with Israel, and even challenging the legitimacy of having the headquarters of the OAU in Addis Ababa in light of the heavy presence of Israeli and U.S. personnel in Ethiopia in civilian, diplomatic, and military institutions. Other African governments cannot help but see Libya as trying to impose its will on them; and, since Libya has made no major political or economic inroads into any of the African states, it is inadvisable for that country to speak as if it could dictate the foreign policies of other African states. Moreover, some of Libya's acts in sub-Saharan Africa seem to reflect a desire on its part for military hegemony. When Kaddafi "stabbed Nyerere in the back" by equipping Idi Amin with arms and manpower during Uganda's crisis with Tanzania, it looked as if this Arab nation was prepared to sacrifice the support of a long-term friend for the whims of a military dictator who had, on the spur of the moment, adopted an anti-Zionist policy. While such acts should not lead sub-Saharan African governments to fall prey to their imperialist detractors, they have not helped to promote Black African–Arab African solidarity.

Libya seems to reckon on the pressures that the Muslim elements

---

13. Israel's aid to Africa is dwindling. Only a few states—for example, the Central African Republic, Ethiopia, and Zaire—had significant aid and trade agreements with Israel in 1973.

14. Mazrui, in quite a different context, has argued that the settlement of the southern Sudan problem, the national nuisance that Israeli manpower in Uganda was becoming, as well as the fear of a coup masterminded by the Israelis, caused General Amin to decide to terminate his friendship with the Zionist state long before he visited Libya. See "Nation-Building and Race-Building," p. 9.

in certain sub-Saharan countries will put on their ruling classes on behalf of the Arab cause. But this kind of *jihad* may only create more rifts among OAU members, for no African regime would want a conflict in another area to interfere with the stability of its rule over its own population. Some of the sub-Saharan African states are quite aware of the fact that the Libyan "religious formula" is meant to help, not the Palestinians, but the Arab ruling classes, who will, in turn, oppress their own populations. At this level, then, these sub-Saharan African countries are taking a progressive stand, which would be better if it were concretized in actual political and material support for the Palestinian liberation movements. But so far these countries have shied away from offering such support.

How May the African States Be More Consistent in Their Orientations and Behavior toward the Middle East Conflict?

First, Africans have to define their positions against imperialism much more consistently and firmly. This might mean the loss of certain "favors," like the loss Tanzania experienced in the mid-1960s, but this will lead the imperialists to take the African governments more seriously, and not to take their weakness for granted. Although what the Africans may achieve is limited, consistency and firmness of purpose would be better than oscillation and a general lack of a "line" on those issues where the interests of Africa and the Third World are definitely not concomitant to the interests of the metropolitan powers.

Second, Africans must recognize the state of Israel for what it is, irrespective of its current conflicts with its Arab neighbors. As Maxime Rodinson has sought to establish, Israel is a colonial settler state that is in the same category as other such states in Africa, states that are oppressing African peoples and depleting their resources.[15] Africa cannot seek to ostracize Rhodesia and, at the same time, condone the wickedness of Israel against the Palestinians.

Israel, living up to its role as a "third force,"[16] has acted as a middleman for both Western imperialist and South African apartheid penetration

---

15. Rodinson, *Israel: A Colonial Settler State?* (New York: Monad & Pathfinder Press, 1973).

16. For an analysis of this theory as advanced by U.S. imperialists, see Arnold Rivkin, *Africa and the West* (New York: Praeger, 1961). For progressive critiques of this theory, see *David and Goliath Collaborate in Africa* (Washington, D.C.: Africa Research Group, 1970).

of Africa. Thus, for example, when Israel convened its Third Economic Conference, in 1973, the fifty-member South African delegation created a small furor when its chairman confirmed that South African manufacturers were investing in Israel as a way of circumventing the African boycott of South African products. The chairman announced that a South African group was planning to set up a textile factory in Israel that would import cotton, print it with African patterns, and sell it in "African countries from which we are boycotted."[17] The *New York Times* of June 2, 1973, further commented: "Israel serves as a very useful base for South African factories that cannot supply to the African countries."

Israel has a long history as an accomplice of the apartheid and racist regimes in southern Africa[18] and as a force working against African unity. (One may mention, in passing, Israel's involvement on the Biafran side during the Nigerian crisis; its aid to the southern Sudanese and its wish for that conflict to continue; its involvement in the Uganda coup, shortly after which Israeli embassy cars were seen carrying soldiers in the town of Kampala, and Israeli military personnel were seen on the Makerere campus with Idi Amin.) Thus, in spite of Israel's great concern for cultivating diplomatic and commercial relations with Black Africa, Israeli–South African economic relations have been improving since 1961. It was reported in *Sechaba* that "between 1961 and 1967, Israel's exports to South Africa increased by $1.4 million to $4 million while *imports* in 1967 reached $3.3 million." Moreover, South African and Israeli military relations are also reported to be very close. Following the 1967 June War, it is reported, South African military personnel were flown to the Middle East "to study how Israel did it."[19] Israel and South Africa thus not only find themselves in similar positions but also realize that in these positions, where they regard themselves as "surrounded by enemies," they need each other. From the South African viewpoint, Israel guards the northern gate to Africa, and, from the Israeli angle, South Africa guards the southern gate. After all, consideration for its interests in the Indian Ocean and the Red Sea— among other considerations—first prompted Israel to seek the friend-

---

17. Middle East Research Project, *Report*, no. 19, "Israeli Economic Conference," pp. 17–18. See also *Jerusalem Post Weekly*, May 15, 29, June 5, 1973.

18. For a comprehensive, though not up-to-date, analysis of Israeli—South African complicity with imperialism, see Madison Area Committee on Southern Africa, *Israel and Southern Africa, A Comparison of the Roles of South Africa and Israel in the Third World* (1970).

19. Richard Stevens, "Zionism, South Africa and Apartheid," *Sechaba* (official organ of the African National Congress of South Africa), Vol. V, no. 9 (September, 1971).

ship of independent African states. Thus, while Israel engages the northern African countries in indecisive battles, forcing them to spend their scarce resources on arms, South Africa keeps sub-Saharan African countries fighting drawn-out wars of liberation, delaying the moment when they can concentrate their resources on modernizing their economies.

And, third, African governments must realize that no Western power is going to liberate them. It is by modernizing their own economies and by making these economies viable in the present world that African countries can become effective internationally. Kwame Nkrumah said it long ago, that Africa cannot do this unless it is united; and others have since confirmed it.[20]

But what if the ruling classes in Africa are satisfied with things as they are? What if they are not interested in doing away with the present structural arrangements? This poses a serious problem for Africa. The ruling classes—except for those in a few countries whose members have imaginatively tried to seek alternative avenues to development—are oriented toward enjoying the status, privileges, and power that the present arrangements have bestowed on them. If there are progressive elements within the African populace that would like the African revolution to be carried beyond political independence, they are, as John Saul rightly noted, "terrorized and repressed" by the national and comprador bourgeoisie classes that reign supreme in the neocolonial state. To discuss the participation of the African people in national affairs, let alone in international affairs, as a people, and not through the mediation of the state, is highly insignificant at this moment in time.

With regard to the Middle East conflict, it may be mentioned in passing that the African populace remains ill informed, unconcerned, and dependent on bourgeois propaganda heavily biased toward the Zionists. Even the African states do not have the technology to counteract the imperialist propaganda that is beamed in from powerful radio stations in Washington, London, and Johannesburg. If the OAU wanted to take a stand on some international issue, and wanted to make sure that its position reached the African people without distortion by foreign-owed mass media, it would not be able to do so. Egypt is one of the few African countries with its own news medium, *Al-Ahram*. For the most part, news is disseminated by Western media, dominated by persons with Zionist sentiments. We cannot speak of an African

---

20. See Rodney, *How Europe Underdeveloped Africa*; R. H. Green and Ann Seidman, *Unity or Poverty? The Economics of Pan-Africanism* (Baltimore: Penguin, 1968).

perspective of international affairs from the point of view of the African masses when they are so influenced by non-African forces and propaganda.

What Can Be Done?

Africans who have brought about changes in the first two decades following independence have tried to establish conditions for the survival of Africans within historical structures and modes of behavior—namely, those created and nurtured by capitalist forces. Those who come after them, the new agents of change in Africa, cannot help but see the limitations of these structures and the uncertainty of survival under them. It is much easier to be satisfied with the status quo when one is in a privileged position and relatively well off. But for those who are suffering, for those for whom the status quo is antithetical to their interests and survival, there is little choice but to seek change. This is why the Middle East crisis is not simply a matter of Africans being pro-Arab and anti-Israeli, but one of breaking loose from all those forces, domestic and foreign, that are choking African development and delaying the liberation of productive forces in African countries that would make the Arab and African world a truly modern one.

Hatem I. Hussaini

THE IMPACT OF THE ARAB-ISRAELI CONFLICT ON ARAB COMMUNITIES IN THE UNITED STATES

THE ARAB-ISRAELI WAR of June, 1967, had a significant, but not a decisive, impact on Arab communities in the United States. Psychologically, it led to the emergence of a new consciousness that left an imprint on some Arab communities and their organizations. The Syrian and Lebanese community, for example, began to identify with the Arabs and with "Arabism," and began to rediscover its ethnic nationalist background. The Palestinian community and the Arab student sector developed a more radical and revolutionary consciousness. They began to identify with popular movements rather than with Arab governments in the Middle East. This psychological awareness generated a level of political activity which had not existed in Arab-American communities prior to 1967.

Politically, the Arab defeat of June, 1967, resulted in the emergence of new Arab organizations that began to play an active political role in Arab-American affairs. It also resulted in the reactivation of a number of dormant Arab-American organizations. Organizations that had limited themselves to social and cultural activities began to assume a more active political role.

ARAB-AMERICANS BEFORE 1967: ASSIMILATION
AND NONINVOLVEMENT

There are no precise statistics on the number of Americans of Arab descent in the United States. Some sources have estimated the number at one million, others at two million.[1] Arab-Americans can be classified into two broad categories: the descendants of early immigrants (pre–World War I), mostly Syrians and Lebanese; and recent immigrants (post–World War II), Palestinians, Iraqis, Egyptians, and other Arab nationals. Most Arab-Americans fall into the first category. They are the pioneers, and the children of pioneers, who immigrated to the United States in the early 1900s and who have since established themselves as Americans in the upper and upper-middle classes. They do not refer to themselves as Arab-Americans, but as Americans of Lebanese or Syrian descent. These immigrants carried with them the political and social realities of the Middle East in the late 1800s and early 1900s, when there was no such phenomenon as "Arab nationalism." From their perspective, there was a division between Muslims and Christians, with the Ottomans representing an oppressive regime that denied both Christians and Muslims their political and human rights. These Arab-Americans did not experience the later British and French colonialism, the division of greater Syria, or the Arab struggle for independence and liberation in the 1930s and early 1950s. Therefore, they could not comprehend Arab agitation against the West and against European imperialist powers.

The early immigrants sought freedom and economic well-being in the United States. They came believing in American ideals of democracy and private enterprise, and they moved to establish themselves within the American system.[2] They did not oppose assimilation, and as "white Christians" the system was open to them. They changed their names, adopted American business and behavioral habits, and became part

1. In 1960 the U.S. Immigration Department estimated the number of immigrants of Arab origin at 500,000. See Arab Immigrants Association, *History of Arab Immigrants* (Damascus, 1966), p. 49. Another source indicated that there were 1.5 million Muslims in the United States in 1960, but this figure includes non-Arabs. See U.S. Information Department, *Al-Majal,* no. 48.

2. In discussing motives for Arab immigration, George Tomeh stated that in addition to political factors, the economic factor was most important. See Tomeh, *Arab Immigrants in North America* (Damascus: Ministry of Culture and Guidance, 1965), p. 44. In a study of Muslim communities in Toledo and Detroit, Abdo El-Kholy concluded that the immigrants achieved a high degree of assimilation; they found life in America satisfying, they gained wealth and prestige, and they enjoyed full political freedom. See El-Kholy, *The Arab Muslims in the United States* (New Haven: College and University Press, 1966).

of the American system.³ Their only link with their ancestral country was through food, music, and a few Arabic words.

The second category of immigrants includes not only Lebanese and Syrians but also Palestinians, Egyptians, Iraqis, and individuals from the Arabian Peninsula. These immigrants moved to the United States during and after the independence of the Arab states. They were politicized, aware of Arab nationalism and the struggle for Arab independence. Many of them had experienced the forceful creation of Zionist Israel, with the displacement of the Palestinian people.

In general, the recent immigrants were not assimilated into the American system. Since they viewed their stay in America as temporary, they were concerned primarily with improving their economic situation; ultimately they planned to return to their homeland. They referred to themselves as Arabs or Arab-Americans, rather than Syrians, Egyptians, or Palestinians.

Within this category could be found a hard core of Arab professionals (professors, medical doctors, engineers) and students who were politically conscious and committed to the struggle for Arab liberation and socialism. They represented activists of different political tendencies who were persecuted in the Arab states and who moved to the United States.⁴ However, they kept their political views to themselves and were not involved in American politics.

The early immigrants established a number of clubs and organizations, but along communal lines and for social and religious purposes only. These clubs, such as the Rashid's clubs, Ramallah clubs, Alepo Friendship Club, Phoenician Club, and others, were organized on the basis of family or village ties.⁵ Each group of immigrants from the same village or community established its own club. These clubs were primarily concerned with Arab music and dancing, and with getting the children acquainted so that they would, it was hoped, marry within the group. Thus the most common activity was the *hafli* ("party"), where the immigrants danced traditional folk dances and where their children

---

3. Examples of Arab names and their American versions are Ibrahim (Abraham), Muhammad (Mike), Abdul-Hawa (Howard), Jamil (Jim).

4. These include members of the Syrian Nationalist Socialist party, the Ba'ath party, the Arab Nationalist party, the Communist party, the Nasserist movement, and so on.

5. The Rashid's clubs are the best example of an organization along family lines. Its members, numbering 1,000, meet annually to conduct business and financial affairs of the family and to enjoy Arab dancing and music. They trace their origins to the seventh century, to Beni Ghassan. See "The Rashids in the Land of Opportunity," *Washington Post*, July 4, 1973.

met and got acquainted. The older men discussed business and arranged to assist each other financially.[6]

In the early 1950s some of these clubs were federated at the national level. The most important of those was the Federation of Syrian American Clubs. This federation comprised clubs in four geographic areas of the United States: the West Coast, the East Coast, the South, and the Midwest. Each area elected officers, as well as representatives to the national board. The latter supervised the activities of the federation in the United States. The federation was concerned mostly with cultural and social activities, especially during its annual conventions.

Major political events in the Arab world which shocked Europe and the United States passed unnoticed by these organizations and clubs. The Arab-Israeli War of 1948, the Egyptian Revolution of 1952, and the Suez War of 1956 did not bring them into action or affect their functions. Although a few educated leaders from the Syrian and Lebanese clubs took note of these events, they were unable to rally their communities into action.

These communal organizations were involved in disputes and rivalries along religious and family lines. Thus, if one group of American Lebanese would form a club, another group from a different family or village would form a rival club. Rivalry also existed among the leaders of each club; they competed vigorously for high positions and thus contributed to the ineffectiveness and decline of these organizations.

In contrast, recent immigrants did not attempt to form their own organizations. Some of them, like the Lebanese and the Syrians, joined existing clubs. Others, especially laborers and nonprofessional immigrants, did not join. They lived in closed communities in the major cities, such as Chicago, Detroit, and New York, and devoted their energies to work and to economic survival.

The professional class among recent immigrants, especially professors and medical doctors, did not, prior to 1967, form their own organizations or involve themselves in Arab affairs. Some of these Arab-Americans made valuable contributions in the form of books and articles on the Arabs and their political and socioeconomic systems, but they did nothing to organize or politicize the Arab-American communities. There remained a gap, therefore, between the majority of Arab immigrants and the educated elite, and it was only after 1967 that this gap was narrowed.

---

6. One of the most famous *haflis* for Americans of Lebanese descent is held annually in Danbury, Connecticut, where thousands of immigrants meet and enjoy Arab music and dancing.

The exception to this rule was the Organization of Arab Students in the United States, which, although not necessarily an immigrant organization, did represent a large number of Arabs studying in the United States. Since its establishment, in the early 1950s, it has played an active role in explaining and defending Arab issues and causes, and in raising political awareness in Arab immigrant communities. Its quarterly publication, the *Arab Journal,* containing articles on such issues as Arab nationalism and Arab socialist change, is directed not only to the Arab-American sector but also to the American intellectual and university sectors. But, as a student organization, it had limited resources and means of reaching and mobilizing Arab-Americans.

Neither the early nor the recent immigrants were involved in the American political system as an ethnic or minority group. Despite the fact that there was a surge of ethnic and minority involvement in American politics in the late 1950s and 1960s, especially within the Democratic party, Arab-Americans remained uninvolved as a group.[7]

Some of the early immigrants who became established eventually played a limited role in the political process. As influential businessmen and community leaders, they worked within the local Republican or Democratic party, contributing money and occasionally running for local office. They did this as Americans, on an individual basis, and not as an organized ethnic group. Within the two parties these individuals were divided along conservative and liberal lines. A large number of them were conservative, influential within the Republican party at the local and state levels.[8] They were for free enterprise and were opposed to big government, black radicals, and other minority groups with radical tendencies.

In contrast, recent immigrants did not play such a role within the American political system. They did not have the financial ability to do so, and their political orientation was different. They were critical of the political system as a whole and did not feel that their participation within the established parties could influence the development of

---

7. Tomeh, however, cites the political roles of some early immigrants. He mentions that three Arab-Americans attended the Arab Congress in Paris in 1913. He also documents the role of the Federation of Syrian American Clubs in the early 1950s in contacting members of Congress and explaining the Arab point of view. See Tomeh, *Arab Immigrants in North America,* pp. 26–41.

8. In Cleveland, for example, Arab-Americans have played a key role in local politics. Their leaders have had influence within the Republican party and helped elect a Republican mayor in 1970. A number of Americans of Arab descent have been elected to Congress— among them, Sen. James Abourezk (D., S.D.), Rep. James Abdnor (R., S.D.), and Rep. Abraham Kazen (D., Texas).

pro-Arab policies. While the early immigrants played an active role in the political system for economic and local benefits, and not for Arab issues or causes, the recent immigrants were motivated by Arab national issues and realized that the political process was closed to them on these issues. They understood the power of Zionists and pro-Israeli Jewish Americans within the political parties and realized that it was futile to challenge these powerful forces within a political system that they controlled.[9] Early immigrants and their descendants did not raise Arab or pro-Arab issues within the established political parties and thus avoided challenging Zionists and pro-Israeli Jews. In some instances, Americans of Lebanese descent refused to raise issues related to the Arabs or the Arab-Israeli conflict for fear of antagonizing American Jews with whom they had financial and economic dealings.[10]

Until 1967, then, the majority of recent immigrants, including Palestinians, Iraqis, and Syrians, were not involved in any political or Arab-oriented activities in the United States. This was a result of their evaluation of the power of Zionists, their lack of strong motivation, and their fear of being politically involved in light of their negative political experiences in the Arab states. Political involvement meant persecution and imprisonment; and thus, among lower and lower-middle classes of immigrants, such as workers and technicians, political involvement in the United States was viewed as a liability rather than a guaranteed right. They did not realize that their rights to political participation and free speech were protected by the American Constitution.

THE 1967 JUNE WAR: A TURNING POINT

The 1967 Arab defeat and humiliation had a great impact on the recent immigrants. Arab-Americans who identified with Arab nationalism and Nasserism were stunned by the swift Israeli military victory. Their initial reaction of disbelief was followed by genuine anguish and

---

9. For a detailed study of the influence of Zionist groups within the American political system, see Odeh Aburdeineh, "The Jewish Factor in U.S. Politics," *Journal of Palestine Studies*, I, no. 4, 93–109.

10. In Springfield, Massachusetts, an influential Lebanese businessman refused to contribute money to Palestinian refugees for fear of antagonizing American Jews in the clothing industry with whom he had business dealings. Fawzi Asmar mentions the case of a Lebanese shopkeeper in Connecticut who stopped selling Lebanese food after being intimidated by a rabbi. See Asmar, "Three Snapshots Unframed," *Israel and Palestine* (Paris, 1973), no. 16017.

pain. To those politically conscious Arabs, Israel and the foreign powers supporting it had dealt a heavy blow to the forces of revolutionary and socialist change in the Arab world. The Nasserist and Ba'athist regimes were totally defeated, while the conservative monarchies and pro-Western regimes remained strong and intact. Israel's military victory was a decisive factor in the Arab "revolutionary" versus "conservative" conflict. Egypt and Syria were immobilized; Saudi Arabia and other countries with conservative regimes soon moved to the center of power in the Arab arena.

Among some Arab-Americans, a school of thought emerged which viewed the 1967 June War as a foreign "imperialist" plot against the Arab masses and their "revolutionary" regimes. They viewed Israel as a tool used by foreign powers to halt the Arab revolutionary tide in the Middle East and to establish a new political order in which conservative pro-Western regimes would be dominant. In this view the United States government was regarded not as a peacemaker but as a foreign power that supported Israel and depended on it for the protection of American strategic and economic interests in the area.[11]

These Arab-Americans turned their attention to the shortcomings of the "revolutionary" regimes, the reasons for their defeat, and the ways and means by which these regimes could overcome this "Zionist-imperialist" challenge. Their main interest was to strengthen the revolutionary and popular movements in the Arab world and to assist them in mobilizing the masses to defeat Israeli aggression. One of the first groups to begin this evaluation consisted of student leaders from the Organization of Arab Students who met in July, 1967, and after three days of extensive discussions issued a comprehensive study with detailed proposals for Arab political and economic action. The study was sent to the Arab heads of states involved in the conflict with Israel.

Instead of being demoralized, the Organization of Arab Students, due to the efforts of these leaders, was activated along radical lines. During 1967 and 1968 it held teach-ins at different universities, organized demonstrations and sit-ins at Arab embassies, and published a large number of articles and studies, all of which called for the mobilization of the Arab masses and the use of Arab economic and political power for a long struggle against Zionism and imperialism.[12]

---

11. Arab intellectuals have made this position clear in AAUG resolutions which have stated that the U.S. government has pursued a policy of duplicity and imperialism in the Middle East, and that continued U.S. military support of colonial-fascist regimes has thwarted the principles of liberty, dignity, and equality.

12. At the Egyptian mission to the U.N., Egyptian students led other Arab students in sit-ins protesting Egypt's acceptance of the cease-fire and calling for the mobilization

The emergence of the Palestinian Resistance Movement in 1967 had a decisive impact on the Arab students and on some Arab-Americans. In the midst of total Arab defeat, the resistance movement became the rallying point for all the forces which rejected compromise and settlement and which sought continued revolutionary and socialist struggle. Since 1967, the defense and support of the Palestinian Resistance Movement has been the central theme of the activities of the Organization of Arab Students. It began to communicate with American students and peace groups, urging them to support the Palestinian cause, and held hundreds of teach-ins to inform Americans about the Palestinian struggle. In 1969 the organization, after adopting a political program that gave it a revolutionary identity, changed its constitution to reflect its new commitment. The new constitution stated:

> The Organization of Arab Students will struggle for . . . 1. The liberation of the Arab people, their independence and unity in a democratic popular State through the continuous struggle against world imperialism . . . 2. To organize and politically educate the Arab students and to . . . prepare the students . . . as revolutionary intellectuals who link their struggle with the Arab masses. . . .

The organization purged from its ranks rightist Muslim students who had attempted, in 1969, to take over the executive committee. Since 1970 it has conducted activities in support of the resistance movement and the struggle of the Arab masses. Its 1970 and 1971 annual resolutions called for total commitment to the Palestinian resistance and declared that it represented the vanguard of Arab revolutionary struggle. It criticized Arab regimes and condemned those, such as Jordan, that had attempted to liquidate the resistance movement.

The students began, moreover, to turn their attention to the Arab-American community, especially to Palestinians and other recent immigrants, in an effort to mobilize them for support of the Palestinian resistance. In major cities such as New York, Chicago, Detroit, and San Francisco, students initiated community-oriented programs and activities aimed at educating the immigrants politically and uniting them for effective action.

On the humanitarian level, a number of organizations were formed

---

of the Egyptian people for a long struggle for liberation. In 1971 they published statements critical of the Egyptian government, and in 1973 they again condemned the undemocratic policies followed by the government in harassing progressive writers and students. See *Al-Wattan*, February, 1971; April, 1973.

to provide assistance and aid to the Palestinian refugees. Arab-Americans and Palestinians who were uninvolved and isolated before 1967 became activists and community organizers, and took the lead in establishing these organizations. The most important and effective of these organizations were the United Holy Land Fund and the Palestine Arab Fund, both national organizations, with chapters in different states. The United Fund, a tax-exempt nonprofit organization, was established in 1969 by a group of Arab and Palestinian professionals.[13] It has raised funds for hospitals, orphanages, and other institutions serving the Palestinian refugees. The Palestine Arab Fund, which is not tax-exempt, was established on the West Coast in 1969. It has also raised funds for helping the Palestinians and has been concerned with raising the political consciousness of the Arab-American community and informing Arab-Americans about the achievements of the Palestinian movement. The organization includes professional Arabs as well as students and workers. Both the United Holy Land Fund and the Palestine Arab Fund are community-oriented organizations that feature lectures, films, and panel discussions about the Palestinian and Arab struggles.

Other smaller organizations, such as NAJDA, Project Riayat, and Pal-Aid International, emerged to fulfill similar humanitarian functions. Some were limited to a specific project, such as Riayat's assistance to orphaned Palestinian children. The Palestinian Red Crescent Society, on the other hand, was formed by a group of Arab and Palestinian medical doctors who send medical supplies and equipment to hospitals and clinics serving the refugee camps. Some of these doctors volunteered for medical service in the refugee camps in 1970 and 1971.

These organizations were able to reach thousands of Arab-Americans and to solicit their support for the Palestinians. They represented a new awakening among Arabs in the United States, a willingness to work on a voluntary basis, and a commitment to the Palestinian people and their struggle for survival and liberation. But despite the mobilization efforts of these organizations, they remained essentially fragmented and therefore unable to provide unified and consistent support to the Palestinian refugees. In 1972 and 1973, some of these organizations disappeared because they were dependent on the work of one or two individuals and were unable to continue in a long and sustained manner.

---

13. The United Holy Land Fund had difficulty in obtaining its tax-exempt status but was finally chartered in the state of Missouri. Its charter states that it caters to the needs of Palestinian orphans, widows, injured, and unskilled, and that it supports vocational, civic, health, and rehabilitation programs. It has fourteen chapters in different states. Its headquarters is in Michigan, and it maintains offices in Jordan. See *The United Holy Land Fund* (Clawson, Michigan, 1971).

On the political level, a number of important organizations emerged to mobilize Arab-Americans and to direct their energies toward supporting the Arab and Palestinian cause. They represented the efforts of Arab-American professionals, mostly professors and intellectuals, who responded to the Palestinian struggle and began to involve themselves in Arab activities. The Association of Arab-American University Graduates (AAUG) has been the most successful and effective of these organizations. It was established in 1967 by a few Arab professors who were alarmed by the Arab defeat and inspired by the Palestinian movement. Its first annual meeting, held in Washington, D.C., in 1968, was attended by less than fifty professors. Within two years the association had more than four hundred members, and its 1970 annual convention was attended by a number of prominent Arab and non-Arab writers and intellectuals.[14] The association has criticized Arab regimes severely and has shown consistent and firm support for the Palestinian movement. The 1970 annual resolution stated:

> The AAUG recognizes the Palestine Resistance Movement as the only legitimate liberation movement of the Palestinian people and as the vanguard of the Arab revolution.

At its annual convention of 1972, the AAUG asserted:

> The Association condemns unequivocally the irresolution and the hypocrisy displayed by the regimes in the Arab states in conducting their struggle against Israel and its supporters. This irresolution and hypocrisy have enabled Israel to expand its war of extermination of the Palestinian and Arab people, and have enabled the U.S. government to implement policies in the region calculated to further institutionalize the fragmentation of the Arab world.

Thus, Arab professionals were finally organized and effective in articulating their position and defending the struggle of the Arab masses. Within a few years the AAUG sponsored a number of significant activities: it published a number of important books about Zionism, Palestine, the involvement of colonial powers, and the struggle of the Arab people, and a number of pamphlets to inform Americans about the Arab people and their political problems.

---

14. Among them, Maxime Rodinson, Noam Chomsky, Indian leader Krishna Menon, Egyptian journalist Ahmad Baha El-Din, and Lebanese writers Clovis Maksoud and Munah Solh.

In addition to its academic and informational role, the AAUG played an important function as a pressure group articulating the Arab position in the United States. It vigorously protested American involvement in the Middle East and defended the civil rights of Arabs in the United States. It also developed strong ties with Americans in universities and with some political groups, such as the peace movement and Blacks. Locally, it established a number of active chapters across the country. But it has remained basically an academic professional organization and has not developed grass-roots support within Arab-American communities.

The function of mobilizing Arab-American communities was performed by other newly organized groups of Arab-Americans who were highly motivated after 1967. They established community-oriented clubs and organizations that began to educate Arab-Americans about Palestine and the Palestinian movement, and to mobilize their resources for its support. The most active of these were the American Congress for Palestine, which was established in Detroit, Chicago, and Los Angeles; the Palestine Committee, in Boston; and Palestine House, in Washington, D.C. Their activities have included dinners, films, lectures, and study groups on Palestine and the struggle for its liberation. Many of the activists in these organizations are nonprofessionals, workers, students, and technicians who have volunteered to serve their communities and guide them in activities for Palestine.

These activists also publish a number of magazines and newspapers in English and Arabic in order to bring the Arab communities news about the Palestinian movement. The most successful of these has been *Free Palestine,* a monthly periodical in English that speaks for the Palestinian movement and carries its news and ideas.[15] Publications in Arabic have been published and distributed locally in an effort to mobilize the communities.

EARLY ARAB-AMERICAN IMMIGRANTS: CHANGING ATTITUDES

The early immigrants, especially Americans of Syrian and Lebanese descent, were not immediately affected by the 1967 June War. In contrast to the recent Arab immigrants, who mobilized their energies and developed new organizations, the established Syrian and Lebanese communities remained inactive with regard to the Arab cause and

---

15. Other periodicals and local magazines include *Al-Fidai* (in Arabic), *Tariq al-Talabah* (Arabic), *Fateh* (Arabic), *Al-Nida* (Arabic), and *AMARA Newsletter* (English).

Palestine. They continued their activities on the social and cultural level.

It was not until 1971 that these communities began to show interest in activities for the Arab cause. They were prodded into action by three developments. First, Israel's image in 1971 was totally different from the one that it had in 1967. The state that, in 1967, had appeared weak and surrounded by hostile and superior Arab forces had emerged as a superior and aggressive military power able to impose its will on its weak neighbors. Israel was no longer threatened by "annihilation." Lebanon, Syria, and Egypt were now subjected to continual Israeli military raids and attacks. The massive Israeli military incursions into Lebanon began to move Americans of Lebanese and Syrian descent into action.

Second, the U.S. government policy, which, in 1967, had appeared evenhanded, had become totally one-sided by 1971. Israel, although victorious and unthreatened, continued to receive sophisticated American weapons, including Phantom jets. Furthermore, Prime Minister Golda Meir, with her famous shopping list, had become a regular visitor in Washington. The American commitment to Israeli military superiority, which left Lebanon at the mercy of Israeli generals, enraged the American Lebanese and Syrian communities. The American government, moreover, did nothing to stop Israeli attacks on Lebanon and other Arab countries.

Third, and most important, was the investigation of Arab communities by government agencies in their campaign against so-called terrorism. The Boulder Operation, enacted in 1972 by the White House and the State Department, required that all persons whose parents were Arab would have to be investigated before they would be issued a visa to enter the United States. This policy offended the dignity and pride of Americans of Arab descent. The Syrian and Lebanese communities, whose members viewed themselves as loyal and law-abiding Americans, protested this discriminatory policy and began to organize for political action.

Leaders of Syrian and Lebanese communities moved on two levels of action. First, they created new organizations capable of playing a political role. Thus, in 1972, the National Association of Arab-Americans (NAAA) was established to "engage in political . . . activities for the purpose of maintaining political action and involvement in the United States."[16] Its founders, prominent businessmen and lawyers of Arab

---

16. A brochure of the NAAA, published in Washington, D.C., in 1973, states that the organization was formed because Americans of Arab heritage are proud of that

descent from major American cities, were immediately involved in political action. They met with high government officials, including the secretary of state and White House advisers, to protest and to register their disagreement with American policies of unquestioning support to Israel and total disregard for the security of Arab states in the Middle East. The association held its first annual meeting in Detroit, in June, 1973, elected a board of directors, formulated plans for political action to influence American foreign policy toward the Middle East, and called for raising millions of dollars for its work.[17] The main speaker at the convention was the recently elected senator from South Dakota, James Abourezk, an American of Lebanese descent, who urged them to identify with their Arab heritage and to organize as an ethnic group so that they might play an effective role in the political process.

Second, leaders of Syrian and Lebanese communities began to politicize members of the social organizations and to seek their support for action on Arab issues. The annual meetings and conventions of these organizations were no longer limited to social and cultural activities, but included educational and political seminars and lectures. The convention of the Syrian Lebanese Mid-West Federation held in May, 1973, included for the first time a number of workshops on such topics as Lobbying in Congress, How to Reach the Press and News Media, and History of Palestine. The convention made a number of resolutions calling for political action, and the newly elected officers urged the members to work for protecting the civil rights of Arab-Americans, as well as the rights of Palestinian Arabs in the Middle East.

The Federation of Ramallah Clubs, which, before 1971, had limited itself to cultural and social activities, also initiated programs to assist the Palestinians. At its 1971 annual convention it established scholarships to assist Palestinian students, and at its 1973 convention there were a number of workshops on Palestine and its history.

The Syrian and Lebanese organizations began to cooperate with other Arab organizations in taking unified action. Thus, in protesting American government policies of discrimination against Arabs, the World Lebanese Council and the Syrian and Lebanese clubs joined with the Association of Arab-American University Graduates and the Organization of Arab Students. Together they published an advertisement in

---

heritage and want to maintain the principles of "self-determination and justice for all people."

17. "U.S. Arabs Mobilize to Form Lobby," *Christian Science Monitor*, August 16, 1973.

the *New York Times* calling for the protection of the civil liberties of Americans of Arab descent.[18] In California fourteen Arab-American organizations sent telegrams to President Nixon and the secretary of state protesting government "harassment of Arabs" and calling for an end to the "violation of human liberties of citizens."[19]

These recent activities, however, represent only a small fraction of the energies and resources of Americans of Arab descent and their organizations. The early immigrants who have become assimilated Americans are unaware of the grave problems facing their countries of origin and therefore have been unwilling to direct their energies and resources to political action. A few well-informed leaders have begun working to raise the political awareness of their communities, to inject "Arabism" into the heritage of these communities, and to get their support for political activities.

The activists and leaders among the early immigrants represent a different school of thought on the Middle East problem than that of the recent immigrants. In contrast to the latter, who blame the American government and its imperialist policies, the early immigrants blame Zionism. They have faith in the American system and its ideals of equality, freedom, and democracy; and they argue that Zionism is responsible for corrupting these principles with regard to the Arab-Israeli conflict. Frank Maria, a prominent American of Arab descent, stated this position clearly when he called on American Syrian and Lebanese communities to "join other concerned and informed Americans in a history-making crusade to help free the American people and their government from the harmful influence of political Zionism." He stressed that

> what is needed in the Middle East is a truly American policy, one based on U.S. interest and on "evenhandedness" between Israel and the Arab countries. This can come about if the stranglehold of political Zionism

---

18. The advertisement stated that "singling out people of Arab origin as targets of surveillance, investigation and interrogation can only be interpreted as a deliberate effort to harass and intimidate the members of the community." *New York Times*, October 29, 1972.

19. The telegrams, dated November 20, 1972, were signed by Islamic Foundation of South California, Middle East Fellowship, St. Nicholas Orthodox Cathedral, Our Lady of Mt. Lebanon Church, St. Ane's Melkite Church, U.S. Omen, Palestine War Victims Society, United American Arab Congress, Council of Arab Students, Palestine Arab Fund, Lebanese Syrian American Society, American Jordanian Palestinian Society, Association of Arab-American University Graduates, World Lebanese Council.

or the Israeli lobby on our government and other responsible American organizations can be loosened.[20]

The positions of these two schools of thought can be made clear by examining the reactions of each to Secretary of State Rogers' "peace plan." Activists and leaders of recent immigrants opposed the Rogers Plan because they viewed it as an attempt to divide the Arab states and to create conditions for the liquidation of the resistance movement. Rogers' proposals were also viewed as an attempt to pressure the Arab states to recognize Israel. Thus the Association of Arab-American University Graduates and the Organization of Arab Students, among others, called on Arab governments to reject Rogers' proposals and to continue their struggle for the liberation of Palestine.[21]

Leaders of the early immigrants viewed the Rogers Plan differently. They supported the plan because they felt that it represented an "evenhanded" policy, calling for Israel's withdrawal from Arab-occupied territories and Arab recognition of Israel. Thus, on April 16, 1973, in a letter to Secretary Rogers, the National Association of Arab-Americans called for the implementation of United Nations Resolution 242 and Rogers' proposals. Its president stated that the organization was not anti-Israeli, and that Arab-Americans were not asking the United States to abandon Israel, but simply to develop an evenhanded policy toward the Middle East. He added that "with its wealth and technical knowledge, and with its Arab labor force, Israel can help the whole Middle East."[22]

This position is radically different from that of the Association of Arab-American University Graduates and the Organization of Arab Students. It reflects the ideas of Americans of Arab descent who are seeking to change American foreign policy toward the Middle East without committing themselves to the goals of Arab liberation. They are interested in protecting American interests and in bettering Arab-American relations. The Arab student and graduate organizations, on the other hand, are committed to Arab revolutionary struggle and

20. From Maria's speech to the Syrian Lebanese Mid-West Convention, Cleveland, August 4, 1973.

21. At its Nineteenth Annual Convention in Long Beach, California, August 29–September 1, 1970, the Organization of Arab Students stated that the Rogers Plan was an imperialist attempt to end the crisis in the area and to eliminate the revolutionary growth spearheaded by the Palestinian Resistance Movement.

22. "U.S. Arabs Mobilize to Form Lobby," p. 3.

change, and concern themselves with serving the interests of the Arab masses. Thus, at its Fifth Annual Convention, held in 1972, the AAUG stated its position:

> The Association reaffirms its unconditional support of the Palestinian Revolution and the inalienable right of the Palestinian people to engage in a war of national and social liberation for the establishment of a free, democratic, and secular State in Palestine.

U.S. GOVERNMENT SURVEILLANCE AND HARASSMENT OF ARAB-AMERICANS

By 1970 the Arab-Americans and Arabs in the United States were faced with a comprehensive campaign of investigation and surveillance carried out by a number of government agencies, including the Federal Bureau of Investigation, the Justice Department, and the Immigration Department. This campaign of "spying, wiretapping, and burglaries" was instituted on orders from the White House in an attempt to uncover the activities of so-called Arab saboteurs.[23] Leonard Garment, White House adviser for Jewish affairs, was ordered to contact Jewish intelligence to assist in this campaign of surveillance.

This campaign of harassment and intimidation came as no surprise to Arab activists. Since 1968, Zionist and pro-Israeli Jewish organizations in the United States have been pressing Congress and the White House for action against Arabs and Arab-Americans critical of Israel. The Zionists were not pleased with the activities of Arab-Americans and Arab students who were publicizing facts about Israeli policies in the newly occupied Arab lands. They made every effort to undermine these efforts and to link them to the activities of dissident American groups, such as the Black Panthers and the Students for a Democratic Society, in order to compel the Justice Department to take action against them.

The *Near East Report,* a pro-Israeli newsletter directed to congressmen, published a special survey in October, 1969, about the activities of

---

23. The *New York Times* published details from two White House classified documents about these plans for "counterinsurgency." The documents mentioned Arab students as spies because they were "pushing the Arab position" and gathering information to be used against Israel. The CIA, on the other hand, contradicted these White House documents and reported that it found no evidence that "students were involved in illegal activities." *New York Times,* May 24, 25, 1973.

Arabs in the United States and attempted to link these activities to the Fatah movement and to militant groups such as the Panthers and the SDS. The Anti-Defamation League of B'nai B'rith also waged a propaganda campaign in major newspapers in 1968 and 1969 to undermine Arab activities and to tie them to extremist and communist groups.[24] The Zionists and advocates of Israel were following a clever strategy in which activities critical of Israel were made to appear as if they threatened the security of the United States.

A number of pro-Israeli senators and representatives, pressured by these Zionist groups, began calling for the investigation of Arab students and Arab-American organizations. Rep. J. Burke (R., Fla.), in a letter to the Justice Department, charged that El Fatah was recruiting supporters among the militants.[25] Rep. Gerald Ford (R., Mich.) also made a number of statements, based on B'nai B'rith reports, accusing Arab students of being "Peking agents" and demanding government investigation of their activities.

These smear tactics employed by Zionist organizations were not successful. Arab students and Arab-American organizations were not involved in illegal activities. Their work was oriented toward assisting the Palestinians on the humanitarian level and informing the American public of the plight of the Palestinians under Israeli military rule.

It was not until 1972, as a precautionary reaction to the Munich incident, that the American government enacted the Boulder Operation.[26] The White House, moreover, established a committee headed by Ambassador Arvin Meyer to oversee the investigation of Arab-Americans and to coordinate the different departments involved in the so-called counterterrorism plans.

Leaders of Arab-American organizations, as well as Arab students and community leaders, found themselves subjected to extensive investigation by the FBI, the Immigration Department, and the Internal Revenue Service. These investigations employed extreme forms of harassment. Activist Arab-Americans were subjected to continuous surveillance; students' homes were entered and searched, and the students were put under "docket control" after their student visas had

---

24. "Arab Propaganda Campaign on the Campuses," *Near East Report*, October 29, 1969. Arnold Foster, general counsel of B'nai B'rith, made these allegations in a letter to the editor of the *New York Times*, May 28, 1969. See also *New York Times*, April 21, 1969.

25. *Near East Report*, May 31, 1969.

26. The Boulder Operation was a direct outgrowth of the Munich incident according to the *Sunday Star and Daily News* (Washington, D.C.), October 15, 1972. See also *New York Times*, October 5, 1972.

been revoked; activist students and Arab-Americans were taken to FBI headquarters for questioning.[27] These agencies also cooperated with Israeli intelligence agencies and provided them with information about the Arab-Americans and their activities. The *Washington Post* reported that the Israeli intelligence (Mosad) had the full cooperation of the CIA and the FBI. "According to the Israelis, the United States has shown great initiative in relaying intelligence and coordinating anti-terrorist techniques."[28]

The immediate effects of these policies on the Arab and Arab-American communities in the United States were significant. Many Arab-Americans began to withdraw from activities and organizations for fear of harassment and physical harm. Although Arab-Americans were involved in legal activities and were exercising their right to free speech, they chose to isolate themselves and not to exercise this right when faced with official harassment. The civil liberties and political rights of Arabs and Arab-Americans were thus threatened and, in fact, denied. The American Civil Liberties Union moved to protest these official measures of "investigation, interrogation and surveillance," and asserted in the *Sentinel,* October 17, 1973, that "there must not be the impression in the U.S. Arab community that public statements of support for the Arab position in the Arab-Israeli dispute will be reason enough for federal officers to take official interest in the spokesmen of these views.

A number of Arab-American organizations and Arab activists began a campaign protesting this denial of civil rights and this harassment. They formed committees to assist students and others in legal matters, and they published material to inform the Arab communities of their legal and constitutional rights. A number of American lawyers of Arab descent joined these committes and offered legal advice to Arabs having problems with the Immigration Department.

FUTURE PROBLEMS AND CHALLENGES

Since 1967, Arab Americans, whether assimilated Americans of Arab descent or recent immigrants, have begun to play an increasingly active

27. Larry Mosher documented cases of harassment in an article entitled "Arabs Taste U.S. Terror," *National Observer,* November 18, 1972. *Newsweek* also reported that federal agents broke into the Arab Information Center in Dallas, Texas, and stole a briefcase containing names of Americans "suspected of being pro-Fateh." *Newsweek,* June 18, 1973, p. 32.

28. "Israel Fighting Terror with Terror," *Washington Post,* October 15, 1972.

role in the United States. They have directed their energies and talents toward different, sometimes conflicting, goals ranging from humanitarian aid to the Palestinian refugees to informational work concerning the Arab cause and political support for the Palestinian movement and some of the Arab governments. This is being done through old and new organizations and clubs. Through these groupings Arab-American activists have attempted to mobilize their communities and direct their energies toward these different goals. They have begun to discover their Arab heritage and to rally for the defense and support of the Arab people in the Middle East.

Despite the progress that these organizations have made since 1971, they have been confronted with a number of external factors which have had an adverse effect on their activities. The campaign of surveillance and investigation by government agencies has created fear and confusion in Arab-American communities. Many Arab-Americans, not realizing that their civil rights were being violated, began to withdraw from active involvement in these organizations. The leadership reacted by organizing legal committees, publishing material to inform Arab-Americans of their legal rights, and protesting the anti-Arab policies.

In addition, the decline of the Palestinian movement in the Arab world and its liquidation in Jordan have had a significant effect on the Arab-American communities, which earlier had rallied in support of the Palestinians. By 1972 most Arab governments, including Lebanon, had begun to curb the activities of the Palestinian movement. The resulting clashes between the Arab regimes and the Palestinian resistance had an impact on Arab-American communities. A number of organizations committed to the Palestinian cause on the humanitarian level began to narrow their supportive activities. The decline of publications on Palestine reflected the reduced support for the Palestinian movement. Furthermore, the "energy crisis" in the United States generated a greater interest in Arab oil. Arab governments began to take more diplomatic initiative in solving the Arab-Israeli conflict.

This immediate change in the activities of Arab-Americans should not be interpreted as the beginning of a long-range trend. The basic challenges for Arab-Americans, and for Arabs in general, remain. The key issues continue to be the Israeli occupation of Arab territories and the oppression of Palestinians. American military and political commitment to Israeli superiority in the Middle East seems stronger than ever, while at the same time the Palestinian Resistance Movement and its supporters continue their struggle.

Arab-Americans committed to the goals of Arab liberation will continue to play a role in the United States. The effectiveness of this role, however, will depend on their ability to solve certain problems that have plagued Arab-American communities for a long time. These can be summed up as follows:

1. In order to play a more effective role, Arab-Americans must unify their rapidly multiplying organizations or create some kind of supervisory council to coordinate their activities. The fragmentation that exists in the Arab-American community has been one of the major causes of ineffectiveness and confusion. There are too many Arab and Arab-American organizations duplicating activities and thus wasting needed energy.

2. A number of existing Arab-American organizations have no base of support in the Arab-American communities. Such organizations revolve around one or two individuals. The community remains isolated from these groups, which, in turn, are unable to make full use of the community's financial and political power. Arab-American organizations must therefore give more attention to community-oriented programs and services. They must develop programs for the education and politicization of community members. The introduction of democratic means of participating in these organizations would also help to mobilize the Arab-American community and to make full use of its resources.

3. There is need to develop a broad program of action that would be the basis for unified and coordinated activities, of different orientations and ideas, within the Arab-American communities. Different schools of thought as to what should be done would therefore have to be reconciled. Different organizations could define their special spheres of action: some would concentrate on Congress and other policy-making institutions, others would deal with community-oriented programs, and others with raising funds and resources to support the Arab cause in the Middle East. This program must not be based on compromise that leads to inaction and deadlock, but on a commitment to basic human values and goals. Within this context, Arab-Americans would play a role in criticizing not only Israel but also those Arab governments that deny their citizens human and social rights and use oppressive means against popular movements. Arab-Americans would support the struggle of the Palestinian people for liberation and freedom, as well as the struggle of other people for these same rights. And Arab-Americans would play a role within the American political system reflecting their commitment to these ideals of human justice and freedom.

PART V: ARABS AND JEWS: POSSIBILITY OF CONCORD

Daniel Berrigan, S.J.

RESPONSES TO SETTLER REGIMES

I COME BEFORE YOU this evening as a nonexpert in every field of human expertise, including the subject you have invited me to explore. I wish to include also in my field of inexpertise my own religious tradition; I am a nonexpert Christian, by any conceivable standard.

This admission is in the interests of both clarity of mind and moral conduct. I am interested, as a Christian, in one thing only; in so simple a thing as sane conduct in the world. The experts in my tradition, the theologians, the biblical scholars, and, by and large, the hierarchy, go in another direction than mine. "Sane conduct" (whatever that means) is taken for granted; what really counts is the jot and tittle of the tradition, or its worldly prospering, or its honorable reception among peoples. Sane conduct is taken for granted; are not Christians by definition sane, in touch with the truth, destined to share infallibly in their reward?

I say no. The exemplary conduct of expert Christians, as indeed of most experts in human disciplines, is to fiddle while the world burns. Hardly sane! A kind of lethal fatalism looks equably upon combustible human flesh, shrugs its shoulders the better to nestle the violin and coax from its entrails the immortal (and irrelevant) stroke.

Sane conduct in the world. Let me explain. I do not believe it is the destiny of human flesh to burn; and for that I am in trouble, as are my friends, to this day. I do not believe that a violin concerta, however immortal in execution, is the proper comfort to offer a napalmed child. I believe that the fiddler should come down from the roof, put his violin aside, take up an extinguisher, raise a cry of alarm, break down the intervening door. I believe that he should on occasion of crisis destroy property in favor of human life.

You see, I am a heretic in a consuming and killing culture, as well as in a complicit church.

These are troublesome statements; but do not call them naive, or shrug them off as generally accepted by the civilized—or, in the presence of scholars, as irrelevant. Do not say: It is of course the generals who light fires; we deplore that. I answer: Most scholars, most priests, most Jews, most Arabs, while they would prefer some less horrendous sight than the burning flesh of children, are not seriously shaken in their style of mind, their taxpaying, their consumerism, their spiritual, economic, or political complicity, by such "incidents."

I begin in so odious a way because I do not wish to narrow our question so sharply as to exclude ourselves from its orbit. I do not wish to take us off the hook, even while I wish to say something unequivocal about one instance of cruelty, racism, murder, as political tools.

It is of course scarcely possible to open the moral question of Israeli or Arab conduct today without exciting the most lively passion and risking the most serious charges. A war is under way. We are assured by the Israelis, and by most of the Jewish community throughout the world, that the war is a war of survival. We are assured just as vehemently by the Arabs that the war is one of expansion and aggression by Israel.

Moreover, the interests of the superpowers are deeply imbedded in Near Eastern soil. Those interests include Western oil contracts and, East and West, an impalpable element of outreach, something hard to define, a cold-war afflatus perhaps, something called an "ideological sphere of influence." In any case, both East and West are shoring up their interests with that most concrete and bloody proof of devotion: arms, and more arms.

Certainly these facts must be respected if this evening and the days to follow are to be more than an exercise in national or racial or religious frenzy. A ceasefire has been offered by Egypt; something uprecedented in the history of this conflict. Moreover, the terms of the ceasefire seem reasonable and clear of Arab arms-rattling. The offering includes a declaration of de facto respect for the existence of Israel, a de facto state; it asks for a return to the boundary lines which existed before the 1967 war, and some justice for the Palestinian people.

In the seriousness and sanity of the ceasefire offer, therefore, I believe that events themselves are helping set the stage for a fruitful study.

In supporting the Egyptian proposal, I hope to answer those who would make the present war into an Israeli spasm of survival. Nothing of the sort. Or those who would make the critics of this war into proponents of Israeli extinction. Nothing of the kind. Or those who would make critics of the United States into supporters of the Soviet Union. Nothing of the sort.

In calling attention to this proposal I am simply urging that attention be paid to the first sane option that has arisen in the course of this suicidal adventure. Indeed there are no sides worth talking about tonight. There are indeed immense numbers of people whose lives and rights are being violated, degraded, and denied. Any real solution will take into account these peoples: the Palestinians, a people without a country; the Iraelis, a people in danger; the Arab nations, a people invaded. How carefully one must proceed on these matters if he is not to worsen an already tortured situation. I endorse the Egyptian ceasefire proposal while opposing many aspects of the Egyptian regime, and of the sheikhdoms, and of Jordan and Syria. We must take into account their capacity for deception, which is remarkable even for our world. We must take into account their contempt for their own poor, a contempt that would be called legendary if it were not horrifyingly modern. We must take into account their willingness to oil the war machinery of the superpowers, making them accomplices of the American war criminals. We must take into account their cupidity masked only by their monumental indifference to the facts of their world. No, I offer no apologia tonight for the Arab states any more than I do for Israel.

I do not wish to begin by "taking sides"; nor, indeed, to end by "taking sides." I am sick of "sides"; which is to say, I am sick of war, of wars hot and cold, and all their approximations and metaphors and deceits and ideological ruses. I am sick of the betrayal of the mind and the failure of compassion and the neglect of the poor. I am sick of foreign ministers and all their works and pomps. I am sick of torture and secret police and the apparatus of fascists and the rhetoric of leftists. Like Lazarus staggering from his grave, or the ghost of Trotsky, I can only groan: "We have had enough of that. We have been through all that."

Thus this evening, and my presence here. When I received the invitation some months ago, I winced. Another crisis? If the nerve ends of Israelis and Arabs were raw, so were mine. More, why should I enter their back yard on a cleanup project when my own, America, was a moral shantytown? And the war broke, and I winced again and very nearly begged off. Then a better, second thought occurred, something like this. If it was important to speak while the peace—at least a relative peace—held, then why not when a war broke? Indeed, did not the need for dispassionate and reasonable courage increase while the guns were cutting down whatever rational exchange remained alive? If the first casualty of war was the truth, might it not be important to prevent, at least on one scene, that mortal casualty from occurring?

I do not wish to heap conflict upon conflict. If I seem to concentrate upon the conduct of Israel, it is for reasons which, to me at least, are profound, of long pondering, and finally inescapable. It is not merely because my government, which has brought endless suffering to the world, is supporting Israel. It is not merely because American Jews, as well as Israelis, have, in the main, given their acquiescence or their support to the Nixon ethos. The reasons go deeper and strike harder. They are lodged in my soul, in my conception of faith and the transcendent, in the vision Jews have taught me of human conduct in a human community.

I am (to put the matter as simply as I know how) paying an old debt tonight. It is a debt of love—more properly, a debt of outraged love. I am a Western Christian in resistance against my government and my church. That position, as I read it, makes me something very like a Jew. It is of that uneasy circle, ever changing, widening, contracting, including, excluding, that I wish to speak. I am a Catholic priest in resistance against Rome. I am an American in resistance against Nixon. And I am a Jew in resistance against Israel. But let me begin.

A common assumption exists in the West, buttressed by massive historical and religious argument, to the effect that Israel is exempt from moral criticism. Her people have passed through the Gentile furnace. How then shall the goy judge the suffering servant? And is not the holocaust the definitive argument for the righteousness of this people, heroically determined to begin again, in a promised land, that experiment in survival which so nearly went awry, so often, under such constant assault at our hands?

In such a way, bad history is mightily reinforced by bad faith. The persecutor is a poor critic. His history weighs on him. Like a bad parent, he alternates between cruelty and indulgence without ever striking the mean of love.

In such a way, Christians yield to Israel the right to her myths, to indulge them, to enlarge them, to live by them, even to call them biblical truth. If the Jews are indeed the people of promise, and Israel the land of promise, then it must follow that God has willed the two to coincide. The means? They are swallowed up in the end. They disappear into glory. And if the means include domestic repression, deception, cruelty, militarism? And if the classic refugee people is now creating huge numbers of refugees? And if technological warfare has become the instrument of expansion, and preemptive warfare the instrument of so-called peace? And if this people, so proud, so endowed with intelligence, so purified by suffering, sends its military missioners into every part of the world where minority people are bleeding under the heel of jackboots? (Israeli military advisers in Iran, Israeli military advisers in Ethiopia.) And if these advisers (that cruel euphemism under whose guise America kindled the Viet Nam holocaust) are sought and hired because Israelis have become as skilled in the fashioning of espionage and violence as ever were their oppressors? Are such means as these swallowed in glory? Or do they stick in the throat of those who believe, as Judaism taught the world to believe, Thou shalt not kill?

I started to say something about my own church, and I proceed to talk about Israel. I did so advisedly. I did so because today my church has helped Israel in that project which is almost invariably the project of the settler state—whether of South Africa or Israel or the United States—namely, to seek a biblical justification for crimes against humanity.

For a Christian who is trying to understand and live by his own tradition, the confusion of Bible and imperialism in Israel represents an altogether unique tragedy. We in the U.S.A. learned to bear the filthy weight of South African religious violence, even while we abominated it. We learned to survive the filthy weight of American religious violence, even while we abominated it. In both cases, we tried to separate out the corrupt cultural elements from the truth of a tradition and to live by the latter. We learned to do this because we knew at least something of the history of Christianity, in both its criminal and its saintly aspects.

But you must understand our horror, our sense of impoverishment, almost our sense of amputation. For while we had known criminal Christian communities, and suffered at the hand of our own renegades, and seen Viet Nam assaulted in the name of Christian civilization—we had never known a criminal Jewish community. We had known Jewish communities that were a light to the Gentiles, that were persecuted, all but erased, that remained merciful, eloquent, prophetic. But something new was occurring before our eyes. The Jews arose from the holocaust, a cause of universal joy; but the Jews arose like warriors, armed to the teeth. They took possession of a land. They exiled and destroyed old Arab communities. They (a minority) made outsiders of those who were, in fact, the majority of citizens. Then, they flexed their muscles. Like the goyim, the idolators, the "inhabitants of this earth," like Babylon and Egypt and Assyria, like those kingdoms which Israel's own prophets summoned to judgment, Israel entered the imperial adventure. She took up the imperial weapons. She spread abroad the imperial deceptions.

In the space of 25 years, this metamorphosis took place. The wandering Jew became the settler Jew; the settler ethos became the imperial adventure. More, the thought of Nietzsche, of Camus, and of Fanon was vindicated: the slave became master, and created slaves. The slave master created a "shadowy other." Israel had emerged from the historical shadows determined to take her place in the company of nations, an ambition no decent conscience could object to. But the price of her emergence was bitter and heavy; and it continues. That price, indeed, neither Israel nor ourselves have yet counted up. But we do know a few of the human items who have been placed on the block of Israeli hegemony. They include some one and a half million refugees, whom Israel has created in the process of creating herself.

And let us not hesitate to state the price in Israeli coinage. Something like this: not only a dismal fate for foreign and indigenous victims, but a failure to create new forms of political and social life for her own citizens. The coinage of Israel is stamped with the imperialist faces whose favor she has courted, the creation of an elite of millionaires, generals, and entrepreneurs. And the price is being paid by Israel's Oriental Jews, the poor, the excluded, prisoners. Do we seek analogies for this "sublime adventure of return"? They are not hard to come by. But they do not exist, alas, in the dreams of Zionist rhetoricians; they exist, rather, in the real world, where Zionist violence and repression join the violence and repression of the great (and little) powers. A common method, a common dead end.

It is entirely logical, for instance, that Russia, which crushed the Czechs, is now in the process of crushing the Ukrainians and bottling the brains of political dissidents on the shelves of psychiatric morgues. It is entirely logical that the U.S., which determined to crush the Vietnamese, also spent a considerable part of the sixties "mopping up" political dissidents at home. Imperialism has no favorites; it freezes all it touches. It is thus not to be wondered at that torture has been applied to Israeli citizens as well as to suspect Palestinian terrorists. It is logical that Israeli workers are exploited, even while indigenous peasants are rooted out and their villages destroyed. Logical, too, that racist ideology, which brought the destruction of the Jewish communities at the hands of the Nazis, should now be employed by the state of Israel, fostering the myth of the "barbarian Arab," and of Israel as the "sublime expression of the liberation of the Jewish people."

If only a people could know itself! If only a people could stand back from the welter of claim, the barrage of propaganda, the blood myths of divine election, the rhetoric which assures it that its case before history is unique and virtuous and, in fact, unassailable! If that could happen, Israel would see—as indeed some of her own resisters, some of her own victims, some of her own friends, do see—that she is rapidly evolving into the image of her ancient adversaries; that her historic adventure, which gave her the unassailable right to "judge the nations," has veered off into an imperial misadventure; that she carries, in the world, the stigmata of the settler nation; that she is ranged not at the side of those she once stood with and succored and protected from extinction—the poor, the despised, the victims of the powers of this world.

No. She has closed those books, her sacred books. Her prophets shed no light upon her politics. Or more exactly to the point, she has not passed from a dispossessed people to a democratic state, as she would claim; she has passed from a dispossessed people to an imperial entity.

And this (I say it with a sinking heart) is to the loss of all the world: to her own loss, and to the loss of Palestinians, and Americans, and Jews in the Diaspora, and Jews in Russia, and the Pope in the Vatican, and Vietnamese, and Cambodians, and South Africans, and Chileans. For it is of moment to us all (I almost said of supreme moment) that Jews retain their own soul, their own books, their own vivid sense of alternate paths to the light, so that Jews might be the arbiter and advocate of the downtrodden of the earth. On the scales of the spirit, as the nations are finally judged, it is a tragedy beyond calculating, that the state of Israel should become the repository, and finally the tomb, of the Jewish soul; that in place of Jewish compassion, Israel should legislate armaments and yet more armaments; that in place of Jewish passion for the poor and forgotten, Israel should legislate evictions, uprootings, destruction of goods, imprisonment, terrorism; that in place of Jewish peaceableness, Israel should legislate a law of expanding violence; that in place of Jewish prophetic wisdom, Israel should launch an Orwellian nightmare of double talk, racism, fifth-rate sociological jargon, aimed at proving her racial superiority to the people she has crushed.

My sense of loss here is something more than academic. Let me say this: When an American is resisting the murder of the Vietnamese people, one of his chief sources of strength is the conviction that around the world there exists a spiritual network of those who have put their lives to the same resistance. A network of conscience. One is joined in this way to Blacks and Cubans and Brazilians and Chileans and so many others who have made it their life's work to create a better method than murder for dealing with human conflict.

Now at any moment of my struggle, in the underground or in prison, did resisters such as I take comfort from the conduct of the state of Israel? Could we believe the rhetoric that she was packaging and huckstering in the world? I must answer no, in the name of all. Rather than being comforted, I was tempered and sobered. I knew that I must take into account two bitter facts about Israel: (1) that if I were a conscientious Jew in Israel I would have to live as I was living in America—that is, in resistance against the state; and (2) that the reaction of Israel to my conscience would be exactly the reaction of the United States—that is to say, I would either be hunted by the police or be in prison.

Which brings me to a reflection nearer home: the American Jewish community and the Viet Nam war. By and large, that community's leadership—I stress leadership—fervent in support of Israel, was also fervent in support of Nixon. It was a massive support indeed; and it did not gather in a political vacuum. Nixon is a political manipulator of great astuteness; religion and religious interests are part of the fulcrum he exerts on world events. So he was able to mute the horrific facts of the Viet Nam War in light of Jewish concern for the well-being of Israel. The plain fact was that Mrs. Meir wanted Phantom jets and Nixon wanted re-election. Another fact was also plain, if of less moment to either party: in Nixon's first term alone some six million Southeast Asians had been maimed, bombed, displaced, tortured, imprisoned, or killed. This was one of those peculiar facts which must be called free-floating. It was a statistic; it did not signify. To put the matter brutally, many American Jewish leaders were capable of ignoring the Asian holocaust in favor of economic and military aid to Israel. Those of us who resisted the war had to live with that fact. The fate of the Vietnamese was as unimportant to the Zionists in our midst as was the state of the Palestinians.

But I venture to suggest that it is not merely we, nor the Vietnamese, who must live with that fact. So must Israel. So must the American Jews.

If there is an ultimate hope in all this, one must, of course, pay tribute to the great majority of the Jewish community, which refused the bait offered by Nixon and peddled by their own leaders. Their acute and legitimate concern for Israel never became a weapon against Vietnamese survival. They refused that immoral choice offered them by a leader who would make a price of the safety of one people, the extinction of another. As you may recall, the American Jewish community rejected that choice, and for that we must honor them.

I cannot but reflect how strong is the irony of this occasion: a Jesuit priest speaking of the sins of Israel. A member of the classic oppressor church calls to account the historic victims of Christian persecution. History has spun us about, a game of blind man's buff. In America, in my church, I am a Jew. I am scarcely granted a place to teach, a place to worship, a place to announce the truths I live by. I stand in front of St. Patrick's Cathedral to pray for the victims of our ceaseless rage. I stand in front of the White House. And a question arises from both powers: How shall we deal with this troublesome Jew?

How does a Jesuit, a member of the church elite, come to such trouble? How does the son of the oppressor come to be oppressed—even while the oppressed, the Zionist, the state of Israel, becomes the oppressor? I can offer only the clumsiest of clues.

The power of the Jew, as indeed the power of the priest, arises from the questions which his life raises. It comes from no other source. It cannot come from adherence to the power of this world. When the priest becomes a secular nonentity, his passion for justice is blunted, his sense of the sufferings of the world grows dim and abstract. And the same holds for the Jew.

And, I venture, for the Arab. Human life today, if it means anything, is meant to raise a cry against legitimated murder. Our lives are meant to be a question mark before humanity, whether we are Arab, Jew, or Christian. When a Zionist or an American Catholic or an Arab Apologist loses that momentous dignity, he becomes a zero; his soul is torn in two. Let Amos Kenan, the Israeli writer, speak the bitter truth: "I believe that Zionism came to establish a shelter for a persecuted people, and not to persecute other people. Even when facts strike me in the face and prove to me ex post facto that Zionism was nothing but a useful tool to deprive the Palestinian Arab people of their homeland, I will stick to the lie."

Let him stick to the lie. But let him also know, the lie sticks to him. It sticks in the throat. It sticks to the very soul—to the point where a Christian must continue to ask of Israel those questions which Israel proscribes, ignores, fears. Where indeed are your men of wisdom? Where are your peacemakers? Where are your prophets? Who among you speaks the truth to power? Where are the voices that abhor militarism, torture, bombing, degrading alliances with the great powers? Israel knows the answer. She has dealt with "this people," who are her truest people. Her peacemakers, her men of truth and wisdom, are dispensed with, are disposed of. They have neither power nor voice in the affairs of the Israeli state. Many of them are in prison or, hounded from the scene, are living in exile. They are equivalent to Palestinians: no voice, no vote—non-persons.

These are among the most sorrowful facts of the world we live in. Israel, that millennial dream, belonged not only to Jews but to all of mankind—it belonged to me. But the dream has become a nightmare. Israel has not abolished poverty and misery; rather, she manufactures human waste, the by-products of her entrepreneurs, her military-industrial complex. Israel has not written justice into law; she has turned the law of nature into a mockery, creating ghettos, disenfranchised peoples, exiles, hopeless minorities, cheap labor forces, Palestinian migrant workers. Israel has not freed the captives; she has expanded the prison system, perfected her espionage, exported on the world market that expensive bloodridden commodity, the savage triumph of the technologized West—violence and the tools of violence.

In Israel, military might is increasingly both the method and the goal of political existence. Her absurd generals, her military junk, are paraded on national holidays before the narcoticized public. The model is not the kingdom of peace; it is an Orwellian transplant, taken bodily from Big Brother's bloody heart. In Israel, the democratic formula is twisted out of all recognition. The citizens exist for the well-being of the state. It follows, as the imperialist corollary, that that measure of terrorism and violence and murder is applied to dissidents as shall guarantee the "well-being of the state," as the ominous phrase is understood by those in power.

Who will save us from such saviors? I venture to say: neither Egypt nor Libya nor Syria nor Al Fatah nor Golda Meir nor General Dayan; neither Migs nor Phantom jets nor nuclear skills. After such saviors do the Gentiles lust.

The present course, I suggest, leads to the same dead end for both sides. The settler state and the long-settled state, both are in mortal danger, daily increasing, of metamorphosing into slave states, clients of the fascist superpowers. At home, a slave mentality is progressively created: the reduction of rights of citizens, slave labor forces, slave wages, the domination of slave masters, politicized police, the militarization of national goals and policies.

Then the same process is internationalized. Such a nation inevitably becomes the instrument of great-power politics. It serves as a foreign military base for one or another of the world powers; to that purpose everything is mobilized, including the truth itself.

To demobilize the truth may be one useful way of putting our task. Other terms occur: to demilitarize the truth, to demythologize it. In any case, to snatch the truth from its betrayers and belittlers. I wish you well in the task.

Dear Friends, my concluding words are addressed especially to the Arab peoples. My argument with you is also made in a spirit of love and deep concern. You have suffered greatly from colonialism and colonization, and your demand for justice and self-determination deserves more attention than it has received. Yet my central argument with you is ultimately my argument with the Jewish people, in the sense that both of you have ignored your own symbols and history. But in different ways. Israel has betrayed her exodus by turning it into military conquests. And the Arabs have often betrayed their resistance to rhetorical violence and blind terrorism. The question of the weekend is: What else can we do?

Some two or three years ago Eqbal Ahmad suggested—I believe, at one of these meetings—a massive and worldwide reversal of symbols on the part of the Palestinian people. If I understand him correctly, he was saying something like this: What if the Arabs throughout the world would raise a great cry and implement their cry after the manner of Gandhi and Martin Luther King and Cesar Chavez? What if your cry became "Let my people go"? What if your people equipped boats to enter Israeli harbors to speak the truth and implement the Palestinians' right to return? What if you were to begin knocking on doors of the embassies—Russian, American, and Israeli—demanding the restoration of your rights and your homes, taking into account, at the same time, Jewish fears—welcoming Jews to a community of compassion, welcoming Israel's people to your side, among your people?

Edward W. Said

ARABS AND JEWS

During 1970 and 1971, reasonably articulate Arabs in the United States were frequently asked to participate in public discussions on the Middle East question. On one such occasion I was preceded to the lectern by an Israeli speaker who, I thought, had the lack of irony to say that it was the Arabs who had always seen themselves as chosen people. This heedless remark was a later embarrassment to him as a Jew, and it was easy to mock him with his own observation. This incident perhaps is not of tremendous value now; but it does come to mind, particularly during these anxious and confusing days of Arab-Israeli war. You begin to realize that what, as an intellectual of secular persuasion, you have always believed, that there is no such thing as a divinely chosen race, has a disquieting additional meaning. No, the Jews are not a chosen people, but Jews and Arabs together, one as oppressor and the other as oppressed, have chosen each other for a struggle whose roots seem to grow deeper and whose future seems less thinkable and less resolvable with each year. Neither people can develop without the other there, harassing, taunting, fighting; no Arab today has an identity that can be unconscious of the Jew, that can rule out the Jew as a psychic factor in the Arab identity; conversely, I think, no Jew can ignore the Arab in general, nor can he immerse himself in his ancient tradition and so lose the Palestinian Arab in particular and what Zionism has done to him. The more intense these modern struggles for identity become, the more attention is paid by the Arab or the Jew to his chosen opponent, or partner. Each is the other.

I can recall that as a child in Palestine and Egypt, before 1948, the foreigners by whom I was surrounded here and there stood out with a hard and almost cold difference from me. The Englishman, the Frenchman, and the Greek had recognizable patterns of speech, dress, gestures, and so on. Yet the Jew, whether he was Egyptian, Palestinian, Italian, or British, seemed to seep through those harder identities and be mixed up with mine. Usually, of course, nothing was said, but there was a felt correspondence between us nevertheless. Maybe this experience was not common to many Arabs: I do not know. Now, however, there is a corporate Arab-Jewish identity, so overlaid with events, with insults, war, humiliations, and fear, with all those seeming inevitabilities; but there are only the rarest occasions for judging how, in victimizing each other—most often at the instigation of imperialist powers—we have shared little except conflict and a gradually diminished human reality.

Every Arab has his own national identity to protect his spirit from the fraying ordeals of Arabism-Israelism, that ugly padlock of one-against-one tension. For the Egyptian there is an unbroken national history that has endured for eighty centuries; this is a sovereign life whose richness astounded even Herodotus. For the Palestinian, perforce, his national identity is an embattled resistance to dispossession and extinction; yet for most of the world he has seemed like cigarette ash, moved from corner to corner, threatened always with irreversible dispersion. How many partisans of Jewish immigration to Israel recognize that each penny spent for that purpose also buys a Palestinian more time as an exile from his country?

However, all Arabs have suffered, both in the Middle East and in the West. The Arab is seen as the disrupter of Israel's existence, or, in a larger view, as a surmountable obstacle to Israel's creation in 1948. This has been part of the Zionist attitude toward the Arab, especially in the years before 1948, when Israel was being promulgated ideologically. Palestine was imagined as an empty desert waiting to burst into bloom, its inhabitants minimized as inconsequential nomads possessing no stable claim to the land and therefore no cultural permanence. At worst, the Arab today is conceived of as a bloody-minded shadow that dogs the Jew and that interrupts the smoothly flowing "democracy" of Israeli life. In that shadow—because Arab and Jew are Semites—can be placed whatever latent mistrust the Westerner still feels toward the Jew. The Jew of pre-Nazi Europe has split in two: a Jewish hero, constructed out of a revived cult of the adventurer-pioneer, and the Arab, his creeping, mysteriously fearsome shadow. Thus isolated from his past, the Arab has seemed condemned to provide local color, to be chastised at the hands of Israeli soldiers and tourists, to be kept in his place by American Phantom jets, American cluster bombs and napalm, and UJA money.

Let me digress here for a moment to point out that the Arabs and Islam have always been a singular problem for the largely Christian West. As an intance there is the attitude of the West to Islam during the Middle Ages, the great age of Islamic civilization, roughly from the ninth through the eleventh centuries. This attitude is the subject of a book by the Chichele Professor of Modern History at Oxford, R. W. Southern, *Western Views of Islam during the Middle Ages* (Cambridge, Mass: Harvard University Press, 1962). To the Western thinkers who tried to understand Islam and the Arab achievement, a great problem constantly supervened: how to explain a religion, a society, a civilization which in many ways paralleled that of the Christian West, yet which was, on the one hand, immeasurably more mature and powerful, and, on the other hand, immeasurably different and non-Christian. "In understanding Islam," Southern says,

> the West could get no help from antiquity, and no comfort from the present. For an age avowedly dependent on the past for its materials, this was a serious matter. Intellectually the nearest parallel to the position of Islam was the position of the Jews. They shared many of the same tenets and brought forward many of the same objections to Christianity. But Christian thinkers had at their disposal an embarrassing wealth of material for answering the Jewish case; and the economic and social inferiority of the Jews encouraged the view that their case could be treated with disdain. Nothing is easier than to brush aside the arguments of the socially unsuccessful, and we can see this verified in the melancholy history of the Jewish controversy in the Middle Ages. . . . But Islam stubbornly resisted this treatment. It was immensely successful. Every period of incipient breakdown was succeeded by a period of astonishing and menacing growth. Islam resisted both conquest and conversion, and it refused to wither away [pp. 4–5].

Even during the comparatively remote period of which Southern speaks we have the Western habit of associating the unfamiliar with the inferior—how ironically prophetic of the Arab-Israeli conflict of today, and of the implicit attitude of identifying Jew with Arab.

I point this out with the intention only of showing that the relation between Islam and Arabs on the one hand and the West on the other has a long and unhappy history. Not infrequently, as Southern says, Judaism and Islam were considered together, as more or less interchangeable problems. In referring to all this it is by no means my intention to characterize the present political relationship between Arabs, Jews, and the West as something reducible to a doctrinal problem in the Middle Ages. I wish only to show that the impoverishment of the Arab and of Islam, as well as of Judaism, at the hands of the Christian West has behind it a long and complex background of unsatisfactory dealings. In part it is this background which illuminates the commonly accepted view of the Arab that is found in the West today, where the Israeli appears as the champion of Westernism and modernity and democracy, while the Arab is subservient, obscure, and strangely to be feared.

Even though, as I write these remarks, the war from the Arab viewpoint seems to be going better than one had expected—and it would be hypocritical for an Arab to deny his sense of restored self-esteem—there are strong reasons for thinking of this war in particular as a very dangerous business indeed. I am not thinking exclusively, or even principally, about dangers of its escalating into World War III, or of the increased risk of superpower confrontation. It is entirely to have been expected that the United States would request funds for aid to Israel and for Cambodia simultaneously, and that President Nixon would use the war to divert attention from his shady misadventures. The risks taken by superpowers, the mindlessness and the lack of respect for human issues, are risks, of course; but at this point they seem to me less immediate than other ones. For so unusual and eccentric a conflict as the one between the Arabs and Israel breeds unusual and eccentric consequences. In the past, and even now, one such consequence has been the total absence of engagement; each side has denied the other, each in its own way. Since 1967 this has been far less true of the Arabs than of the Israelis; I think that one can say this as an Arab quite honestly, without fear of being accused of being biased by nationalist pride. From the governments to the people, there seemed to be a growing willingness, perhaps because there was no real option, to deal with the unpleasant fact of Israel's presence. It is probably this willingness that accounts for the far more popular and determined sort of struggle that Arabs are presently waging on the field. At last the Arabs have discovered that Israel, and Israel's strength, are *real*, which means that Israel can be fought, and can be fought bravely if necessary. There is no mythology here.

For the Israeli since 1967 there seemed to have emerged two kinds of Arabs: one, the intransigent, rebellious type of fellow, the so-called terrorist, the wicked enemy of Israel; and, two, the good Arab, the reasonable man, with whom it was always pleasant to flirt, to exchange left-wing ideas, dovish sentiment, and so on. Yet in neither case was there a determination to open up the questions about which the conflict, from the Arab side at least, turned; there was no willingness, for example, to discuss seriously the rights of the Palestinians, except after all the pieties about Jewish statehood had been pronounced, all the necessities of maintaining the Law of Return and other undiscussable privileges of that sort. All talk of the rights of Palestinians was thereafter invalidated, and such talk seemed only to be a way of standing with Israel's strength and, at the same time, maintaining a good conscience.

If this seems too harsh a statement, and if it discounts too much the often courageous stand of those Israelis who were critical of their government policy of illegal occupation of Arab territories, denial of the Palestinians' existence, and so on, nevertheless I believe it is right to say that such positions were always hampered in Israel by something called "realism." "Realism" dictated that to talk at all of seriously modifying the immigration laws and the completely Jewish institutions of the state was tantamount to being a fool or a knave or a traitor or all three. To be realistic, one was very often told by realists, was to take into consideration the country's mood, the fervent nationalism, the unchangeable characteristics of the state of Israel as it was presently constituted, and even Jewish racism. Those were things about which one was not supposed to argue since they had the force of reality, of history, and—even though it was not always mentioned—the force of military power. Realism, therefore, was the uncrossable line, rather like that formidable Bar-Lev line, which assured one that here, at last, was something absolutely secure and powerful; and this line—far more than Arab good intentions or promises or whatever—guaranteed reality. So one could discuss Palestinian rights as one could discuss the question of the annexation of the Sinai, as a choice one might or might not make, depending on the attractiveness of the argument put forward on its behalf, and, above all, depending on its realism.

Many former doves in Israel, and perhaps in America, now see that they were wrong and unrealistic—that is, if what they had argued for had become state policy, then Israel (so they say) would now be fighting Arabs in the streets of Tel Aviv. As an instance, there appeared in the *New York Times* of October 17, 1973, a letter signed by a whole team of former doves, including Shlomo Avineri, Jacob Talmon, and Gershom Scholem. Here are some typical excerpts:

> We, the undersigned, have always used our right as free men to express our views on our country's policies, both external and internal; and some of us have disagreed with some of these policies in the past. The real

issue today, as it was in 1967, is the determination by Egypt and Syria to destroy Israel. . . .

The Egyptian and Syrian attack against us on the Day of Atonement has led us to the painful conclusion that the policy of the present governments of the Arab states is to go to any length to destroy Israel. . . .

The Arab doctrine of prior agreement by Israel to withdraw from territory is illogical and unacceptable. Every one of us is wholly convinced that our very existence today is due to the fact that this doctrine was rejected by us. The way in which the Egyptian and Syrian attack was prepared and launched must convince the world that this rejection was thoroughly justified.

This is a very strange realism indeed. For the state policy was precisely *not* to yield an inch, not to engage the Arabs in any serious way except as bodies to be raped and spaces to be entered violently at will; and it was that same realistic policy that led to the present war. For instead of seeing that the realism of the situation since 1967 is that one cannot, by sheer sightless force, impose one's will on anyone, no matter how badly beaten, the neorealists call for more, not less, stubbornness and realism of the old variety. As if all the bombing done by the Nazis in World War II, and all the U.S. bombing in Viet Nam, had any effect but to strengthen the people's will to resist. As if the Bar-Lev line was anything more than an invitation to Egypt to cross it and to attempt, rightfully, to retake its occupied territory. *This* realism is missing from the conflict even now. And it is this missing realism, this missing chapter in the history of Israel's existence among the Arabs, that is very dangerous.

All of us in the United States have witnessed the sometimes appalling spectacle and sound of media coverage of the present conflict. Most of the time it seems as if we are watching a football game, with favorites and villains, home teams and visitors, or as if we are watching a horse opera, with marshals, Indians, and bad guys. Language is completely out of touch with reality. Arabs, always mobs of them, faceless, voiceless, dark, and frightening, are always *claiming* to have done something. Israelis, who look like Bohemians of some sort, are *doing* things; the interviews are uniformly of some clever glib fellow, like General Herzog, or a friendly infantryman from the Bronx. Bombing, napalming, strafing of Arabs is perfectly acceptable, for is it not with Arabs, as with subhuman others, that American bombs were designed to deal, keeping American hands clean? How hard it is to watch the silent faces of Arab suffering on the anonymous, ruthless face of American TV! When the Israelis cross the Golan Heights, they are going "into Syria," as if the Golan was somewhere else. One is constantly struck by one theme: the hardship endured by the Israelis, and always their hope and optimism. This is no war; it is a pastime: at least that is the impression one gets, that fighting Arabs is like ridding the back yard of a few miscellaneous pests. On one occasion during the second week of the war, an irrepressible CBS reporter stepped up to an obviously dead-tired Israeli soldier (an American) and asked him whether, after eleven days in the field, it was worth it. "Yes," came back the answer. "If it's the last time, anything is worth it." Earlier in the war the answer was not quite so weary; one heard remarks like, "It'll be over in a couple of days," "We'll break their bones," "We'll be home for the weekend." But later, a more resigned note crept in: for the last time, anything is worth the effort. There are several possible interpretations of this change in tone. But mainly, I think, one gets the feeling that the realism of the present situation is that once we beat the Arabs this time, they will never dare come near us again.

Let me give one more example of this realism, or, rather, this extraordinary absence of realism. One of the classical texts on Zionism is Arthur Hertzberg's anthology, *The Zionist Idea, A Historical Analysis and Reader* (New York: Meridian Books, 1960). The book is a six-hundred-page compilation of excerpts from the principal figures in the history of Zionism, from Alkali and Kalischer to Ben Gurion, Silver, and Weizmann. The readings cover a span of about a hundred years, precisely those years during which Zionism went from a theory to a movement. An astounding fact is that in this six-hundred-page book there are scarcely a dozen pages that refer to Arabs, that so much as mention them as in some way constituting, for a part of the hundred years in question, half and more than half of the question of Palestine. This book was not hastily thrown together. It was intended to provide a reliable and scholarly guide to the most representative as well as the best of Zionist thought. Yet this book, like the major thrust of Zionism, has practically nothing to say about the Arabs, whose presence in Palestine must have reminded the Zionists from time to time of another people on the land, and there for a long time. Aside from Magnes, Jabotinsky, and Buber, the thinkers, ideologists, and theorists whom Hertzberg anthologizes consider Arabs as less than an incidental difficulty to the Jewish question, which is remarkable for the sustained and often profound attention it receives.

This is "realism." And behind this sort of thought and practice is an even more intensified disengagement from reality. Can anyone seriously believe that another defeat will make all Arabs stop bothering

Israel and go away? Yes, people seriously believe that. Even a whole nation believes that. Has it occurred to no one to say to those people that if you beat the Arabs this time, the next time will be sooner than you expect; that continued tyranny does not break the will or the back of a people, but that popular resistance grows, rather than lessens, with every blow? Even American intellectuals, who had the freedom to make these truths apparent, never, or very rarely, did—once again, because in the interests of realism it was better to repeat the tired truths of official Israeli realism.

But to be honest with ourselves as well, we must state what, in this war, is a threat to us. It is not that we might lose, for we have learned how to deal with defeat. It is that, like the Israelis, we will start to believe that our Middle East can be restored to us, either by war or by negotiation, as a pristine, unspotted land, free of its past enemies, ours for the taking. That is out of the question. There is no future that is entirely free of the past; and, without an adequate understanding of the present, there is no future at all. For the Arab today there must be an understanding that years and years of war with the Israelis, possibly with the great powers as well, will not, in the end, bring a utopia. Certain processes which inhere in the struggle must be acknowledged. First of all, any struggle on the popular or on the individual level involves drastic changes. This is a truism. Among those changes, the giving up of certain ideas, at very great cost, is one of the most difficult to endure. We must give up, once and for all, the idea that we shall have a Middle East existing as if Zionism had never happened. The Israeli Jew is there, in the Middle East; and we cannot—I might even say that we must not—pretend that he will be gone tomorrow, after the struggle is over. This is something to be faced directly and immediately by the Palestinian who has always fought for his right to be there. It is not for me to say what the right of the Israeli Jew is or should be; but *that* he is, that he exists with a special attachment to the land, is something we must face. We must face it directly, and not through the distorting glasses of an imperialist project which, alas, is the only way we have had to face it; quite justly we have rejected it on the grounds that such a vision scants us. But how then do we face it? We cannot avoid the continued presence between us and the Israelis of distrust, war, and even the deepest hate. Those cannot be wished away simply. But they can be isolated and seen as secondary attributes of the struggle, the result of a situation in which Palestinian Arabs and Diaspora Jews were victims of powers and historical circumstances that made violence or the total absence of any sort of meaningful engagement the only two alternatives.

The present war is a result of such conditions and circumstances. It has made violence on the field of battle the only acceptable language to both sides and the only language understood by the world at large. This idea is not mine alone, for I find it in the editorial declaration, in more approving terms than I would use, on the front page of *Al-Nahar,* October 8, 1973. The violence of war, however, brings very limited results, despite the heady feeling that combatants get as they fight. I myself despise the violence of war. It would seem that one of the perceptions Israelis should now have about violence in the past is that violence of that kind obstructs vision and impedes understanding. These limitations of war apply no less to Arabs. War leaves the major tasks undone. But for the past several years, particularly in the West and generally among Diaspora Jews and expatriate Palestinians and Arabs, there have been taking place other sorts of violence which are more productive and perhaps even creative. I am not speaking of hijacking, kidnaping, robbery, or other forms of free enterprise of that kind; those, I think, lead politically and morally to nothing. The violence I have in mind is the activity that takes place, for instance, when a Jew or an Israeli is forced psychologically and morally to confront the fact of the Palestinian's presence before him, his presence as a human and political and national and moral entity with which he, as a Jew and as an Israeli, must deal, and to which he must answer. War today has made such a confrontation possible, of course—not since 1948 has the possibility been greater. But I believe that we cannot stop there, just as we must not forget that during those black years after 1967 it was mainly the Palestinians who kept our spirits alive. There has to be acknowledgment of the human and the political reality which includes both Arabs and Israelis for the simple reason that their day-to-day reality includes the other as foe and as presence. This is the kind of realism that I would oppose to the Israeli pseudorealism of which I spoke earlier. It is a realism that takes in as much as possible of what has happened, of what has been felt and experienced, on both sides. It takes in the dense human reality which one side has hitherto denied the other, and it encompasses not only the discovery of this reality but also the political and emotional pressures—of memory, of war, of threats, of humiliation, and, above all, of fear—whose impressions on all our spirits are very deep. In the United States such confrontations, such interhuman violence of a constructive type, have taken place; and I would urge no Arab to shrink from them. Without the Israeli and the Jew, most of our twentieth-century Arab history is not fully intelligible. Israel has made us clearer to ourselves in ways that we have not liked, in ways that we have justly resisted—but the fact of Israel's role is to be acknowledged nevertheless. If Israel cannot rise to such challenges, if it is doomed to the moral and political dullness that every day violates the Judaic prophetic traditions, *there is no reason at all* why we should so fail! We must not fail.

Thus a major and dangerous consequence of this war is that these reckonings of Arabs with Israelis and Jews might not take place. One reason, as I have said, is the hindering violence of war itself, which gives a combatant the sense that all is solved, or solvable, by war. A second is the setting of this war, which is not simply in the Middle East, but in the media, on the world stage, amid great-power rivalry, and up and down the great, even unlimited, dimensions of history. In other words the danger in this war is not that it will spread to include more participants, but that it will spread to include more elements and perspectives that will obscure the vision, impede understanding, and finally blunt one's humanity. I mean, quite frankly, that this war takes on the symmetry of a blood feud, one side retaliating for the evils of the other, while the roots of the struggle get forgotten and become unknown to those who struggle the hardest. An Arab becomes only a reaction to an Israeli, and an Israeli only a killer of Arabs. As Yeats put it, speaking of such a situation: "The best lack all conviction, while the worst / Are full of passionate intensity." Such a war can appeal, and indeed often does appeal, to the worst in one—I have already spoken of the base feelings of latent anti-Semitism that emerge as the world watches us, the sense that in watching Jews and Arabs killing each other one is watching a gladiatorial contest, the feeling that there is "our" side and "their" side, and so on. We must not forget that the loss of life, the terrible expenditure of blood and treasure on both sides, is taking place now; and, however much it concerns an idea in conflict with another, the struggle is over a land whose place is central and absolute for both the Arab and the Jew. One of Mahmoud Darwish's short poems can be read as a reminder to both sides that the land is in some measure theirs together: the excerpt below comes from a collection entitled "Diary of a Palestinian Wound," and it is dedicated to Fadwa Toukan.

> This is the land that sucks in the flesh of martyrs;
> Summer's returns are wheat and flowers.
> Worship the land!
> In its bowels we are salt and water:
> But on its breast we are a wound, warring.

The perspective of the poem is a broad one, almost a cyclical one;

I take it as an invitation to see the struggle in Palestine as twofold, as a struggle that devastates, but one that, from this broad perspective, also enriches the land's moral and human worth to its people.

For those of us who, for one reason or another, have lived at some geographical distance from the struggle, there is no need to consider ourselves outside the struggle or apart from it in any serious way. Those of us who believe very strongly that there can be no long-term solution to the problem of Palestine without the reckonings of which I have been speaking must, in our perspective, include ourselves as participants in the struggle, in its devastating and enriching aspects, in certain very specific ways. In the first place, I believe that each of us must feel called to contribute to the discussion on the crucial issues facing the Arabs at large. By this I mean that we must avoid following party lines and, more important, espousing vague, general ideas—like Arab unity or peace with justice—but must turn instead to a committed investigation of and involvement in precisely the kind of Arab world in which we would like to live. This is especially true, it would seem, for Palestinians, who have not often realized, I think, that the Palestine for which they have struggled and continue to struggle is yet to be made, is still in the making. For most people Palestine is but a word or an idea; it must descend from that ideal world and enter the world of actuality without much more delay. And only the potential citizens of Palestine can initiate and sustain such a process, give it precise shape, and determine its content.

In the second place, I would say that we must work at establishing a system of relationships that will enable us profitably to connect our past with our present and our future. My feeling is that too many of us have felt that our past is too distant, our present too unpalatable, and our future too hazy; we have felt that our traditions are cumbersome and worn out, our daily life too trivial, and our potential much beyond our capacities for realization. Perhaps the problem is that we rely too heavily upon the perceptual modes which we have learned, under stress, from the West. Who today can seriously say that he is not thoroughly tired of the sterile debates on such subjects as the conservative and the orthodox movements in Islam, or the Westernizers and the reactionaries, or British interests versus Russian interests, and on and on? The answer is not simply to speak happily of Arab development and Arab oil, but to put ourselves politically and spiritually in the closest touch with our resources, which may be orthodox or modern or neither, but which cannot be something toward which we are sullenly hostile. Of such resources I would say the principal one is neither oil nor money but rather our staggeringly complex cultural system, which accommodates an infinite series of particular experiences, experiences sectarian, topographical, political, religious, historical, and sociological, with a general Arab-Islamic world view. A second principal resource is the almost unparalleled access that we have as a modern people to the traditions of a rich past. There can be no people whose modern birth took place in so short a time and with such remarkable natural and material wealth, and who, at the same time, incorporated within their modern life so much of their stable traditionalism. These two resources alone require human, social, and political exploitation of a sort that will occupy many future generations.

In the last place, and at the risk of sounding perhaps a little conservative, I would say that a broad perspective must necessarily take into account the present state of affairs, not as something to be lamented or joked about, but as something to be concerned about. There are institutions, from governments to school systems to legal processes, in the Arab world and among Arab communities in the West, whose functioning at present may be unsatisfactory but which are, nevertheless, essential. I think, for example, of those Arab Palestinian institutions, such as Bir Zeit College, now functioning in the occupied territories. Such institutions cannot be abandoned while we research the theory of revolutionary practice in the New Jerusalem. There are realities of power and government which we, as the most revolutionary group perhaps, cannot afford to misunderstand or be ignorant of. I think that we face a real test of our vision as we set about dealing with these presences, not as something to be put aside until the correct plan or the most perfect solution happens upon us, but more or less as a call upon our inventiveness and generosity and our intelligence. Each one of us, I suppose, has a hold on him of some urgency in the present Arab world or in contemporary Arab life; it is that hold with which one must begin, not with a vague theoretical desire to reform the world, nor, as I have been saying about the Israeli, with a very definite wish to exclude all but the small part of reality which obsesses one. From that beginning on, our involvement gets more specific and more strong, and this takes place in ways that I will not describe here. What I have tried to describe is the fairly complex and rich process which connects Arabs with each other and with Jews in what is now a terrible and costly struggle but which, one can hope, will turn out to have been a step made during the long revolution.

Israel Shahak

EQUAL JUSTICE FOR EVERY HUMAN BEING

I WANT TO ARGUE a thesis which may appear most paradoxical and improbable: that it is possible to establish a lasting concord between Jews and Palestinians, between the Jewish community and Arab communities of the Middle East. And I am convinced that the way to establish such a concord is really quite simple. I believe that the principle of equal justice for every human being, if taken seriously and not merely declaimed, can form the basis of such a concord.

I must distinguish between a slogan and a principle. A slogan is shouted at demonstrations, or perhaps is repeated to journalists, but it is not adopted as a doctrine. People who have shouted slogans return home and act in many ways contrary to what they shouted. They never criticize their friends and allies, their leaders, or themselves in the name of the slogan they shouted, but only their enemies. A principle is different. People reform their own lives and their traditional opinions in support of a certain principle; they argue with their friends about it; in short, they are true to it. At present, only very small minority groups in the Middle East believe in equal justice for every human being as a principle.

Therefore, my first task is one of ruthless criticism. A principle, if it is a principle and not a slogan, must serve as a yardstick for everyone's behavior, and for the behavior of friends and potential friends first of all. I see such criticism as my most important duty; and only after such criticism does a lasting concord based on agreement to a commonly held principle become possible and, indeed, probable.

However, in criticizing, I do not pretend to be "symmetrical." I distinguish very sharply indeed between the conqueror and the conquered, between the power that denies freedom, and the people who struggle for freedom. And because I am not "symmetrical," I am going to be ruthless in criticizing both sides. Those who want to abolish oppression must adopt the way of principle; experience has shown that with muddled thinking nothing can be achieved. I want to examine three particular problems in light of the principle of equal justice for every human being: the problem of terror, the problem of conditions for any "political solution," and the problem of possible allies of any movement that believes in this principle.

When speaking of "terror" I am referring to any indiscriminate act of power, on behalf of a state, a group, or a movement, which causes death to civilians. It does not matter whether the act is carried out by people in or out of uniform. I am quite conscious, as an Israeli citizen, that the Israeli government is responsible for the greater part of deaths caused by terror in the Middle East. I condemn such acts of terror—for example, the Beirut raids of April, 1973—as war crimes, and it is my hope that those responsible will yet be brought to trial as war criminals. Not in the interest of any "symmetry," but in the interest of honesty and truth, I condemn also, on the same terms, any and every act of indiscriminate terror carried out by Palestinian organizations.

When Israeli forces have committed an act of terror against a Palestinian or an Arab population, the usual excuse has been that "Arabs understand only the language of force." But no group of human beings submits for a long time to force. The bombing of London by the Nazis and the bombing of the Vietnamese by the United States are only two cases in which the use of indiscriminate terror has only hardened the will of the population to resist, has only united the people behind the government. And the same is true for the other side. To suppose that bombs in the cinemas of Israel will persuade Jews not to support the oppression of Palestinians is absurd. Any movement which accepts the principle of equal justice for every human being, which looks on the people of the Middle East, whoever they may be, as human beings, must dissociate itself completely from acts of indiscriminate terror, and must support instead the common political struggle of Jews and Arabs alike on behalf of this principle.

The second problem concerns the conditions for a political solution. All parties involved spend much effort advocating various "solutions," various "states," present or future, and little if any effort deciding what the lot of human beings in such states is or will be. This is, for me, the most important question; and I will examine both the existing and the proposed structures in the light of my principle. Any state or states which are just, and which will lead to a lasting concord, must belong only to their citizens, with no restrictions placed on any race, religion, or nationality. On that principle I condemn the whole idea of the so-called Jewish state as unjust, as leading necessarily to subjection, oppression, and unlimited war. I especially condemn the infamous Law of Return, which, with other similar laws, causes the greatest discord between Jews and Palestinians. As long as such unjust and inhuman laws exist—as long as a Palestinian born, let us say, in Haifa is prohibited from returning to his home town, while a recently converted Mexican Jew is readily admitted to that city—there is, in my opinion, no possibility for a just and lasting solution.

But I must add that I am not fighting to replace one injustice with another. I oppose the Law of Return. And, by the same token, I oppose the notorious Paragraph Six of the 1968 Palestinian Covenant, which states that only Jews who arrived in Palestine "before the beginning of the Zionist aggression" will be offered Palestinian citizenship. Just as I am against a "Jewish state," I am against an Arab state as well. Any movement committed to equal justice for all human beings must repudiate this paragraph, just as it must repudiate the Law of Return and similar laws. And I tell you that in Jerusalem and Nazareth, in Tel Aviv and Haifa, there do exist various groups, integrated groups of Palestinians and Jews who, however they differ in ideology, apply the same standards of justice to every human being, and that these groups oppose both the Law of Return of the state of Israel and Paragraph Six of the 1968 Palestinian Covenant. I differ from them in many points, but I do not differ in this: I can entertain many possible political solutions, and I can and will take my place in any common struggle, but the struggle must be common in humanity, common in principle, common in equality. Only such a way is possible.

The last problem I want to discuss is the problem of possible allies of any movement based on the principle of equal justice for every human being. One thing must be made clear: principles are not to be given up for the sake of any alliance, no matter how profitable that alliance may be in terms of money or other material help. The experience of the Jewish community has shown time and again that any alliance with Zionists, any tolerance of racism, leads straight to disaster, and the "profits," in terms of long-range objectives, turn out to be imaginary. A Zionist party cannot be part of a positive movement;

a *kibbutz* has to be criticized for the anti-Arab, racist organization that it is; and those who support the Israeli government support all the crimes of Dayan.

I trust that it is axiomatic in this forum that women are human beings, entitled to equal justice. Every movement which believes in this as a principle, and not as a slogan, should act on it. Declarations like that of President Kaddafi about the "biological inequality of women" should not be overlooked. Moreover, any movement devoted to human rights for men and women must fight for women's rights as an inherent part of its struggle. Women must participate fully in demonstrations, in elections, in all activities. In short, no consideration of money or other help should prevent any movement based on this principle from fighting for equal rights for women, or from resolutely and openly opposing all those who deny this principle.

Another factor that sometimes leads to the pardoning of unworthy allies is to rely on the past, and to entertain foolish ideas of bringing back some imaginary "golden era." The principle of equal justice for all human beings is not found in the Jewish past; nor is it found in the Arab past. The roots of this principle do not go further back than the American and the French revolutions. I am devoted to many aspects of the Jewish past and culture, but political theory is not one of them. King David and King Solomon may have been poets and prophets, but they were also tyrants; and all who idealize them politically are dangerous as political allies. I admire many aspects of the Arab heritage, but I do not accept the rule of Caliph Haroun al-Rashid, or that of any other caliph, as a model to be followed. We all are the children of modern times; our beginnings are in "liberty, equality, fraternity," and "government of the people, for the people, and by the people." Allies who are devoted exclusively to the past are dangerous and must be repudiated.

Many other problems can be discussed in the light of this principle, but I think that the way I propose has been made clear. It is a hard way, one that demands that we all—Jews, Palestinians, Israelis, and Arabs—fight against the mores of our own societies and our own peoples, and that we carry out this fight first of all in our own minds and in our own hearts. I think that this way, which perhaps seems to you long, will turn out to be long but short. Let me conclude by telling you my favorite Talmudic story. Rabbi Yehoshua Ben-Hananya used to tell how once, as he was walking on his way, he came to a crossroad where a small boy was sitting. He asked the boy, "Which is the best way to town?" The boy answered, "One way is short but long, and the other is long but short." The rabbi took the short but long way and found that close to the town the road got lost among the orchards. He returned and rebuked the boy, but the boy answered, "Did I not tell you that that way is short but long? You should have taken the long but short way!" And, indeed, when the rabbi took this advice, he arrived safely in town.

I offer you the advice of this small boy. The way of the principle of equal justice for every human being, of being true to it in all its consequences, may be the hard way, may be the long way, but it is the long but short way and will lead us to our common aim: to lasting concord between Palestinians and Jews, to lasting cooperation between the Jewish community and the Arabs in the Middle East.

INDEX

Abbas, Abdul Halim, 87
Abbas, Ferhat, 73–74, 75
Abboushi, Burhan al-Din al-, 87–89
Abbud, Bulos, 89
Africa: and Middle East conflict, 189–200. *See also individual countries*
African Party for the Independence of Guinea and Cape Verde (PAIGC), 33
Algeria: European settlement in, 76–77, 127–28, 134; French military in, 77–78, 79
Algerian literature, 125–35
Algerian nationalism, 73–75
Angola, 32–33
Anti-Semitism, 237–38; in South Africa, 169–72; and Zionism, 25
Arab-Americans: humanitarian organizations of, 209; and Middle East conflict, 201–20; participation of, in U.S. politics, 205–6, 213–14; political organizations of, 210–11, 212; and Rogers Plan, 215; social clubs of, 203–4, 213–14; U.S. government harassment of, 212, 216–18
Arab Executive, 101, 106–7
Arab Higher Committee (AHC), 109–10
Arab nationalism, 83, 89–93, 99–100
Arif, al-Arif, 92–93
Arriaga, Kaulza de, 36, 38–39, 41
Azoury, Najib, 83

Balfour Declaration, 183–86
Ben Gurion, David, 8
Bible and Zionism, 3–6, 227
Boulder Operation, 212, 217
British: in Middle East, 95–97, 109–12, 187; in South Africa, 175, 178
Brune, Jean, 128–29

Caetano, Marcello, 34, 35, 41
Camus, Albert, 130–31
Canaanites, 11, 14–19
Circassians in Ottoman state, 64–65

Dajani, Sidqi al-, 90
Darwazah, Izzat, 87
Darwazah, Muhammad Izzat, 89–90, 92

Eban, Abba, 9
Eliav, Arie, 8

Feraoun, Mouloud, 130, 131–32
French in Algeria, 76–78, 79, 127–28
Front for the Liberation of Mozambique (FRELIMO), 33, 136, 138–45

General Syrian Congress (1919), 97–98, 101
Guinea (Bissau), 32–33

Hajj, Messali, 75

Herzl, Theodor, 27, 29, 95–96
Husayni, Ishaq Musal al-, 87
Husayni, Muhammad Yunis al-, 90

Ibn Badis, Shaykh Abdul Hamid, 73–74, 75
Israel: and Black Africa, 193–95; geographical extent of, defined in Bible, 9–14; militarism in, 30, 232; and South Africa, 198. *See also* Zionism

Jerusalem: Arif's history of, 92–93; attachment of Jews for, 10
Jewish National Fund (JNF), 43–53, 104
Judaism, spiritualized, 6–7

Kabyle literature, 132
Kawakji, Fawzi ad-Din al-, 99, 110
Khalidi, Yusuf Diya al-, 82
King-Crane Commission, 98
Kremenetzky, Johann, 45

Libya and Middle East conflict, 196–97
Literature: Algerian, 125–35; Mozambican, 145–46; Palestinian, 86–93

Mammeri, Mouloud, 132–33
Mendes, Alfonso, 39
Middle East, British in, 95–97, 109–12, 187
Middle East conflict: and Africa, 187–200; and Arab-Americans, 201–20; and Libya, 196–97; and Palestinians, 189
Mozambique, 32–33, 136–46
Mozambique Liberation Front. *See* Front for the Liberation of Mozambique
Muslim Brotherhood, 99

Nationalism: Algerian, 73–75; Arab, 83, 89–93, 99–100; Jewish. *See* Zionism; Palestinian, 101, 108–9, 111–15
National party (South Africa), 168, 169–72
Natonek, Rabbi Joseph, 66–68
Nixon, Richard M., 230

Organization of Arab Students, 205, 207, 208
Ottoman state, immigration policy of, 57–72, 84, 85

Palestine: economic transformation of, during mandate, 101–6; European settlement in, during nineteenth century, 57–72; resistance to European settlement in, 100–15, 150–61; settlement of Jews in, 62–63, 66–71, 72, 81–82, 84, 85, 103; traditional leadership in, during mandate, 102, 107–8; Zionist land-acquisition in, 43–53, 84, 104
Palestine Arab Congress: Seventh (1928), 106; Third (1920), 101
Palestinian literature, 86–93
Palestinian nationalism, 101, 108–9, 111–15, 149–50, 159
Palestinians: alienation of, 119–24, 236; and Arab-Americans, 219; and Middle East conflict, 189. *See also* Canaanites
Popular Movement for the Liberation of Angola (MPLA), 33
Portuguese "overseas territories" in Africa, 32, 34, 36; and South Africa, 33; counterinsurgency in, 37, 39

Qassam, Izz ad-Din al-, 99, 108

Return, concept of, 10–11
Rhodes, Cecil, 23–24, 176–77
Rothschild, Edmond de, 27–28

Schapira, Hermann, 44
Shiloach, Zwi, 13
Smuts, Jan Christian, 173–83, 185–86
South Africa: and Israel, 198; and Portuguese "overseas territories," 33
South African Jews, 165–72, 179–80, 181–82

Tuqan, Ibrahim, 87–88
Tuqan, Qadri, 91–92

Weizmann, Chaim, 173–76, 183–85
White supremacy: and Jewish South Africans, 168–69; in Portuguese "overseas territories," 36–40; in South Africa, 179–80
World Zionist Organization (WZO), 45, 46, 51

Yacine, Kateb, 134

Zionism: and anti-Semitism, 25; and Bible, 3–6, 227; and counterrevolution, 24–26, 114; and European imperialism, 21–24,

95, 113, 176, 182–83, 197–98; and Jewish big bourgeoisie, 26–28; and land-acquisition in Palestine, 43–53, 84, 104; and Palestinian literature; 89–93; and South African Jews, 165–72